RUDOLF II

Books in the RENAISSANCE LIVES series explore and illustrate the life histories and achievements of significant artists, rulers, intellectuals and scientists in the early modern world. They delve into literature, philosophy, the history of art, science and natural history and cover narratives of exploration, statecraft and technology.

Series Editor: François Quiviger

RUDOLF II

The Life and Legend of the Mad Emperor

THOMAS DACOSTA KAUFMANN

REAKTION BOOKS

Roberto Orpheo Carolo Francisoque neopotibus dilectissimis

Published by Reaktion Books Ltd
Unit 32, Waterside
44–48 Wharf Road
London N1 7UX, UK
www.reaktionbooks.co.uk

First published 2025

Printed and bound in India by Replika Press Pvt. Ltd

A catalogue record for this book is available from the British Library

ISBN 978 1 83639 061 9

COVER: Hans von Aachen, *Rudolf II*, 1606–8, oil on canvas.
Kunsthistorisches Museum, Vienna (GG 6438), photo
Bridgeman Images.

CONTENTS

Introduction: Countering the Black Legend of the Mad Emperor

udolf II Habsburg (1552–1612; illus. 1) is a figure of legend. He was King of Hungary (including Slovakia, Croatia and nominally Transylvania, now part of Romania) from 1572; King of the Romans, presumptive emperor, from 1575; King of Bohemia (including the present Czechia, Lusatia, now in southeastern Germany, and Silesia, now in southwestern Poland) from 1576; and when his father, Maximilian II (1527–1576), died in the same year, he succeeded him in reigning over the hereditary Habsburg lands of Upper and Lower Austria. In 1576 Rudolf was also crowned Holy Roman Emperor of the German Nation, thereby obtaining what was the highest position in the protocol of European rulers. Yet by the end of his life all that remained was, it has been said, the bare shadow of the imperial crown. All his other titles had been stripped away: Rudolf sat powerless in Hradčany Castle in Prague, where he had resided since 1583.[1]

Rudolf II's fate as a ruler contrasts with his renown as a patron of art and science. He acquired the largest painting collection of his time and one of the greatest in European history. He owned a *Kunstkammer* (cabinet of art and wonders of nature) that was the greatest of its time and one of the most important ever assembled. He attracted to his court scores of painters, sculptors, goldsmiths and masters of stone and ivory carving, and patronized many other artists. He had in his employ the famed astronomers Tycho

1 Hans von Aachen, *Rudolf II*, 1606–8, oil on canvas.

Brahe and Johannes Kepler, who made numerous observations and several momentous discoveries while in imperial service. Alchemists, magicians and others who have been described as practising the occult arts also flocked to Prague while Rudolf resided there.

Rudolf's involvement with the arts and sciences, moreover, has long been linked to the causes of his downfall.[2] A familiar version of this story relates how the emperor shut himself up in Prague Castle, neglecting affairs of state to pursue his personal passions. His flight into the arcane and obsession with collecting are said to be symptomatic of someone on the verge of complete mental and physical collapse.[3] Rudolf's idiosyncrasies are supposed to indicate that he was not just an incompetent ruler but insane.[4]

Imputations of instability and insanity may be traced back to Rudolf's II's lifetime. Some contemporaries claimed he was possessed, and many others claimed that he displayed the effects of melancholy.[5] His melancholy has been said to have been expressed in a moody and mysterious personality that inclined him to madness. This ascription of melancholy derives from the ancient doctrines of Hippocratic medicine which held that a mixture of the humours (phlegm, blood, black bile, yellow bile or choler) determines the composition of four basic temperaments (phlegmatic, sanguine, melancholic, choleric) affecting the constitution of human beings. An excess of any one of the humours may cause illness. The humours and temperaments are also related to the planets (seven in traditional count, including the moon) under whose influence they stand in astrological theory. Influence here literally means outpourings from the heavenly bodies that induce both general effects and specific ones in individuals.[6] The location of planets in the sky at someone's time of birth, their location in one of the twelve houses, or divisions in the older form of a horoscope, also affect the course of a person's life.

Rudolf II's melancholy was exacerbated because he was born while the planet Saturn was rising on the horizon of the night sky: the planet increased the effects of those 'born under Saturn' (and Rudolf has been dubbed the Saturnine emperor).[7]

Melancholy is only one of the unfavourable characterizations of the emperor that originated in his own time. The Swiss-born English agent Paulus Lesieur wrote in a dispatch of 17 November 1610 that Rudolf 'ought to be walled up in a cloister with a necromancer, an alchemist, a painter and a whore'.[8] This slander echoes a vignette in what is perhaps the first *roman à clef* in European literature. In *Euphormionis Lusini Satyricon* of 1607 the Franco-Scottish author (and sometime ambassador) John Barclay depicted Rudolf II as a doddering fool, Emperor Aquilius.[9] Weak and unsteady on his feet, Aquilius avoids human contact and implicitly the duties of his office; instead, he spends his time indulging his sexual fantasies and his obsession with art and the occult. Reflecting descriptions of ancient painters of prostitutes, Barclay says that Aquilius paints images of the women he desires, sleeping with those who match his dreams. Along with the paintings he produces and displays, the emperor collects curiosities, studies astrology intensely, possesses magical objects, and carries out alchemical research in the company of a Jewish adept.[10] His folly is dramatized when he drops the fruit of his labours, a vial containing a fluid (probably the elixir of life, whose production was a goal of alchemical endeavours), and then collapses.

Other contemporary rumours helped entrench the lasting image of Rudolf II as a lustful, physically and mentally weak ruler who preferred painting and alchemy to governing and lost power because of his personal pursuits. Rudolf's own papers, which seem to have vanished when Prague Castle was sacked in 1648, might have altered this view, but in their absence scholars have been left with what has been described as a 'buzzing and chaotic cloud of often ill-informed diplomatic rumors, on the one hand, or with the echo-chamber of retrospectively biased literature on the other'.[11] Propaganda spread by the emperor's antagonists helped tilt opinions even further in a negative direction.[12]

Unfavourable impressions of Rudolf II were picked up in succeeding centuries. In the eighteenth century a comprehensive historical survey, while making some positive remarks about the emperor, repeated the comments found in Barclay's slanderous satire and in a report of a Tuscan ambassador.[13] In the nineteenth century the touchstone for such treatments of Rudolf II was firmly established. Even the comparatively sympathetic treatment found in the best known literary work featuring Rudolf, Franz Grillparzer's *Ein Bruderzwist in Habsburg*, staged his fall as an outcome of the emperor's instability. Grillparzer (1791–1872) dramatized Rudolf's condition as the result of struggles both within himself and with members of his family, which the title of the play calls a 'fraternal quarrel in [the House of] Habsburg'. In Grillparzer's drama Rudolf took refuge in the study of the stars because he believed they revealed an ideal order above the vagaries of human conduct and foretold a forthcoming disaster – the Thirty Years War (1618–48). The emperor tried to fend off calamity by avoiding decisions that would have intensified mounting divisions between Catholics and Protestants. But his irresolution pleased no one, and his failure to wed caused alarm among his Habsburg relatives who worried about the continuation of their dynasty's reign. Rudolf's brothers and cousin used their concerns as a pretext to advance their own interests and undermine his authority. They made peace with the Turks (while Rudolf is shown hoping that war with the 'infidel' would help unify Christians) without his knowledge or consent. They then conspired to take away his power, forcing Rudolf to cede most of his positions to his brother: a more general tragedy, the onset of the disastrous Thirty Years War that the relatively tolerant emperor had tried to avoid, is manifest at the end of the play.

Based on research from his 'day job' as archivist, Grillparzer's drama gave some of Rudolf II's biographical details accurately, but it was first published the year of his death when views of the emperor were becoming increasingly unfavourable.[14] Grillparzer's depiction of Rudolf II as a relatively tolerant ruler was readily contradicted.[15] And the publication of the play also coincided with the popularization of the idea that Rudolf II was an ineffective ruler whose ineptitude in one way or another led to the Thirty Years War.

The view of Rudolf as erratic and incompetent dominated both popular and scholarly accounts during the first three-quarters of the twentieth century. Historians treated him as unstable or odd, an enigmatic emperor who was 'the strangeling in the imperial castle'.[16] Rudolf was indecisive and incapable of action: he dithered rather than marrying, putting his sexual passions above Habsburg dynastic interests. He preferred art and science to politics and the demands of rulership, and shut himself up in the castle to enjoy art, alchemy and necromancy. Reclusive, perverse, depraved, he was more than merely melancholic: he was mad.

Several other long-standing prejudices seem to have encouraged the entrenchment of this view. One is the belief that rulers are successful because they win wars, not because they promote the arts and sciences. Another is the tendency, especially in Anglophone historiography, to disparage the Habsburgs and suggest that they lacked any coherent approach to rulership. They have often been described as reactive, subject to the whims of fortune or, as in the case of Philip II of Spain, prone to naked aggression.[17] Rather than having rational plans, caprice and passion have often been said to have dominated the Habsburgs of the sixteenth and seventeenth centuries.

Rumours about Rudolf's illness and instability, including his celibacy, thus not only caused him injury during his lifetime but shaped his reputation. Seemingly 'starkly opposed images of Rudolf'

– mad and apathetic emperor and 'archetypical Renaissance Maecenas' – have combined to construct a legend.[18] Although Rudolf II did not share their policies, he has been treated in the same way as several Spanish monarchs and especially Philip II, though probably for less substantial reasons and with more direct impact on what happened to him in his lifetime and how he has been viewed by posterity. In short, Rudolf II has been the victim of a black legend.[19]

In order to separate history from legend, threads of what can be more securely determined about Rudolf II must be disentangled from the misunderstandings and misinterpretations that continue to be wound around them. Already in the seventeenth century, Benedikt Hopffer, philosophy professor at the university in Tübingen and its rector in 1683, argued the year before that one of the most important diplomatic accounts of Rudolf II was biased, slanderous and unfair.[20] It took 250 years, however, for a convincing argument to appear that demonstrated many of the accounts of Rudolf II rested on shaky foundations. In 1932 the Czech historian Jan Matoušek showed that much of the information about Rudolf's purported physical and mental instability, inactivity and indecision derived from reports that were at best second hand and that other contemporary accounts contradicted. For example, Matoušek adduced eyewitness accounts that described Rudolf as having a firm stance and clear speech when he was supposed to have been unsteady on his feet and prone to angry outbursts. He also demonstrated that the negative comments about Rudolf appeared in dispatches from ambassadors who felt they had been received unpleasantly, had failed to achieve their ends, or had failed to gain any access to the emperor whatsoever while other visitors had audiences with him.[21] Many negative comments were also made by papal legates or other unsympathetic and even antagonistic envoys, including those from Spain, who were at best suspicious of Rudolf II.[22]

A more recent review of the question of Rudolf's madness offers reasons why derogatory impressions of the emperor were shaped by those who were working for a ruler who was an antagonist of Spain and the papacy.[23] These were namely Lesieur and Barclay, who were working for King James when he was beginning to engage with Central Europe. It has been argued convincingly that Lesieur and Barclay sought to rise in English diplomatic circles; ridiculing Rudolf may have helped because James I was known to be wary of the Habsburgs. Although James completed a peace treaty with Spain in 1603, the date of Lesieur's mission to Prague, Britain remained a close ally of the rebels in Holland, for whom many British fought (including the poet Philip Sidney, who died in the Netherlands). Barclay's depiction of Rudolf II of 1607 also complemented the widespread British view of Spanish Habsburgs as grasping despots. At the same time, slandering Rudolf would have appealed to the supporters of Rudolf's antagonist and successor Archduke Matthias, who – along with his allies like Archduke Maximilian III – was on the ascendant when Barclay and Lesieur (who spoke well of Maximilian III) made their comments.[24] Ultimately, James's daughter Elizabeth was married to Frederick V of the Palatinate, an antagonist of the Habsburgs.

Barclay's depiction of the emperor could, in any case, not have been based on first-hand information. His visit to Prague came in 1609, two years after he published his satire of Rudolf. Lesieur also wrote his negative comments seven years after he had visited Prague; he did not spend much time in the imperial capital, and his comments were published after Rudolf II had died. Both may have learned about Prague from an imperial ambassador who visited Britain, while many other conduits for information about Prague existed for British writers.[25] Lesieur and Barclay may have had further reasons not to speak well of Rudolf which resemble those of other ambassadors who complained about him. Although he was received within five days of his arrival and obtained his goal of obtaining imperial support to lift trade restrictions favouring the Hanseatic League, Lesieur says he had a 'sour' audience with the emperor and was not treated courteously by 'imperialists' – probably because it was evident that he did not have the social status that an ambassador to the emperor was expected to possess.[26] Barclay may have been treated similarly.

Regardless of the role of the British ambassadors in the reception of Rudolf II, Matoušek convincingly traced the source of many negative rumours to Archduke Matthias. Grillparzer portrayed Matthias as ambitious, opportunistic and scheming, and there is evidence to support this view.[27] Negative rumours about Rudolf intensified just at the times that Matthias was in conflict with him. Spreading rumours about Rudolf provided propaganda for the cause of Matthias and his allies.[28]

A reading of the proposition for the meeting of Archdukes Matthias, Ferdinand (of Styria) and Maximilian III in Vienna in April 1606 is instructive. The protocol claimed that Rudolf neglects political affairs, fails to provide audiences to papal and Spanish ambassadors and refuses to marry or to name one of the archdukes as his successor. His melancholy and the angry outbursts associated with it are uncontrollable, leading Rudolf to believe that he is being punished or possessed by the Devil. He is interested only in wizards and their ilk, and constantly seeks to eliminate God and serve a different master. These criticisms provided a source for propaganda (and have formed the basis for many subsequent interpretations) and, significantly, an excuse for the archdukes to dispose of matters themselves: they made peace with the Turks without consulting the emperor, and progressively deprived Rudolf of most of his realms.[29]

Forty years after Matoušek's essay was published, a groundbreaking work offered another approach to considering questions of Rudolf's character. In 1973 R. J. W. Evans introduced Rudolf II to English speakers in a masterly book that shifted emphasis from excessive concentration on the emperor's personality and on him as an individual. Re-evaluating previous historiography, Evans set Rudolf into the broader cultural context of his time.[30]

Although Evans recognized that the burden of eminence and responsibility on Rudolf II was a difficult subject to study, as was his character, he continued nevertheless to interpret the emperor's actions through what he himself regarded as the problematic lens of the emperor's personality.[31] And while in 1973 he did not treat Rudolf II as a madman,[32] granted much attention to the importance of his patronage as symptomatic of his time and place, and argued against separating aspects of his character, he, like many writers on Rudolf II, has never treated patronage and interest in the arts as essential components of Renaissance rulership. In 1991 Evans moreover stated that Rudolf suffered from 'deeper psychological disorder', that his reactions to his family's predations bore 'the hallmark of paranoia' and insinuated that the emperor's patronage was megalomaniacal.[33] While he was initially sceptical about psycho-analytic approaches to Rudolf, he thus appears to have adopted its language. Evans followed Arnold Hauser in discussing Rudolfine art and science as marks of 'Prague Mannerism': Hauser compared Rudolf II with Philip II by linking their apparent isolation and interests in art and artists and collecting with Mannerism, and in treating the emperor as a psychopath. In 2005 Evans stated that Rudolf's 'occult inclinations' and 'collecting mania' were 'forms of appearance of his deepening madness'.[34]

Despite his initial caution, Evans's later comments are characteristic of the continuing treatment of Rudolf II through the template of mental illness.[35] For instance, while offering a serious assessment of the evidence, one important historian of the period calls Rudolf the 'most prominent example' of the 'mad princes of Renaissance Germany' and states that 'The Thirty Years' War was ultimately due in part to his madness.'[36] Psychologically oriented

analyses continue to provide diagnoses for Rudolf's supposed
failure to act: he supposedly suffered persecution anxiety, megalomania, schizophrenia and schizo-affective psychosis.[37] When
new information is published that may shed light on Rudolf, it
is often fitted into this framework.[38]

But the evidence for Rudolf's persecution mania is shaky,
the accusation of megalomania misunderstands how early modern rulers thought of and presented themselves, more grounded
analyses discount the imputation of schizophrenia, and a careful
review of the evidence has contradicted the analysis of schizo-
affective psychosis.[39] Furthermore, to call Rudolf II mentally ill,
as some psychiatrists on whom historians have relied have done,[40]
is to ignore some of the basic principles of psychoanalysis that
Sigmund Freud himself enunciated. In his essay on 'Wild Analysis',
Freud argued: 'Psycho-analytic intervention absolutely requires
a fairly long period of contact with the patient.'[41]

Significantly, in the same year that Evans's important book
on Rudolf II appeared, the American Psychiatric Association
promulgated the 'Goldwater Rule' in response to what had happened during the 1964 presidential election in the United States,
when many American psychiatrists called Barry Goldwater, the
losing candidate of the Republican party, insane. Psychoanalysts
were thenceforth to adhere to the rule that 'it is unethical for a
psychiatrist to offer a professional opinion unless he or she has
conducted an examination and has been granted proper author-
ization for such a statement.'[42] American psychologists soon
followed their proscription by making a similar rule. Unethical
means unprofessional and unscientific. Having died more than
four hundred years ago, Rudolf is not available for psychoanalysis, unless one subscribes to the charge falsely raised against him
and his entourage and practises necromancy.

While there are some grains of truth in what has been presented as a major cause of Rudolf II's decline and fall – his illness

(or illnesses) – the actual evidence for his maladies, including the question of his supposed mental illness, must be reassessed. Rudolf's madness is rooted in early descriptions of him as melancholic. Yet melancholy is only one of the ways the emperor was characterized according to humoural qualities at the time, and the grounds for this description are questionable. While it was said that he was 'above all so melancholic that he wishes to exile himself and be seen by few, and he only delights in hunt, ball games, handling horses, and in arms', at the same time this description mentions these activities are for his health as much as his pleasure (and as we shall see in the next chapter, these were all standard princely pursuits) and that Rudolf was temperate in his pastimes. Moreover, the very same report uses other humoural qualities to characterize Rudolf, saying that he was 'by nature rather more phlegmatic and meek than choleric, rather timid'.[43] While the term melancholy may include the possibility of madness, this early description of Rudolf suggests that melancholy may mean little more than saying someone seems gloomy or shy.

According to Richard Burton's *Anatomy of Melancholy* (first published in 1621), the most extensive contemporaneous compendium on the subject, many symptoms, causes and cures relate to melancholy. Among the causes are illness, family, heredity, study, incarceration and old age. Several of these might fit Rudolf II. However, Burton, who probably had some information about the emperor – he specifically refers to the imperial printmaker, Aegidius Sadeler[44] – and who in any event was familiar with English contemporaries who had visited or worked in Prague, did not mention him in any of these contexts. For Burton it was not Rudolf II but his grandfather Emperor Charles V (1501–1558) who served as the example of a melancholic emperor. Burton also says old age was the cause of Charles V's melancholy.

But being melancholic does not mean being mad. Rulers like Philip II of Spain may have been melancholic, but they were not mad even when they displayed behavioural traits that have been used to bolster diagnosis of the emperor as insane, such as outbursts of anger (*furia*) as well as what might be termed depression, or have been diagnosed, as has Philip II, as having an obsessive personality.[45] While ancient philosophers and physicians did consider anger as a kind of madness – being mad in one sense was mad in another – this diagnosis has long lost its validity and is effectively a cliché. Indeed, to apply the categories of traditional humoural psychology that include melancholy, angry outbursts primarily exemplify choleric (not melancholic) behaviour.

To call Rudolf the Saturnine emperor means even less than to say, as one might do now, that he was a Leo (his actual birth sign, as he was born in July – he adopted the Capricorn sign of the Roman emperor Augustus). 'Saturnine' properly applies to all those people who were supposedly affected by Saturn regardless of the year in which they were born. Leo is one of the twelve signs of the zodiac into which a person's horoscope is divided. Fitting a person into the seven categories, including Saturnine, according to what were known as the seven planets (Moon, Sun, Jupiter, Saturn, Venus, Mercury, Mars) during Rudolf's lifetime thus reduces from twelve to seven even the limited possibilities provided by the zodiacal signs and makes this sort of analysis even more vague.

From a more recent viewpoint, some people may seem to be momentarily depressed or gloomy (supposedly of 'Saturnine' disposition) without being chronically so. Someone may 'feel down' or even appear temporarily depressed without having a depressive (or manic-depressive) personality, labels that have been applied to Rudolf II. A person may become suspicious without being 'paranoid', as the emperor has also been called. In any case, it is not correct to claim that Rudolf II was being paranoiac or suffering from persecution mania (another diagnosis) in being on his guard or suspecting that people were working against him.

The emperor's enemies (most notably his brothers and cousin) did plot against him and did work to take his power away. Spanish and papal ambassadors also connived against him and were involved in having his trusted advisors and administrators removed from their offices around 1600 and replacing them with people who undermined him; some of the advisors who angered him also schemed with his enemies; and his antagonists did spread nasty rumours about him. If Rudolf had outbursts of anger or was suspicious, he may have had good reasons.

On the other hand, in the past melancholy and a Saturnine disposition were also regarded as having positive as well as negative aspects. Melancholy may pertain to positive qualities of a ruler, philosopher or poet. According to the ancient book of *Problems* attributed to Aristotle, those gifted in 'philosophy or politics or poetry or the arts are clearly melancholics'. Almost two millennia later, the fifteenth-century Florentine philosopher Marsilio Ficino spoke of melancholy as a 'unique and divine gift'. According to Ficino, the children of Saturn are more disposed to intellectual work; people capable of deep and lofty contemplation are drawn into Saturn's sphere of influence. Heinrich Cornelius Agrippa von Nettesheim introduced these ideas into Central Europe.[46] Agrippa served Rudolf II's ancestor Maximilian I in several capacities including secretary, and his theories were well known at Rudolf's own court. Maximilian I was much interested in such matters.[47] Agrippa's notions have also been thought to have inspired the famed engraving of *Melencolia* by Albrecht Dürer, one of Rudolf II's favourite artists (illus. 2).[48]

In a recent analysis of Rudolf's health, melancholy has moreover been called a disease of the Renaissance elite.[49] One supporting example: Duke Francesco de' Medici has been regarded as melancholic.[50] A recent historian of the Habsburgs has even speculated that 'it is entirely possible that Rudolf's depressive demeanour was a pose.'[51]

In any case, it seems significant that reports about Rudolf II's melancholy appear especially around those times when he was physically ill. Rudolf reportedly suffered from serious illnesses in 1578, 1580, 1582, 1600 and perhaps in 1606. It was during these times of greatest illness that he also may have withdrawn from the public. In addition to the political reasons for making personal access difficult, it seems that he – quite reasonably, one

2 Albrecht Dürer, *Melencolia I*, 1514, engraving.

might add, if one considers what is still called 'keeping up appearances' – did not want to be seen when he did not feel well. He was also afraid of the plague, and on occasion fled Prague from fear of catching it. It appears that it was as a result of recurrent morbidity, and not because of his imagination (an excess of which is also attributed to melancholics), that many physicians were called into imperial service and that Rudolf may have occasionally secluded himself. One scholar has recently suggested, 'given the grave dynastic and religious consequences his heirless death entailed, Rudolf's self-isolation could be considered highly rational.'[52]

To sum up: convincing evidence does not exist for Rudolf II's madness. His interest in astronomical discoveries and his artistic discernment and collecting of great works of art certainly cannot be called insane. Rudolf II displayed keen aesthetic judgement, as demonstrated by his patronage and collecting. He continued to be active and resourceful as a ruler until almost the end of his life. He does not seem to have ruled according to his whims or passions of the moment. His decisions followed their own logic of reason of state (to be discussed), which do not match those of a madman. While he may have had moments of doubt or even depression, was repeatedly physically ill (reasons for which will be discussed presently) and his physical ailments may have affected his mental state, there is no evidence that he was unstable for an extended period of time. His actions around 1600 and thereafter do not clearly indicate, as some historians have argued, that he experienced a mental breakdown at that time which caused lasting damage; he certainly did not subsequently change his behaviour substantially.[53] He continued to exhibit a sharp mind until near the very end of his life, despite his physical ailments: indeed, in 1609 a critical papal nuncio who was not well disposed to him and made negative insinuations about the emperor said that Rudolf II's *ingegno* or mental acuity was greater than that of his brother and rival Matthias. Rudolf remained intellectually curious about and comprehended discoveries: in 1610 Kepler compared him to Galileo Galilei.[54] Almost until the very end the emperor struggled to maintain or regain his positions and to maintain his dignity. He did not shut himself up as a recluse in the palace: until almost the end of his life he held audiences and was seen in public. There are good reasons why Rudolf II put some people off or delayed access, and this behaviour has also been called shrewd.[55]

It is possible that the physical reasons for Rudolf II's illness may have had an effect on his mental state. But the sources are mostly taken at second or third hand, conveyed largely through ambassadors' reports and rumours. At best, the reports may refer to opinions of physicians, but these are also inconsistent. Some physicians mention stomach and digestive ailments; others report 'his heart was being eaten away,' and it is also said that the emperor felt dizzy.[56]

Descriptions of dizziness correspond to accounts that he was unsteady on his feet: they may also be related to Rudolf's being called *Blödsinnig* (feeble-minded). While in the absence of more precise data and sustained medical historical analysis it remains speculation to say what could have ailed him, Rudolf was certainly not feeble-minded. Mentions of dizziness and possible heart trouble point to other possible diagnoses than the repeated accusation that he was mad or had a schizophrenic personality.[57] Such references to his physical ailments relate to each other: they suggest that Rudolf II may have been bothered by a variety of medical problems.

While retrospective diagnosis of medical evidence is always risky, recent reviews of Rudolf's illnesses have reconsidered some evidence of such a specific and unusual nature that some reasonable hypotheses may be proposed. In 1577 undigested pieces of food were found in his diarrhoea. This suggests that he had trouble chewing his food, and Rudolf's pronounced underbite, hardly disguised by portraits, could have been a cause. This would have been a chronic problem, and could have led to malnourishment, with noticeable side effects. Another chronic problem may have been venereal disease. Syphilis was widespread in the early modern period, and many people, including rulers, seem to have suffered from it. Repeated and recurrent reports of treatment for Rudolf's genital sores and swelling from circa 1580 provide evidence for the possibility that he was so affected. While syphilis did not ultimately cause Rudolf's death, it may have been responsible for the hallucinations that he is reported to have had, and for other signs of growing dementia: these may be symptoms of tertiary syphilis, in which blood being cut off from the brain may slur speech, alter behaviour, cause memory loss and create difficulty coordinating muscle movements. In tertiary syphilis such symptoms may coincide with the time, 20–25 years on, that clinically such disturbances become apparent. In Rudolf's case these symptoms match the period around 1600 and after. A third possible ailment is heart disease. The autopsy on Rudolf's body found scars on his heart, indicating that the immediate cause of his death was a heart attack. His pericardium was also filled with an immense amount of fluid, suggesting that he had a cardiac infection and heart disease. His heart condition may be related to problems with circulation, blood pressure and consequently unsteadiness.[58]

Some previously overlooked material evidence may also point to Rudolf's problems with circulation. As they now appear on display in Prague Castle, the stockings in which he was buried are broader at the top. This suggests that his legs may have been swollen. Swelling may be related to gout, from which many rulers including Philip II suffered, or to general circulatory problems of the sort that might have led to congestive heart disease or heart failure. Reports that at the end of his life Rudolf had to stay in bed because his lower limbs were swollen – presumably with oedema – are also common signs of congestive heart failure.[59] Low blood pressure and circulatory problems may also have led to aphasic attacks or even stroke, accounting for some of the recorded lapses from which Rudolf is said to have suffered.

Rudolf may have inherited some of his health problems. His father, Maximilian II, was chronically ill with heart disease; it is generally believed that heart trouble shortened Maximilian's life.[60] (Rudolf, despite his many recorded bouts with illness, lived ten years longer than his father.) Maximilian II and Rudolf II were in any case not the only members of the Habsburg dynasty who suffered from serious physical illnesses. It may be that many Habsburg maladies, including possibly Rudolf's, were hereditary. They probably resulted from or were intensified by endogamy, excessive intermarriage: many Habsburgs married their close relatives. Rudolf's parents were first cousins, and Philip II, his mother's brother, was not only his uncle but his first cousin and at one point his brother-in-law. Philip's daughter, Isabella, was proposed at different times to Rudolf and to his younger brothers Ernst and Albrecht, the latter of whom she eventually married. Like many other Habsburgs, Albrecht and Isabella never had children: endogamy has been suggested as the probable reason for the infertility of the last Spanish Habsburg king, Charles II, as well as his many maladies. Certainly, they account for the famous pronounced underbite.[61]

However, this again does not mean that the Habsburgs passed on some strain of insanity that they inherited from Queen Juana of Castile and Aragon, who since the sixteenth century has been called 'Juana la loca', Joanna the Mad. Recent biographers have debunked this calumny of the queen. They have demonstrated that Juana was well spoken and could write eloquently. Accusations of her madness lack real substance and were used by Charles V to deprive the queen of power and to shut her up, quite literally, much like what happened to Rudolf II.[62]

In the end it seems that slanders about Rudolf's health grew out of rumours that dwelled on his physical ailments and turned them into mental ones. Together they contributed to making Rudolf fit the image of a violent, lustful, irrational despot that was taking shape during his lifetime. Contemporary sources indicate it was feared that accusations of disease and the diagnosis of melancholy would be used by Rudolf's enemies and rivals to malign the emperor and gain advantage. This is exactly what happened.

While much of Rudolf II's activity might be related to his personality, in the absence of many direct sources and reliance on second-hand reports of him, it is difficult to determine how his personality affected his actions, and for that matter what his intentions really were. Given the nature of early modern princely rule, Rudolf's attitudes can be related instead to his ancestry and upbringing and the standards they embodied. Rudolf's apparent pursuit of what seem to be personal interests corresponds to contemporary conceptions of rulership. While one prominent historian dismissed the problem of connecting collecting and patronage of art and science to politics as overly theoretical, anachronistic and ideologically motivated,[63] the connection of patronage and collecting with concerns of power, politics and religion is evident and is emphasized in this book. The visual arts and the sciences, including those called 'occult', provided more than pastimes, or forms of entertainment, resources for contemplation and signs of curiosity, although they may also have been these things too. They do not furnish evidence for personal aberrations, nor can they be treated simply as expressions of the spirit of the times or of the place, nor treated in relation to 'Mannerism' or 'the Baroque' (as Evans did), characterizations that critics were already regarding as 'rather second-hand generalizations' and questioning five decades ago.[64] Long regarded as irrelevant to, distractions from or even antithetical to concerns with power, politics and religion, Rudolf's interests in the arts and sciences are inextricably connected with them. Understanding how these connections worked is fundamental for any comprehensive biography. Rudolf's personality had many aspects, but it was not schizoid. This book thus offers an account of a crucial question: how Rudolf II's interests and actions intersect with the histories of art, architecture, collecting and with the history of science (including the supposedly occult).

The first chapter plots Rudolf's biography against the key political and religious issues of his time. As titular head of both the House of Habsburg and the Holy Roman Empire, Rudolf II was conscious of his position in Europe and more broadly the world, and pursued similar concerns to his dynastic predecessors. Early experiences at the court of Spain reinforced his appropriation of the imperial ambition and attitudes of his grandfather Charles V, as communicated by Rudolf's uncle, brother-in-law, and first cousin, Philip II of Spain. In contrast with Philip II, Rudolf's father, Maximilian II, who like Rudolf II has been treated as enigmatic, assumed a moderate stance towards religious issues, and hence to political questions. Maximilian II and Rudolf II found themselves in a complicated and much different situation in Central Europe from Philip II. Constraints, challenges and outright opposition created difficulties for them. Maximilian II and Rudolf II attempted to follow a course of action that projected imperial authority and protected the Habsburg lands while securing peace and unity in the Holy Roman Empire – but not exclusively by force of arms or suppression of ideas.

The next chapter deals with the importance of collecting for Rudolf II, treating it not as a personal idiosyncrasy but in a broader context. Rudolf's collecting can be related to a long family tradition and to contemporary princely interests and ideology. Having a *Kunstkammer* and other collections that complemented it were intrinsic to the conduct of diplomacy and politics in the early modern period (the Renaissance). Gift giving, collecting and representative imagery (in various senses of the term) suggest how having collections was important for rulers. Contemporary discussions indicate that the imperial *Kunstkammer* and Rudolf's painting collection had both symbolic and actual importance.

While Rudolf II has long been recognized as one of the great patrons and collectors in European history, opinions differ not only about his involvement with the arts but about the character of works made for him. The third chapter examines his personal involvement and what was made for him. It counters what has not been recognized as a critical commonplace. For example, before Rudolf II, another great patron of the arts, King Manuel of Portugal (r. 1495–1521), was similarly accused at the end of his reign of paying more attention to buildings than to affairs of state.[65] However, there are many reasons why rulers patronized art and architecture. Art and architecture could serve – as did collections – as forms of propaganda. They could mark rulers as exalted. They could otherwise serve as forms of self-presentation. And among other things, they could be used for diplomatic purposes. In short, works of art and architecture were key instruments in the exercise of power. Rudolf's patronage may be compared with that of his predecessors and contemporaries, as a background to reconsidering what may be distinctive about art made for him.

The following chapter addresses Rudolf II's interests in the occult and other sciences. It is true that many practitioners of alchemy, astrology and the Kabbalah did find employment in Prague, but Rudolf II was also actively involved with studies of natural history and astronomy, and these interests often intermingled. Supposedly scientific concerns were expressed in objects with allegorical content and mystical character. In addition, imperial artists made nature studies that not only assisted scholarship in natural history but helped to stimulate the development of new pictorial genres. Mechanics and technology simulating natural processes were implicit in the manufacture of automata. In the end, the knowledge that occult and other sciences delivered was believed to provide sources of power. The ruler possessed singular ability to understand themes in art that correspond to the desire both to seek out and to conceal secrets of nature: these secrets provided keys to power over nature and hence the world. And this is why there was good reason for many rulers, not just Rudolf II, to be interested in these pursuits.

Rudolf's aspiration to mastery of the world reflects one aspect of the global reach of Rudolfine Prague, the subject of the final chapter. Animals, birds, plants and artefacts from all over the world were found at the imperial residence. Diplomacy, trade and armed conflict brought the imperial court into contact with the wider world. Many gifts flowed to Prague, while Rudolf II himself – along with the gifts he gave, the works his artists made and their status – provided models for many rulers and artists. The impact of Prague spread from the Americas to East Asia.

Another book might deal with still more aspects of Rudolf's life and personality.[66] But this one tackles what seem to be central issues in understanding him. Seeking to revise some central impressions of the emperor, this text presents an interpretation of a singular Renaissance life that may offer more general lessons.

ONE

Rudolf II:
Politics and Religion

udolf II was born in Vienna on 18 July 1552, the third of sixteen children; he was the eldest surviving son of Emperor Maximilian II (r. 1564–1576) and Archduchess (and Infanta, Princess of Spain) Maria. His father was the eldest son of Emperor Ferdinand I (r. 1558–1564), and his mother the eldest daughter of Emperor Charles V (r. 1519–1558; r. 1516–1556 as King Charles I of Spain). Rudolf was thus the grandson of two emperors and the son of another.

This chapter summarizes the events of Rudolf II's life, relating his actions to the principles his predecessors set, the political (and religious) pressures he faced, and his own goals and strategies. It begins with the model of Charles V, and then briefly discusses how Ferdinand I transmitted and transmuted similar ideals in mid-sixteenth-century Central Europe. Ferdinand's son and Rudolf's father, Maximilian II, and Charles's son, Philip II, King of Spain and Rudolf's uncle on his mother's side, took different approaches to issues. Though raised at the court of Philip II, whose influence he felt in many ways, Rudolf followed Maximilian II in attempting to consolidate his reign, to secure peace in the empire amid growing tensions, to defend his realms against the Turks, and ultimately to protect his own position. But the middle course that (like Maximilian II) he pursued was not successful in a time of increasing religious and related political antagonisms, and he faced further problems none of his predecessors had to contend with, chief among which were the machinations of family members and their allies that ultimately led to his downfall.

IN 1516 CHARLES SEIZED control of the kingdoms of Castile and Aragon along with their possessions in Italy from his mother, Joanna (Juana), daughter of Ferdinand of Aragon and Isabel of Castile, and became King Charles I of Spain.[1] From his father, Philip the Fair, son of Emperor Maximilian I Habsburg and Mary of Burgundy, he had also inherited Habsburg lands that spread from the Rhine to the Danube in Central Europe and Burgundian holdings that reached from the Low Countries through what is now central France. He became Emperor Charles V in 1519 at the death of Maximilian I. During the first decades of his reign, Hernán Cortés, Francisco Pizarro and other conquistadors conquered extensive territories in the Americas. Habsburg imperial ambitions grew even more when in 1526 Charles's brother Ferdinand became King of Hungary and Bohemia.

The myth of world empire revived.[2] It appeared as if the imperial idea expressed by the 'AEIOU' device of the House of Austria (Habsburg) was being realized. Charles's great-grandfather Emperor Frederick III (r. 1452–1493) had coined this acronym and used it on many objects: it stands for 'All the earth is Österreich's [Austria's] underling' (*Alles Erdreich ist Österreich untertan*) or 'Austria's end is [to rule] over the universe' (*Austriae est imperare orbi universo*).[3] The title 'Catholic king' borne by Spanish monarchs (including Charles V) since Ferdinand and Isabel seemed to become political reality as well. This title carries obvious religious overtones, but as suggested by the meaning of the word 'Catholic' in the belief that the Roman Catholic Church was universal (the pope made similar claims in the secular domain, contesting the emperor as universal monarch), it also posits the existence of a universal monarchy with a religious as well as secular character (as is also implied in the notion of the 'Holy Roman Empire'). Propagandists for Charles V asserted that he incorporated in his person the ideal of the universal monarch. The emperor-king was styled a new Charlemagne, a Christian emperor (Charlemagne was thought to be the first Holy Roman Emperor), or a new Augustus, the emperor who had expanded the Roman Empire and brought it peace after civil wars.[4]

These notions informed Charles's attitudes towards what he felt were his basic obligations. As universal monarch he was to assure the survival of the human community by preserving peace and order in Europe and the wider world. As ruler over the world and protector and defender of the Church, he was to guarantee the existence of civil society leading to the re-establishment of the golden age of peace and prosperity prophesied by the return of Justice with the realm of Augustus. He was tasked, in particular, with maintaining harmony and prosperity within the Holy Roman Empire and protecting lands under Habsburg control. In order to carry out his duties, he could use force when the unity of Christian Europe or the Habsburg lands were threatened.[5]

The Ottoman Turks posed such a threat. They took Constantinople in 1453, putting an end to the Eastern Roman (Christian) Empire of the Byzantines. In the next seven decades they conquered the Levant and Egypt, the northern coast of the Black Sea, and the parts of the Balkans that were not already under their control. During the reign of Sultan Suleiman ('the Magnificent'; r. 1520–1566), Turkish armies swept further across North Africa to Morocco and drove into Europe. In 1526 the Jagiellonian King of Hungary and Bohemia Lajos (Ludvík, Ludwig) II died fighting them at the Battle of Mohács, ending the rule of the Jagiellonian dynasty and precipitating Habsburg accession to the thrones of these large realms. The Turks then gained control over large tracts of historic Hungary, including Buda and Pest, and advanced as far as the walls of Vienna, the imperial residence, which they besieged unsuccessfully in 1529. Turkish threats to the Mediterranean, the Habsburg lands in Central Europe and beyond them to the rest of Central and Western Europe did not cease with this setback: the Habsburgs fought the Ottomans until the mid-eighteenth century.

While Habsburgs and other European Christians were confronting the Ottoman Turks, the unity of Western Christendom shattered. Disagreements had long existed about religious doctrines, especially in the Czech lands. Several dissident sects originated in Bohemia, most notable among them a movement catalysed by Jan Hus in the early fifteenth century that demanded the laity partake along with the clergy in both bread and wine in the central Christian sacrament of communion (Utraquism). In 1517 Martin Luther initiated what became the decisive schism of Christian churches in Central and Northern Europe when he tacked his 95 Theses criticizing practices of the Church of Rome on to the doors of the Castle Church in Wittenberg, Germany. New theological beliefs, confessions and practices arose, and with them calls for change in Christian doctrine and practice. Zwinglians, Anabaptists, Socinians, Unitarians and the Unity of the Czech and Moravian Brethren all came into being. Jean Calvin (Cauvin), in particular, gained many followers: Calvinists were numerous in Germany and elsewhere in Central Europe, especially Hungary. Europe fragmented into Christian confessions that were often antagonistic to each other. The later sixteenth century has consequently been termed an age of confessionalization, a time in which religious camps opposed each other according to their profession of different confessions.[6]

Because of their position as emperors and their role as rulers of lands in East-Central Europe, the Habsburgs had to tackle both sets of problems simultaneously. On the one hand, the Ottoman threat intensified their sense of duty as defenders of Christendom. Several Habsburg emperors from Charles V through to Rudolf II took up this task as if it were a crusade: this is best exemplified by Charles V's assault on Tunis in 1535 and the way it was exploited politically.[7] During the later sixteenth century the Habsburgs managed to hold the Turks in check, most importantly by the victory at the Battle of Lepanto (1571) won by a 'Holy Alliance' headed by the Spanish fleets of Philip II under Don Juan of Austria. It was not, however, until the later seventeenth century that they caused Turkish control over Hungary and the Balkans to recede definitively.

At the same time, several emperors, including both Charles V and Ferdinand I, believed that they had a mission to maintain – or, as did King Philip II of Spain and later Emperors Matthias and Ferdinand II (1578–1637; r. 1620–1637), Rudolf's successors, to restore – the unity of Christianity in response to what they regarded as Protestant heresy. They believed that the Protestants had disrupted the internal peace of the empire, and because of what they regarded as sedition used this as a pretext to wage war against them.[8] Charles V and his brother King (later Emperor) Ferdinand I upheld the Church of Rome and tried to stamp out religious and political disunity in the empire through force of arms. At the Battle of Mühlberg in 1547 Charles V (with Ferdinand I) appeared to have done so when they decisively defeated the Schmalkaldic League of Protestant princes.

Charles V served as a model for Rudolf II, as seen in works of art. For example, the famous Venetian artist Titian painted Charles on horseback to commemorate him as victor at Mülhberg. Titian's equestrian portrait (illus. 3) represents Charles wearing the sash of command and carrying a spear or lance, an ancient Roman symbol of power. His lance also evokes the lance that was supposed to have pierced the side of Jesus, one of the regalia of the Holy Roman Emperor, an object that was regarded as an inalienable possession of the Habsburgs. Charles is shown in the armour that he actually had worn in the battle – it is now displayed

in the new Royal Collections Gallery in Madrid. The presence of
the lance in one version of an engraving of an armoured Rudolf II
wearing a sash and riding on a curvetting horse – a horse standing
on its hind legs – by Sadeler, after a model by Adriaen de Vries
that was possibly for a relief, plays off this depiction of Charles
V (illus. 4).[9] In such images of rulers, the rider's control of a horse
symbolizes the ability to control the world of affairs. Rudolf's
head is uncovered, adorned with a laurel wreath designating him
as victor over the Turkish forces that are seen being routed in

3 Titian, *Charles V at the Battle of Mühlberg*, 1548, oil on canvas.

the engraving. While the scene is purely fictitious as Rudolf never led troops into battle, the portrait type with curvetting horse relates to other equestrian rulers' portraits, and Turks are substituted for Protestants, who were the Habsburgs' enemies over whom Charles triumphed in Titian's painting. It suggests both similarities with Charles V and implicitly a different attitude towards Protestantism.

4 Aegidius Sadeler II, after Adriaen de Vries, *Emperor Rudolf II on Horseback*, 1586–1629, engraving.

Unlike the Turks, the spread of Protestantism in Central and Northern Europe could not be stopped. The imperial forces had already had to rely on support from a Lutheran leader, Duke Maurice (Moritz) of Saxony, at Mühlberg. Maurice was rewarded by having the position of imperial prince-elector transferred to his seat in Dresden from his rival cousins at Wittenberg. But Maurice quickly turned against the Habsburgs. He led a coalition that pushed Charles and Ferdinand I into agreeing to terms that were outlined in the Treaty of Augsburg in 1555. Ferdinand had been put in charge of negotiations for the imperial side and reached a compromise, which was also realized in part through the intervention of Maurice's successor Duke-Elector Augustus, who had spent time at Ferdinand's court when he was young. The provisions of the peace treaty effectively recognized the legality of Lutheranism (but not other Protestant confessions) in the empire. An important proviso established the principle that the ruler of a region could determine its religion.

Ferdinand's handling of negotiations leading to the Treaty of Augsburg demonstrates he could display some flexibility towards Protestants in that he reached a compromise. This approach may be related to the fact that as youths Ferdinand and Charles had learned some of the teachings of the moderate Christian humanist Desiderius Erasmus. But Ferdinand's sense that some of his underlings were committing the affront of *lèse majesté*, as well as what seems to have been his established belief that a ruler could determine his subjects' religion (later established in the Augsburg agreement), led him to respond with force when the Bohemian estates contested his authority. This also occurred in 1547, when the Bohemian estates resisted Ferdinand's attempts to raise monies for Charles V against the Schmalkaldic League. The resistance stemmed from the fact that the population of Bohemia was itself largely not Catholic, and from the Bohemian estates' resistance to granting monies to be used outside the Czech lands.

Ferdinand's reaction to resistance – he saw Bohemians as engaged in a seditious revolt – may also be related to the belief he shared with Charles V that as a ruler he had absolute, unquestionable authority. Ferdinand crushed the uprising and cracked down on freedom of religious practice in Bohemia.[10]

Both within and beyond his own domains Ferdinand also spurred renewal within the Catholic Church. From 1546 to 1563 a church council was held in Trent, a prince-bishopric surrounded by Habsburg-controlled Tyrol, to respond to continuing Protestant challenges. It devised newer Catholic doctrines, which Ferdinand helped to put into effect. Ferdinand also supported the advent into Central Europe of the Jesuits, a new order designed to win back people for the old Church.

Ferdinand became emperor when Charles died in 1558. Nevertheless, after the Habsburgs' realms were split in 1556 when Philip II became King of Spain, the Spanish and 'Austrian' (Central European) branches of the dynasty continued to work in tandem towards achieving common goals, among them the defence of the Catholic Church and the imposition of the provisions of the Council of Trent. However, Ferdinand had to deal with conditions in the Holy Roman Empire that differed from those in Philip's realms. In some regards, these resembled the circumstances in Bohemia that had led to the uprising there. The Augsburg settlement had deliberately ignored the existence of confessional groups among the Protestants other than the Lutherans (including most religious dissenters in Bohemia as well as many others in other parts of Central Europe). All such groups (including Lutherans) continued to press for their rights. Moreover, Protestantism continued to expand in the later sixteenth century. And although his actions in Bohemia demonstrate that Ferdinand had a freer hand in his own domains than he did elsewhere, the wars of the 1540s and 1550s showed that in the end this was not the case in many other parts of the Holy Roman Empire.[11]

With the nomination and subsequent accession of Ferdinand's son Maximilian II to the imperial throne in the 1560s, the hopes Philip II had to succeed to the imperial throne as well as that of Spain were dashed. Philip II's approach to power politics, what has been called his 'grand strategy', also differed from the as yet inchoate version of what has more recently been interpreted as the grand strategy of the (Central European) Habsburgs, certainly from that of Maximilian II, and from that of Rudolf II as well.[12] Philip II was in a much stronger position than his cousins: his vision of empire could be more realistically founded on the claim to be a universal ruler. Philip ruled over possessions in the Low Countries, Franche Comté in what is now France, large regions of Italy (the entire south, Sicily, Sardinia, Lombardy, Mantua, Parma and strongpoints in Tuscany) and huge tracts of the Americas from Chile to Arizona. Through his marriage to Queen Mary (r. 1553–1558), Elizabeth's older half-sister and predecessor, Philip could also claim to be King of England. The Philippines were added to his empire in the 1570s. When Spain annexed Portugal in 1580, it gained complete control of the Iberian Peninsula except for a sliver of Navarre. Even if it did not do so in practice, Spain could claim to rule over Portugal's overseas empire, which comprised Brazil as well as lands that stretched from Africa through India, Southeast Asia and Indonesia to Macao. The sun truly never set on Philip II's empire.[13]

Secure in his Iberian heartland, Philip could draw on vast resources in the defence of his realms. Although he still had to appeal for financial support to the Cortes, and to the individual assemblies of the constituent kingdoms of Spain, he enjoyed direct access to the vast wealth of the Americas. Spanish monarchs from Charles V onwards took advantage of the unparalleled discovery of silver in 1545 in Potosí, Upper Peru (now Bolivia), as they later did of silver from mines in New Spain (Mexico). Even though the importation of silver led to widespread inflation that a famous interpretation holds to have hastened the economic decline of Spain, silver from the New World provided a major source of funding both for peaceful activities such as Philip II's extensive building projects and collecting, and for equipping the fleets and raising the armies that the king (and his successors) sent against their enemies.[14] Like Charles V, Philip projected force outwards to fight the Turks and to crush Protestantism. He acted vigorously in what he regarded as his domains – Spain and Portugal, the Low Countries, and against England.

The Central European Habsburgs did not possess such extraordinary resources and did not enjoy such freedom to act. To be sure, silver mines in Bohemia lay directly in royal hands, but these were far surpassed by silver flowing from the Western Hemisphere. And while Emperor Ferdinand could also call on revenues from silver mines in Tyrol, he granted the Tyrol with its wealth to his second son, Archduke Ferdinand (1529–1595), not to Maximilian II (and hence not by immediate succession to Rudolf): the Tyrol remained separate from the other hereditary Austrian lands until 1809. Another major source of revenue, the salt mines in present-day Austria near Salzburg (salt was important for the preservation of food), was located in lands ruled by the Prince-Archbishop of Salzburg, and they also were not absorbed into Austria until 1816. Otherwise, the hereditary lands of Upper and Lower Austria (Austria above and below the river Enns) over which Maximilian II (and then Rudolf II) did have dominion were largely agricultural; they could be taxed either directly or through forced labour, but only to a limited extent until the prospect of peasant insurrection arose – fourteen such revolts occurred in Upper Austria during the sixteenth century. (Rudolf II learned his lesson: he ordered that unpaid work for peasants be limited to fourteen days per year.) The kingdoms of Bohemia and Hungary (particularly Upper Hungary, modern Slovakia) had, as noted, substantial mineral resources, but these lands were both elected monarchies (until the 1620s in the former case) with their own assemblies. In the Czech lands (and in Hungary) Maximilian II and later Rudolf II thus had to make appeals for monies to the general Bohemian Landtag (Sněm) as well as to the local diets of Bohemia, Moravia, Silesia and Lusatia.

Furthermore, during the reigns of Maximilian II and Rudolf II, religious dissent remained rife in the lands of Central Europe, and religious differences exacerbated the demands of the local estates from the Habsburg point of view. At the end of the sixteenth century an estimated 90 per cent of the population of Lower and Upper Austria was Protestant; large majorities of non-Catholics, perhaps as many as 75 per cent, were also found in the Czech lands and in royal Hungary (meaning the parts of Croatia, Slovakia and cis-Danubian Hungary remaining under Habsburg rule). In order to attain his ends Maximilian II had to make (or seem to make) concessions to local diets, which chiefly involved issues concerning religion. To assure Rudolf's accession to the Bohemian crown in 1575, for instance, he had to appear to accept a joint religious confession (the so-called Bohemian Confession) that allowed freedom of religious practice to Catholics, Utraquists and the Bohemian Brethren. He did not, however, sign the document: only in 1609 in seeking the estates' support to avoid being deposed as King of Bohemia did Rudolf grant a Letter of Majesty that permitted religious freedom there.

During the late sixteenth and early seventeenth centuries the Habsburgs faced several more difficulties within the Holy Roman Empire. Although some judicial agency was officially reserved to the emperor, by Maximilian II's and especially Rudolf II's time the imperial throne had become a position to which it has been said honour and prestige were attached more than authority.[15] To be elected, to retain rule and to defend the empire (and their own crown lands) against external enemies like the Turks required the Habsburgs to have troops and allies. Gaining friends and allies involved bribery, making and receiving gifts, and patronizing works of art or wonders to impress others. To carry out these ends meant having substantial financial resources. Waging war in the sixteenth century necessitated building fortifications as well as assembling fleets and raising armies, and this – along with the maintenance of an appropriately magnificent court – called for significant financing, which the Habsburgs did not have on their own. To obtain funds needed for their ends, the Habsburg emperors appealed to the Imperial Diet, the Reichstag, the assembly of the German polities, for special taxes that were primarily to be used in defence against the Turks, but often provided a ruse to raise monies that were diverted to other purposes like paying court painters.[16] Rudolf's attendance at a Reichstag meeting is a major reason why he was not at his father's side when Maximilian II died in 1576. Later Rudolf II himself repeatedly called for such assemblies: in 1582, 1594, 1598, 1603 and 1608.

Another potential problem lay in the electoral college of princes that existed to select the emperor. From the mid-sixteenth century it consisted of three electors who were Catholic (the Archbishops of Cologne, Mainz and Trier) and three who were Protestant (the Margrave of Brandenburg, the Count Palatine of the Rhine and the Duke of Saxony). The King of Bohemia – a position the Habsburgs occupied since 1526 – held a key vote. Should any elector change his religion, the status quo would be upset. Significantly, Duke-Elector Augustus of Saxony, who had helped to effect the Treaty of Augsburg, broke Protestant ranks by supporting Maximilian II's election as emperor, as he did that of Rudolf II.

Friendship with the Saxon electors, starting with Elector Augustus – who had been a close associate of Maximilian II since childhood and maintained what has been described as a good, almost paternal relation to Rudolf II[17] – thus long constituted a key element in Habsburg strategy, for which there were further grounds. While Switzerland to the west and the lands ruled by the Spanish Habsburgs to the south shielded them in these directions, Saxony not only provided a key vote in the electoral college but helped to shield Austrian Habsburg possessions to the north-west. But threats remained to the east, which in part explains Habsburg efforts to obtain the throne of Poland. (Poland stood in the way of the expansion of both the Turks and Muscovy: accommodation was made with both Poland and Muscovy under Rudolf II.) In 1575 Maximilian II was one of the candidates for the throne of Poland, as was his son Archduke Maximilian III in the 1580s.[18] Maximilian II's resistance to the Turks, most pronounced in 1566, can also be understood as a defence of the southeastern frontier of his realms.

During the later sixteenth century, gaining financial support, succeeding to royal and imperial thrones, assuring peace in the Holy Roman Empire as well as in their own lands and protecting these lands therefore called for prudent behaviour by the Habsburgs in dealing with the complicated religious and interrelated political questions of Central Europe. Restraint, caution and diplomatic agility were called for in a world of polarized religious and political camps,

These conditions help to explain why Maximilian II did not openly reveal his opinions about religion when he became King of Bohemia from 1562, of Hungary from 1563 and emperor in 1564. He gave no public sign of disloyalty to the Roman Church, and there is no doubt about Maximilian's general commitment to Christianity and his opposition to non-Christian religions. Though desire to protect his own lands may also have been a factor, he sent troops against the Turks in 1566, and in 1571 supported the Holy League that fought the Battle of Lepanto. But privately his participation in the Catholic rite of confession was sporadic, as was his attendance at Mass, and he refused the last rites of the Church on his deathbed. Beyond being friendly with Protestant princes like Augustus of Saxony, he allowed the presence at the imperial court of some Lutheran preachers.

Whatever his personal beliefs may have been, it has been argued convincingly that – along with other contemporary rulers like Elector Augustus of Saxony – Maximilian II was concerned with maintaining peace, security and the political unity of the Holy Roman Empire. Maximilian tried to stand above the fray in religious matters. He never clearly supported the dynastic interests of Philip II in suppressing Protestantism in the Low Countries, which formally belonged to the empire. Such support would have been inimical to peace and could (and did eventually) lead to the independence of the United Provinces of the (northern) Netherlands and the consequent dissolution of their link to the empire. Maximilian's position has been described as Compromise Catholicism, and his approach as irenic.[19] In any case his policies seem to have been successful, because sustained warfare was avoided during his reign (except in the Netherlands, which Philip II controlled and where he continued to send armies and fleets). The coherence of the empire was preserved.[20]

These goals became increasingly difficult to attain as the rival confessional camps became ever more militant with the passage of time: Rudolf II faced even more problematic conditions than Maximilian II. Like his father, Rudolf II seems to have tried to take a lofty position and not to commit himself to either side. However, Rudolf's moderate approach conflicted with that of Philip II, who pursued a militant policy that complemented the Inquisition's efforts to suppress beliefs and practices deemed heretical. Rudolf had grown up at Philip's court, and Philip directly and indirectly pressured him to follow this course.

Conflicts over Rudolf's upbringing reveal the differences between Maximilian II and Philip II. Like those contemporary critics who suspected Maximilian II of being crypto-Lutheran, Philip had misgivings about Maximilian's commitment to the

Catholic cause. Philip's sister Mary, Maximilian's devout wife (and Rudolf's mother), was an outspoken proponent of pro-Catholic and pro-papal policies, which she openly advanced at the imperial court during both Maximilian's and Rudolf's reigns.[21] Philip and Mary became determined that Maximilian's successor to the imperial throne should be a firm partisan of the Church of Rome. Rudolf and his brother Ernst spent their first years at the imperial court, but in 1561 Philip began to importune Maximilian to send his oldest sons to be educated in Spain. Despite his initial resistance, and perhaps also to placate Philip, whose aspirations to the imperial title had been thwarted in 1562 when Maximilian was designated imperial successor by being crowned King of the Romans (of Germany), in 1563 Maximilian II finally agreed.

In March 1564 the eleven-year-old Archduke Rudolf arrived in Spain with Archduke Ernst. There they were to spend the next seven formative years of their late childhood, adolescence and early adulthood. Philip II kept them close, receiving them in private every day they resided at court. The young princes' formation as religious Catholics was closely supervised. Rudolf's notebooks and letters from Spain, some of the few directly personal surviving sources on his life, also indicate that the archdukes received a humanistic education – they learned Latin, Greek and the classic literature written in these ancient languages. Rudolf's command of languages, like Maximilian's, was later noted: he spoke French, Spanish, German, Italian and some Czech in addition to the ancient languages.

Rudolf could have observed Philip's conduct of affairs of state during a period that was crucial in Spanish religious and political history. He would have known how Philip instituted the provisions of the Council of Trent in his lands, how he sought to stamp out what he considered to be heresy. The young princes would have directly witnessed how the king and the Inquisition tried to extirpate even moderate Erasmian impulses and to eradicate any supposed backsliders among numerous Spanish converts from Judaism and Islam. Rudolf and Ernst were, for instance, sent to observe how these policies were implemented: they had to witness an *auto da fe*, a burning at the stake.[22]

Rudolf II and Ernst would also have learned how Philip II carried out his 'crusades' with a 'messianic vision'.[23] They would have known how from 1568 to 1571 the king put down an uprising of Moriscos (former Muslims and their descendants) that his repressive policies had provoked. They could have learned how in the same years Spanish forces and fleets were being mustered for war against the Turks, leading to the Battle of Lepanto in 1571. Since they belonged to the close entourage of the court, the young archdukes would also have seen how Philip handled religious dissent in the Low Countries as it grew from 1564. In 1565 Rudolf would no doubt have witnessed the visit to the Spanish court by Lamoral, Count Egmont: Egmont came to plead with Philip against imposing the Inquisition in the Low Countries. But his intercession was in vain, and despite their moderate position and evident respect for the crown, Counts Hoorn and Egmont were beheaded as rebels in Brussels in 1568. This was one of the causes of the revolt in the Low Countries, which Philip II tried unsuccessfully to quell throughout the rest of his long reign. Nominally King of England through his marriage to Queen Mary, Philip was similarly committed to reinstituting Catholicism in England when her half-sister, Elizabeth I, succeeded to the throne in 1558. His antagonism to Elizabeth's England and desire to win the country back to the Roman faith eventually led him to dispatch the ill-fated Spanish Armada thirty years later.

Philip's handling of affairs of state and religion would have familiarized the young archdukes with attitudes that modern critics have called ruthless. Contemporaries might have applied another less anachronistic name to them: Machiavellian. In *The Prince*

Niccolò Machiavelli had famously proposed that 'it is better to be feared than to be loved, if you cannot have both.' Philip might well have seemed to put this policy into practice. Even though *The Prince*, which was first published in 1532, was placed on the Index of Books forbidden by the Catholic Church in 1559, Machiavelli's works were known at the Spanish court. The library of the Escorial contained copies that belonged to Philip II (the books have his binding), and even if they are marked with censuring notes, this indicates they were read.[24]

While Machiavellism was much discussed at the time and applied to various rulers, another political theory fits Philip even better: *prudentia política* or political prudence. This theory was, moreover, openly developed in Central Europe by Jakob Bornitz, a Silesian in imperial service under Rudolf II.[25] According to the general notion, policies that seemed to be severe but were carried out with pious intent like those meant to maintain the Church and the state were not Machiavellian. They were prudent. An epithet by which Philip II is often known — the prudent king — is apposite here. Prudence has been used to describe the deliberate behaviour which characterized Philip's decision making — a process that often infuriated ambassadors or others who wished to have quick decisions made, and that some historians have called lethargic — much as they have described Rudolf's behaviour similarly, and for similar reasons.[26] But prudence, and what it meant as far as delaying decisions and putting off importuning ambassadors is concerned, was even more needed in Central Europe, as previously remarked.

Philip's II's prudence constituted one aspect of his approach to kingship. Another was his sense of the unimpeachable dignity of the monarch. This attitude (which lay behind his and other rulers' comprehension of *lèse majesté*) followed that of his father, Charles V. It may also be associated with an approach to rulership transmitted through the Habsburgs' Burgundian heritage.

Charles V had introduced Burgundian court ceremonial and attire into mid-sixteenth-century Spain while Ferdinand I was introducing them into Central Europe. Rudolf II would have observed directly how this tradition was developed in Philip II's Spain. The Spanish monarch protected himself by a mass of lower personnel who were called upon for services. Sumptuous jewellery and clothing, elaborate carpets, baldachins, steps and platforms, various levels of genuflection and bowing, and terms of

5 Sofonisba Anguissola, *Philip II*, 1564–73, oil on canvas.

address 'set rulers off as a special order of humanity'.[27] This was made clearly visible in the adoption by the Spanish court of black attire with tight tunics, culottes and waistcoats for formal dress, and capes that emulated Burgundian dress of a century earlier.

One of the best known portraits of Philip II by noted artist Sofonisba Anguissola – completed 1573 but originating in 1564 when Rudolf had recently arrived in Spain – gives a good impression of how this affected the appearance of the king (illus. 5).[28] Seated in a chair that might well have functioned like a throne, Philip is dressed in a black tunic and cape, which to judge from its sheen may be made of satin or silk. Their deeply saturated colour is striking, as black was the most difficult colour to dye. White cuffs and collar, probably of expensive Flemish manufacture and themselves status signs, set off the black. The restriction of jewellery to the gold and enamel pendant Philip wears corresponds to a taste related to the 'disornamented' style of architecture created for him. The pendant also has symbolic significance. The sheepskin hanging from the chord indicates that it is the device of the Golden Fleece: this is the most exclusive European chivalric order, which the Burgundian dukes had founded and the Habsburgs adopted as their 'house order'. Philip also has on black headgear. It recalls that while he would have worn a hat, visitors would have had to take off theirs in his presence, just as he could have remained seated while visitors would have had to stand and bow or curtsy. It has been aptly suggested that understated portraits of the king in simple black dress, wearing just the insignia of the Golden Fleece, conveyed the majesty of the king 'not through the outward symbols of kingship but through dignity and "serenity"'.[29]

Making access difficult, particularly at a time when so much hinged on personal decisions (every important paper crossed Philip's desk, and he often signed them 'Yo, el Rey'), may be regarded as what now would be called a winning power play. The king's apparent remoteness seemed to exalt his status and increase the aura of mystery around him. An air of mystery is also redolent of an idea well known in the sixteenth century that Roman writers like Tacitus mentioned and that was applied to rulers from the Middle Ages to the modern age: *mysterium imperii* or mystery of rule. A veil of mystery was believed to enshroud the prince, whose source of power was not immediately apparent. (It was regarded as God-given.) Reformulated during the later Middle Ages, this grounded the absolutist concept of mysteries of state.[30] Instruments by which the state and the person of the ruler were symbolized were considered to be *arcana imperii* or secrets of rule.[31] These symbols could be incorporated in regalia, ceremonies, works of art and other forms of propaganda, including portraits; as we shall discuss in this and subsequent chapters, Rudolf learned these lessons well.

During their stay with Philip, Rudolf II and his siblings were drawn ever closer to the Spanish throne. In July 1568 Don Carlos, Philip II's only legitimate and probably deranged son, died.[32] As Philip was lacking a male heir, Rudolf was promised the hand of the two-year-old Infanta Isabella (1566–1633), who was Philip II's elder daughter (and hence Rudolf's first cousin).[33]

A path seemed to open to the reunification of the Spanish and imperial crowns that Charles V had held simultaneously (although had never administered as such), because it was expected that Rudolf would succeed Maximilian II as emperor and might succeed Philip II as King of Spain as well. Most children of the Spanish king did not survive to adulthood (despite having been married four times, Philip II had only three children who outlived him), and in the early 1580s Philip II's health was often suspect. Until the birth of a male heir, Philip III (1578–1621), and his survival through infancy, Rudolf was in line to inherit Philip II's domains. In 1570 Rudolf's sister Archduchess Anna arrived in Spain to become Philip's fourth (and final) wife. (After she gave birth to Philip III, she died in childbirth two years later.) Rudolf's younger brothers Wenceslas and Albrecht accompanied her to Spain, where they replaced, as it were, Rudolf and Ernst. In May 1571, during his nineteenth year, Rudolf returned to Central Europe.

It seems significant that Rudolf appeared as a personification of Spain at the first major event he attended after his return. This was at a tournament held in Vienna in August 1571 as part of the celebrations of the marriage of his uncle Archduke Karl (Charles) of Inner Austria, one of three inheritors along with Emperor Maximilian II and Archduke Ferdinand 'of the Tyrol' of Ferdinand I's domains. This role seems appropriate, because even though Rudolf later wrote joyfully about his return to Central Europe, he had thoroughly imbibed Spanish models from Philip II's court. These included attitudes, pastimes, dress and demeanour, but as we shall see also significant elements of taste in art, architecture and collecting and some aspects of scientific and alchemical investigations as well. The 'Spanish' traits Rudolf exhibited outwardly may also have corresponded to features of his ingrown character (as Maximilian II seems to have suggested). In any case, Rudolf's Spanish manner was soon observed. His stiffness of gait and gestures, laconic speech (a Venetian ambassador called him 'Rodolfo di poche parole' – Rudolf of few words),[34] and what appeared to be arrogant demeanour were all noted as signs of his Spanish *humores*. Another obvious outward sign is that many later portraits of Rudolf indicate that he had not only adopted but continued to wear attire that resembled Philip's: portraits dateable thirty years later still show Rudolf wearing a similar black hat and black garments with white lace trim, adorned in later years with the Order of the Golden Fleece (after he had received it in a ceremony of 1585; see illus. 1).

In 1571 the Venetian ambassador to the imperial court also offered a physical description of Rudolf II. He was of middling height (for the time – to judge from surviving suits of armour he was probably about 1.6 metres (5 ft 2 in.) tall), and of good corporeal complexion and strength. The ambassador says he displayed his bodily strength to good effect in the jousts and tourneys of the festival. These details are important, because they provide an impression, albeit of Rudolf as a young man, that differs from the characterization of him as a doddering fool, and that relates better to the more favourable physical description given by some later visitors.

Tourneys were among the court entertainments that revived (or continued) chivalric traditions of the Middle Ages, especially relevant for the Habsburgs as the Burgundians had promoted them. The tournaments of 1571 were only the first of many in which Rudolf participated during the decade of the 1570s. Several other such events were held to accompany the ceremonies that constituted Maximilian II's chief preoccupation during the 1570s: to assure Rudolf's succession as ruler (illus. 6).[35]

6 Procession to tournament in Vienna, 1571, detail showing costumes designed by Giuseppe Arcimboldo, hand-coloured woodcut from Heinrich Wirrich, *Ordenliche Beschreibung . . .* (1571).

The coronations of Rudolf II realized Maximilian's ambitions. As noted in the Introduction, Rudolf II was crowned King of Hungary in Bratislava (Pressburg, Poszony) in 1572, King of Bohemia in Prague in 1575, and he was designated heir apparent by being named King of the Romans in the same year. Rudolf's assumption of these titles was celebrated by festivals including tourneys. The coronation ceremonies invested him with authority, while their symbolism and that of the tournaments as well as the objects used in the coronations indicate their ideological underpinnings.[36] The ceremonials of coronation followed regulations of the Roman Pontifical, a book of liturgical rites, and thus had a sacramental aspect. Like his predecessors and successors, Rudolf was anointed king with sanctified oil. In the monarchical theory of the time, acts of unction involved in coronation may again be related to the notion of *mysterium imperii* (mystery of rule): *mysterium imperii* here parallels the idea of *mysterium fidei* (mystery of faith), the foundation of Catholic belief, with which it became intertwined in philosophies of kingship. *Mysterium fidei* are the words uttered at the key moment of the Mass when the Body and Blood of Christ were believed to become bread and wine. Like the paten and chalice, the sacred vessels used to hold bread and wine in the Mass, or like relics of saints, the crowns bore a holy aura. The royal crown of St Stephen of Hungary (called the visible crown, to distinguish it from the idea of the lands of the crown) has long been believed to be a sacred relic of this royal saint; that of the Holy Roman Emperor was believed to have belonged to an emperor who was also canonized as a saint, Charlemagne; and that of Bohemia was thought to have belonged to the patron saint of the kingdom, Wenceslas. The crowns of the emperor and of the king were in fact kept in chapels along with other regalia and treated as if they were holy relics. Royal regalia consequently may further be regarded as being *arcana imperii*, in the tradition of the concept as discussed by Tacitus in reference to state secrets and the unaccountable acts of the Roman imperial government.

The ideology of rule that the coronations expressed remained important for Rudolf II, who was not only preoccupied with the expression of imperial and royal dignity at the beginning of his reign but concerned with them his entire life. The production decades later of one of the single most important objects made for the emperor demonstrates how Rudolf continued to believe in and promote imperial ideas through symbolism.[37] This is the personal crown the emperor commissioned from the Antwerp goldsmith Jan Vermeyen, whom he had brought to Prague in 1602 specifically to make it (illus. 7). Because the crowns of Bohemia and the empire were not usually available except for coronations (as suggested, they were kept respectively in a chapel in Prague's St Vitus Cathedral and in a chapel in Nuremberg; that of Hungary was kept shut in an iron box), a personal crown, like those that may have been made for his predecessors, also served a practical purpose (beyond being able to fit the head of the person who wore it). A personal crown could, for example, be used when the ruler attended a meeting of the estates of the empire, the Imperial Diet (or Reichstag), as Rudolf II did in 1582 and 1594. A miniature by Joris Hoefnagel suggests such a meeting in ideal form. It depicts the emperor with the college of imperial prince-electors: all sit wearing their respective crowns, the electors with their hats, Rudolf with his personal crown (illus. 8).

The design of Rudolf II's personal crown is full of symbolism. The form of the crown resembles that seen in (perhaps idealized) portraits of Rudolf's predecessors. It consists of a circlet capped by panels suggesting a mitre and is spanned by a high ring-like arch. The mitre shape evokes the sacred side of the office of (Holy Roman) emperor as a mitre is a bishop's crown. The pearl-encrusted band running from front to back recalls the band on the imperial crown of Charlemagne, with which the Holy Roman

Emperor had been crowned since Ottonian times, because it also has eight pearls. The circlet itself comprises eight lily-like forms, corresponding as well to the number of panels in the crown of Charlemagne. In addition, the lily shapes probably emulate those on the Bohemian crown of St Wenceslas.

These symbolic allusions suggest that the composition of Rudolf's personal crown incorporates several of the crowns,

7 Crown of Emperor Rudolf II, 1602, gold, enamel, diamonds, rubies, spinels, sapphires, pearls, velvet.

literally and metaphorically, that were used in the coronations. Scenes on the three of the four gold reliefs adorning the crown refer to his realms and the coronation ceremonies, while the fourth allegorizes him as victor over the Turks. The reliefs show a scene of the coronation of Rudolf as emperor; a ritual attending

8 Georg (Joris) Hoefnagel, *Rudolf II and Electors*, miniature from Georg Bocskay, *Schriftmusterbuch*, c. 1571–94.

the Bohemian coronation; the king's progression through Prague
on the way to or from St Vitus's Cathedral where he was crowned;
and part of the royal Hungarian coronation, when Rudolf as
Hungarian king rode up a hill in each of four directions while
waving his sword to suggest he would preserve and extend the
lands of Hungary. The fourth, allegorical panel represents Rudolf
being crowned as victor over the Ottoman Turks, who are symbolized by the quivers, curved bows, turban and war club at his
feet. Rudolf's crown retained an iconic status that lasted long
after it ceased to bear any personal references to him: his Habsburg
successors as emperor used it as their personal crown. After the
Holy Roman Empire itself was dissolved in 1806, the crown
served as the official crown of the Austrian Empire until that
entity too was dissolved in 1918.[38]

The coronation ceremonies, the individual crowns and their
symbolism all promoted the idea that the title of Holy Roman
Emperor announces itself: the crowned monarch is a sacred
ruler. The inclusion of a mitre emulating the form of a bishop's
crown suggests the emperor was invested with ultimate authority:
he rules by God-given right, according to the theory of divine
right of kings shared by many premodern European rulers. The
combination of sacred and secular, Christian and Roman, in the
ceremony, crowns and imperial title further proclaim that as head
of the empire the emperor was like the pontiff, the Bishop of
Rome, who as pope claimed to be head of a universal church. This
claim suggests that Rudolf had thoroughly assimilated political
doctrines associated with the ideas of universal monarchy and
world empire.

The design of Rudolf's crown may moreover be related to
what may be called a competition of crowns. The Ottoman
sultans also claimed that they had universal authority: Suleiman
('the Magnificent') had had his own pearl- and jewel-encrusted
crown-helmet made in Venice to express this claim. It had four

tiers of circlets, one more than the pope's tiara, and it was carried like a relic on the Turkish campaign against Vienna in 1529. As a sultan did not normally wear a crown, its creation for Suleiman may be regarded as having a propagandistic purpose. To respond to such a claim and present an object that served to counter this propaganda, as Rudolf was a rival and enemy of the Ottoman sultan, no doubt provided other reasons why the Habsburg ruler had his crown made.[39]

To be sure, such claims – which were expressed in many ways throughout Rudolf's long reign – are not the same as reality, as was to prove all too true for Rudolf II. Like the Turks, many other European rulers contested his monopoly on imperial authority and power. While the institution of the Holy Roman Empire literally proclaimed continuity with the Roman Empire as a sanctified (Christian) realm, other European rulers maintained that the transference of the seat of empire (*translatio imperii*) had not been passed from the empires of the East to the Greeks (under Alexander) to the Romans and then to the Habsburgs as Holy Roman Emperors: they asserted that empire had been passed to other nations such as France and their rulers. The kings of France and other European sovereigns asserted accordingly that their authority was absolute, that they too ruled by divine right, that they served like the pope as vicars of God on earth – and that they thus had the right to control the Church within their domains. The Russian tsars also adopted a title derived from that of Caesar: they asserted that after the fall of Rome and Constantinople, Moscow was the Third Rome.

These counterclaims provide a reminder that the Russian, French, English and other monarchies could pose threats to the Habsburgs. Charles V and Philip II were embroiled in conflicts with the French, who intrigued with the Turks against them: during the period of Rudolf's reign, only the French wars of religion somewhat diminished this threat. In addition, the Turks,

Protestant antagonists, and in general the particularistic interests
of German princes, who also made claims to rule as sovereigns
over their own individual polities, threatened the continuing
existence and coherence of the Holy Roman Empire (as well as
of Hungary, Bohemia and the Austrian heartland).

Rudolf adopted a stance informed by imperial ideology, and
in the face of real and potential challenges took his position as
emperor extremely seriously. This attitude provides a context for
interpreting his involvement in major events at the start of his
reign. Solemn funeral ceremonies were held for Maximilian II
in Prague and Vienna. They marked the transition of power and
authority, which was further emphasized by Rudolf II's embar-
kation on royal progresses to major cities in his realms. In 1576
and 1577 the new ruler travelled to and was greeted by processions
and triumphal arches in entries into Olomouc, Wrocław (Breslau),
Bautzen (all 'capital' cities of the Czech lands: respectively,
Moravia, Silesia and Lusatia) and Vienna. Involving musicians
and artists, these events belonged to a tradition of celebration
of the entry of a ruler into a city that stemmed from the Low
Countries, where the Burgundians had initiated such progresses
and Spanish and Austrian Habsburgs adapted them.[40] Royal
progresses and entries, conducted by monarchs in Britain, France,
Poland and elsewhere, were not simply merely matters of show.[41]
When he entered cities in his domains, Rudolf II would have
received the homage of the estates of the regions he was visiting.
These celebratory acts of commemoration and fealty contributed
to the process of consolidation of his reign, the demonstration
that rule – imperium – had passed on to him.[42]

Rudolf II was thus hardly inactive at the beginning of his
reign. Not only did he go on progresses as a part of his traditional
duties, but he engaged in tournaments not specifically related
to them and participated in hunts and ball games. These were
entertainments in which nobles and rulers throughout Europe

participated. Referring to older sources, some of which can be verified, the famous seventeenth-century Bohemian Jesuit historian Bohuslav Balbin, for example, declared that 'in the first years of his Empire no occupation of Emperor Rudolf was more frequent or pleased him [more] than tourneys.'[43] Balbin adds that such events took place every year. Rudolf is documented as participating in jousts and other forms of tournaments in Prague in 1578 and 1579. These events were held for celebrations of the marriage of important Bohemian aristocrats and court officials, and Rudolf spent extensive sums on them. In addition, in January 1579 he led a procession of horse-drawn sleighs in which he is said to have delighted. Costumes and the apparatus for these last events were both designed by Arcimboldo, from whose hand such drawings exist. In July 1579 Rudolf is also documented as having participated in a tournament for which Prince Ferdinand of Bavaria (1550–1608) and Ludovico Colloredo, a court chamberlain, served as officials: in it he appeared on a triumphal chariot pulled by two swans with two personages appearing as Venus and Cupid.[44] Tournaments like hunts were, moreover, of a public nature and were used as parts of festivals that the Habsburgs and other rulers utilized for propaganda purposes.[45]

Rudolf continued to participate in public progresses, tournaments, banquets and other celebrations well into the 1580s and beyond. He went on royal progresses and was greeted by elaborate entries when he attended an Imperial Diet at Augsburg in 1582 and one at Regensburg in 1594. In 1584 Rudolf invited several imperial princes to Prague, where he held a banquet for them on 21 September.[46] In 1585 a meeting of the Order of the Golden Fleece took place in Prague where the emperor, Archduke Ernst and Archduke Charles were all inducted into the order. Its formal ceremonies had a quasi-sacral character like coronations, and banquets and tournaments accompanied them. Printed descriptions and pseudo-manuscripts made up like medieval tournament rolls were produced to celebrate the events.[47] Another ceremony of the Golden Fleece occurred in June 1597; Rudolf also attended yet another tournament in Vienna the same year.[48] There is evidence for tournaments, ballets and masquerades held at the imperial court in 1581, 1585, 1597 and 1604.[49] It should also be emphasized that these events occurred during periods when Rudolf was supposed to have shut himself off from the world or been ill. Three more imperial diets met during his reign, a number that amounts to the entire total of diets held during the reigns of his three successors, none of whom attended such meetings. All this further belies the impression that Rudolf was inactive.

There is also little evidence to support the idea that Rudolf neglected affairs of state as more narrowly conceived during the first three decades of his reign. In November 1577 he promulgated a *Polizeiordnung* that prescribed laws for civil conduct in his realms.[50] He foresaw measures to protect and increase trade and to encourage mining, and expanded a network of roads.[51] Sources demonstrate that he wrote on many documents that he diligently read, corrected, changed and improved. While not controlling all papers pertaining to affairs of state as it seems Philip II tried to do, a recent assessment says that he ruled competently and even energetically, at least until 1600, and was engaged in affairs of state and exhibited political cunning in delaying responses thereafter.[52]

Delays in the execution of orders and complaints that he was difficult to access can be laid in part to the administrators who served him, although this is a matter of debate. What especially in Central European circumstances might be regarded as an effective tactic may rather account for this behaviour. In a confessionally and politically fractious environment where every decision had profound repercussions, where information trickled in unreliably, and where imperial finances were perpetually strapped, procrastination had its virtues. Rudolf has rightly been called a master of *weise Zögern* (wise hesitation).[53]

One major concern was continuing strife among Christian confessions. Although, depending on one's confessional affiliation and loyalties, hopes and fears existed that Rudolf II would act like Philip II in religious matters when he became emperor, this proved largely untrue. Rudolf was no religious zealot. It has been said that he was equally turned off by militant Protestants (such as the Calvinists) and Jesuits and mistrusted the papacy.[54] He certainly resembled Maximilian II much more than Philip II in his toleration and indeed cooperation with Protestants. And he was unlike both Maximilian II and Philip II in his treatment of Jews.

Like Maximilian II, Rudolf II seems to have tried to keep matters in balance by receiving Catholic dukes like Ferdinand (in 1579) and Maximilian I of Bavaria (in 1593), while he continued to cultivate close relations with a succession of Saxon electors, all of whom were committed Lutherans. It is, however, unimaginable that a Lutheran lord like Duke Heinrich Julius of Braunschweig-Wolfenbüttel could have served as Philip's advisor and resided in Madrid or become director of his court council, as Heinrich Julius did in Prague, where from 1600 he served the emperor as an advisor and then from 1607 as director of the Geheimrat, the imperial Privy Council. It is even harder to imagine that one of Philip's principal art agents in the Low Countries, where Philip sought to stamp out Calvinism, would have been, as was Rudolf's, the Calvinist Count Simon VI of Lippe.[55]

It is also impossible to imagine that either Maximilian II, who was antagonistic to Jews, or Philip II, who persecuted Jews and *conversos*, would have taken into his closest service and had as a confidant a converted Jew like Philipp Lang, who influenced him from around 1600 until Lang fell into disfavour in 1608. It is also inconceivable that Maximilian or particularly Philip would have allowed, much less fostered, the growth and prosperity of the Jewish population in their realms. In contrast with Maximilian II's and Philip II's antisemitism, Rudolf's toleration of Jews is evident from the beginning of his reign. The Jewish population and its well-being increased in Prague and in many other cities in Bohemia during his reign. There are good reasons to associate these developments with Rudolf II. Already in 1577 the emperor granted a Jewish goldsmith the right to practise freely in Prague. The High Synagogue and Jewish Town Hall were also completed at this time, and in 1591 Rudolf granted the right to build another synagogue to Rabbi Maisel, who was his banker and supplied artworks to him. In 1582 the emperor created an official position for a Jew that freed its holder from special taxes and discriminatory clothing, and allowed him the right to live wherever the court was: this eventually became the position of court Jew. The emperor had an extraordinary meeting with Judah Loew ben Bezalel (the Maharal) in 1592, something neither Philip nor Maximilian would ever have done. He also mediated conflicts between Jews and gentiles, and in 1598 renewed the permit for a Jewish printing house in Prague. These are some of the reasons why the Rudolfine era is considered to have been a golden age for Jews in Bohemia and especially in Prague.[56]

During the early years of Rudolf II's reign, construction and especially decoration of palaces literally embodied the process of consolidation that progresses and tourneys suggest. At first, Rudolf had construction and decoration continued and extended in the Vienna Hofburg, which he also planned to fortify. Imperial artists were at work there on what is now known as the Amalienburg, then called the Rudolfstracht. Maximilian II had intended this building as a residence for Rudolf, but Rudolf turned it over to Ernst, who from 1576 was governor (*Staathalter*) of Lower Austria, of which Vienna was the capital.[57] But in 1579 Rudolf suspended work by artists on the interior decoration of what had been one of his father's chief projects, the Neugebäude outside Vienna, on which work had continued, because he had another place of residence in mind.[58]

Rudolf II does not at first seem to have chosen a fixed residence: the royal progresses suggest that, like many early monarchs, he might have led a peripatetic existence. However, during the later 1570s his eyes turned to Prague. Charles IV of Luxembourg had preceded him in making Prague the imperial capital in addition to its role as capital of Bohemia. This fourteenth-century monarch had founded a university in Prague, arranged for it to become an archbishopric, and made several improvements and extensions to the royal palace. Charles's Jagiellonian successors and Rudolf's Habsburg predecessors in Prague had enlarged them, making Prague Castle arguably a much more sumptuous residence than what Vienna had to offer at the time of Rudolf's accession. Prague was also a much bigger and livelier city than Vienna, and it lay at several crossroads of trade. And as the need to fortify the Vienna Hofburg suggests, Prague was further away and hence safer from the Turks. Finally, in 1583 Rudolf spoke about Prague Castle's cheerful, seasonable situation and its clean air.[59]

By 1583 Rudolf had established his residence in Prague. He had previously given an order to refurbish the interior of the so-called Summer House in the Royal Palace on the Hradčany, and work on construction and connection of the Summer House to the rest of the palace within the castle went on until circa 1585.[60] Around this time he also had work done on the decoration and construction of a room in the White Tower in the palace. Decoration, construction and maintenance of the court were probably among the reasons why in 1582 Rudolf might have been seeking funding from a Reichstag in addition to those monies he could obtain from the Bohemian estates. Whatever the case may be, except for attending imperial or royal meetings, ceremonies or visiting country retreats, Rudolf II remained in Prague for much of the rest of his reign.

Large-scale planning and construction of additions to
Prague Castle started anew in 1588 and continued through the
rest of his reign. This contradicts an older view that Rudolf II
was not concerned with architecture.[61] While his attention
seems at first to have involved designs for interiors, he also had
many new buildings constructed. This misunderstanding of
Rudolf's interest in architecture is important to counter, because
it forms part of a larger misinterpretation. Much as it is believed
that the emperor did not concern himself with external signs of
splendour like architecture, it has been supposed that an overview of sixteenth- and seventeenth-century court culture failed
to include Rudolf II because demonstration of splendour as a sign
of power in the forms of festivals, entries and royal progresses is
a model that does not apply to him.[62] But they do – as discussed
here, Rudolf was much involved with such forms: representation,
as a demonstration of power, splendour and importance, was a
major motivation for them, and as later chapters will show, also
for his collecting and patronage. Certainly, his efforts in palace
building and decoration may be regarded as representational in
the sense of providing a place for and expressing royal majesty.
This mistake about architecture relates again to the legend that
Rudolf was a recluse – a legend that evidence presented in this
chapter contradicts.

Consolidation also involved shoring up alliances. In 1566
Maximilian II had decreed that the title of Duke of Saxony be
granted to Johann Wilhelm of Saxe-Weimar, and that the lands
ruled by separate lines of the (Ernestine branch) of the Wettin
dynasty be unified in his person. Rudolf II reached an agreement
on 20 April 1579 in which Elector Augustus repeated this
Erbvereinigung or *Erbvertrag*, as the constitutional law of the Holy
Roman Empire calls this form of hereditary unification.[63] This
agreement applied to Augustus's own Albertine branch of the
Wettins, not to the Ernestine branch as in the earlier decree: it

unified the lands of Albertine Saxony under his rule, and by
being cloaked as an *Erbvereinigung* tacitly transferred the official
title from the Ernestines to the Albertines represented by
Augustus and his line. Another provision of the treaty established
mutual military aid between the emperor and the elector in
times of war. This is what Rudolf II gained in exchange for the
benefits to Augustus, suggesting that the emperor was not only
continuing the Habsburgs' alliance with Saxony, but including
an important military provision. Rudolf was thus continuing
the long-standing strategy of military cooperation with the
Saxons that had been pursued by Maximilian II, Ferdinand and
Charles V.

Other events that occurred during the earlier years of Rudolf's
reign, including the installation of Catholic advisors and administrators and interactions with the estates of Lower Austria, may
be interpreted better as pertaining to his consolidation of authority than as simple implementations of the Catholic Counter-
Reformation. When Rudolf II appointed Adam Dietrichstein
and Wolfgang von Rumpf to important advisory positions, he was
calling on men who had accompanied him to Spain and whom
he knew well, not because they were devout Catholics. Similarly,
Paulus Sixtus Trautson was appointed because he was a competent
administrator, not because he was Catholic.[64] Archduke Ernst,
who had been entrusted with administering Lower Austria, and
then Bishop Melchior Klesl seem to have been rough in dealings
with Protestants in Lower (and later in Upper) Austria, but not
Rudolf II himself: the emperor was not directly in charge there.[65]
Rudolf's close relations with the Lutheran Saxon electors further
illuminate the issue. A reasonable inference is that, like Duke-
Elector Augustus, the emperor was committed to upholding the
principles of the Augsburg settlement: because the Austrian
estates had overstepped agreements with Maximilian II and with
Rudolf II and had acted aggressively in making their claims,

Rudolf was provoked into thinking that they were challenging the terms of the treaty and were being disrespectful, even guilty of *lèse majesté*.[66]

Irregardless, the distinction between Rudolf II's and Philip II's way of treating Protestants is manifest in their different approaches to religious differences in the Low Countries. The Spanish king believed Netherlandish Protestants had not only committed *lèse majesté* but fostered heresy. But contrary to the belief some historians have expressed that the emperor was an advocate of the Counter-Reformation, as Archdukes Ernst and Matthias seem to have been, Rudolf did not cooperate with Philip in instrumenting Spanish policies of religious suppression in the Low Countries. In fact, he forced Philip to negotiate with the Protestant rebels at an (unsuccessful) peace conference in 1579. This effort disrupted the previously close collaboration between the Spanish and Austrian Habsburgs, and the rulers of Spain and the empire did not closely collaborate until after Rudolf's death.[67]

In addition to his dealings with Jews, his relations with Saxony, and his attempts to promote peace in the Netherlands, by circa 1580 there were good reasons to suggest that Rudolf was deviating from orthodox Catholic and Spanish concerns. This may explain why the first Spanish ambassador to Rudolf's court, Juan de Borja, misrepresented Rudolf's supposed inactivity and preference for ball games over politics, which his involvement in political affairs belies. It may also explain why Spanish envoys (and others in their camp) emphasized Rudolf's illnesses circa 1580. In any case, in 1581 the dowager empress Maria began openly to express her worries about the delays Rudolf was creating in becoming betrothed to Infanta Isabel, the daughter of Philip II. It is telling that the imperial ambassador in Spain, Hans Khevenhüller, who was closely connected to Maria, blamed the delay in betrothing Isabel on Rudolf's courtiers, chiefly Wolfgang von Rumpf, and later on Count Trautson. He wrote that Rumpf took hold of the management of the business of the entire empire: Rumpf distracted the emperor from the tasks of government through recreations and diversions such as alchemy, painting, sculpture and other things of this kind.[68]

Along with Borja's mention of ball games, this claim seems to be one of the first expressions of the black legend that Rudolf neglected the affairs of state for other supposedly trivial pursuits. The absurdity of claiming that Rumpf distracted Rudolf with art and science, which moreover runs against other assertions that Rudolf's own inclinations and interests led him to these pursuits, should be obvious. As would have been very well known by anyone at the Spanish court, Philip II was himself interested in the same things, not only in art but in alchemy and astrology.[69] This excuse was often repeated, as we have seen: the Tuscan ambassador Eremita also said that Rudolf was distracted by art and science, while Eremita contradicted himself in remarking that Rudolf continued to exercise sharp judgement, just as envoys cloaked their failures in accusations about Rudolf's melancholy and indolence.

In 1582–3 what is now called 'science' did, however, function as a component of imperial politics and propaganda. In October 1582 Pope Gregory XIII promulgated the adaptation of a new calendar to replace the ancient Julian calendar that had made the calculation of Easter difficult if not impossible. In 1583 Rudolf II had the Gregorian calendar decreed as the official calendar in the Holy Roman Empire (as well as Bohemia). This decree and other imperial publications that propagated the calendar did not mention religious considerations or their source in the papacy, but emphasized their scientific accomplishment and the accuracy involved in calendrical reckoning.[70]

Furthermore, while the question of Rudolf's marriage and succession remained acute throughout his reign, good reasons existed why from the 1570s he would have had little incentive to marry Isabel. With the survival of Philip III, Rudolf's chance of becoming King of Spain declined radically. Beyond keeping marriage in the family, as many Habsburgs did, little would have compelled him to marry his cousin. On the contrary, Rudolf might well have felt that by marrying Philip's daughter he would have subordinated himself to his uncle. In any instance, it does not seem to have been lethargy that held Rudolf back from marrying Isabel, any more than it was lethargy, as some have claimed, that kept Rudolf from offering Philip II effective support for his policies in the Netherlands and the neighbouring German lands.

Rudolf does not seem to have been opposed to marriage per se, but appears to have manipulated it as a tool of diplomacy. He continued to float marital prospects through the 1580s and '90s. After Isabel had been married off to his brother Albrecht in 1599, in the first decade of the seventeenth century, even after Rudolf had passed his fiftieth birthday, he dangled the prospects of marriage before several princely families. From 1603 to 1605 the emperor sent his court painter Hans von Aachen to portray prospective brides in Innsbruck, Turin, Mantua and Modena. The first was his cousin, the granddaughter of the union of the Gonzaga Duke of Mantua to Rudolf's aunt Eleanor of Austria and the daughter of their daughter and his uncle Archduke Ferdinand (of the Tyrol), the second the daughter of the Duke of Savoy, the third another daughter of a later Gonzaga Duke of Mantua, and the fourth a daughter of the Este Duke of Ferrara and Modena. At the same time there was some discussion of Lady Arabella Stuart, a relative of King James of England and Scotland. At various other times in his life matches were rumoured with other candidates, among whom was Marie de' Medici, daughter of the Grand Duke of Tuscany, before she married Henri IV of France in 1600.[71]

Much as Rudolf II would have made difficulties for himself by placing himself firmly in the Spanish camp had he married

Philip II's daughter, marriage to any other potential candidate
would have also indicated where his allegiances lay. This is what
happened when his brothers married an infanta or a Catholic
archduchess, as did Albrecht and Matthias respectively: they
both ended up openly supporting the Catholic cause. Had Rudolf
married one or another Italian princess, he would have disrupted
relations among polities in Italy, where both the Spanish and
Austrian Habsburgs had direct holdings and further interests
as suzerains. It has been said that Rudolf's failure to choose a
wife was a matter of fatal indecision, but it was largely his enemies
who advanced this accusation and used his celibacy to depose him,
as remarked in the Introduction. In reality, almost up to the end
of his life, Rudolf was still contemplating marriage and alluding
to the possibility of potential matches.

What could happen when a politically ill-chosen marriage
occurred was already demonstrated by a crisis that took place
during the early years of Rudolf II's reign, in 1582–3. In 1582 the
Archbishop of Cologne, Gebhard II Truchsess von Waldburg,
converted to Calvinism. This created a crisis because it effected
a possible change of balance of power in the College of Electors.
In 1583 Gebhard married Agnes von Mansfeld-Eisleben and
intended to transform the lands owned by the archbishopric
into a secular territory. But a provision of the Augsburg settlement
prohibited a territory from changing with the conversion of its
ruler. Duke Ernst of Bavaria, a junior member of the pious Catholic
Wittelsbach family who ruled Bavaria, was elected as counter-
bishop. War broke out, and only after five years of armed conflict
was Ernst's victory assured.[72]

This crisis also indicates how conflicts between rival camps
increasingly assumed an armed aspect: the Cologne controversy
is regarded as one of the sparks that led to the conflagration of
the Thirty Years War. The war began following a comparable
change of crowns from one to another confession in 1618 when

the Calvinist Count Palatine Frederick of the Rhine was elected King of Bohemia. This election interrupted Habsburg rule over the Czech lands and endangered their succession as emperor, as it tipped the balance within the College of Electors to the Protestants.[73] The marriage between Frederick and Elizabeth Stuart, daughter of the British king, encouraged the count palatine to make what proved to be a rash decision in accepting the offer of the throne. (In contrast, the moderate and generally reliable pro-Habsburg Lutheran Johann Georg I of Saxony declined the offer.)

Other politico-religious confrontations occurred in the 1580s in the empire. At the Augsburg Reichstag of 1582, Margrave Johann Friedrich, Prince Elector of Brandenburg, attempted to claim his seat and vote in the College of Princes in his position as administrator of the territory of the Archbishopric of Magdeburg.[74] He was rebuffed, as were other Protestant attempts to determine the successor of the Bishop of Strasbourg. Conflict over the Strasbourg succession also began in 1583, sharpened in 1592 when rival bishops were chosen, and ended only in 1604.[75]

As conflicts between Protestants and Catholics in the empire were becoming increasingly open in the 1580s, Rudolf seems to have tried to stay a middle course like the one Maximilian II had pursued. He exhibited an even more tolerant disposition than his father. In 1584 an English writer noted that relative tolerance had allowed peace to be maintained in Poland, Hungary, Bohemia and Germany.[76] Four hundred years later, R.J.W. Evans gave a good summary of Rudolf's policies at the time: 'In other respects too the new monarch showed himself largely conciliatory, disinclined to make enemies, and with a dignified respect for the sensibilities of vested interests in the state.'[77] Rudolf's continuation of diplomatic engagement with Saxony in the later 1580s exemplifies this approach. Soon after the death of Elector Augustus, in 1587 the testamentary contract between his successor as duke elector, Christian I (r. 1586–1591), with Rudolf as King of Bohemia was renewed.

While Rudolf dealt with actual and potential conflicts within the Holy Roman Empire, other problems arose in the East. A ceasefire with the Ottomans lasted through the 1580s, though it was punctuated by skirmishes along the Balkan and Hungarian frontiers. However, when the Turkish Sultan made peace with Persia in 1590, the Ottomans became free to concentrate their efforts on Europe. In 1591 they doubled their demands for tribute (which the Habsburgs called an *Ehrengeschenk* or honorary gift to save face) from the emperor, and in 1592 declared war. Full-scale combat began in 1593 and ended only in 1606.

Diplomatic activity during the war, however, suggests that Rudolf, like earlier and later Habsburgs, pursued a strategy that cannot simply be deemed reactive, whether or not it can be called a grand strategy. He continued to try to maintain good relations with leaders of different confessional camps in Europe. At the beginning of the war with the Turks in 1593, he received Maximilian of Bavaria in Prague: Maximilian was a staunch Catholic. After the death in 1591 of Christian I of Saxony, who had increasingly turned to Calvinism, Rudolf also renewed imperial diplomatic engagement with Saxony. After Christian I's death, regents governed for his son Christian II (1583–1611) until he came of age in 1601, and Christian II's formal accession (on 23 September 1601) to the duchy provided an occasion for Rudolf to demonstrate his preferences. He responded to the case of Nikolaus Krell, who had been a chief advisor of Christian I and had been suspected of Calvinism and of turning Saxony away from the Habsburgs. The case had been referred to the emperor for final judgement: Krell was sentenced to death and decapitated in Dresden on 2 October 1601. This suggests imperial support for a moderate Lutheran course in Saxony and marks a renewal of closer collaboration on religious matters between the imperial and Saxon courts. Diplomatic missions to Saxony followed in 1602 and 1603, when the painter Hans von Aachen was sent to Dresden and Wittenberg. During the same years he was going to Saxony, von Aachen visited another allied Lutheran court, that of Braunschweig-Wolfenbüttel, while from 1600 Heinrich Julius of Braunschweig-Wolfenbüttel made frequent visits to Prague.

Rudolf also responded to a delegation from King James of Scotland and England headed by Lesieur that came to Prague in 1603, discussed in the Introduction, when in 1605 an imperial mission led by Georg Landgraf von Leuchtenberg was sent to London. Leuchtenberg was instructed to follow up on conversations in Prague in which British emissaries had seemed to present James as sympathetic about offering support against the Turks, to deal with issues involving Hanseatic trade, and to mention the possibility of a marriage with Lady Arabella Stuart. Although, because James did not want to commit himself to more than his own realm's commercial interests, Rudolf II did not gain what he had wanted, this mission demonstrates that the emperor continued to make efforts even on an apparently unlikely front.[78]

During these years Rudolf II patched up differences with the branch of the Swedish Vasa dynasty that ruled Poland. In 1587–8 Archduke Maximilian III had exacerbated relations with Poland by waging an unsuccessful military campaign to win the Polish crown. But while the Habsburgs were waging open war with the Turks, in 1597 the imperial court signed a treaty with Poland. Rudolf II also became proxy godfather for two of Sigismund III Vasa's daughters; daughters of Archduke Ferdinand, the later Emperor Ferdinand II, married the Swedish king and his sons.[79]

There were good geopolitical reasons for the changes in imperial policies towards Poland. Improved relations helped to secure the northern flank of the Habsburg Empire. Through their control of Ukraine, Poland had extensive borders with the

Ottomans and their vassals in Moldavia, Crimea and the lands north of the Black Sea. Polish magnates intervened in Transylvania and Moldavia while imperial forces were fighting there, and Poles were repeatedly to battle Turks in the seventeenth century in these and other areas.

The emperor also improved diplomatic relations with Muscovy for similar reasons. Better relations served Habsburg interests, not only in relieving the threat that the Muscovites were thought to pose, but also in adding an ally against the Turks, with whom Muscovy had frequently been in conflict. Tsar Ivan IV ('the Terrible') had pushed the borders of Muscovy southward, and fought a war with the Turks in 1568–70. At the beginning of Rudolf's reign, Muscovy was impinging on the sensitive and conflicted area of the Caucasus that was also disputed between the Persians and Turks, and conceived of an anti-Ottoman alliance that was to include the Holy Roman Emperor. After Ivan's death in 1584 and during the time of the Polish crisis, Rudolf sent an embassy to Russia. At the beginning of the Turkish War, another imperial embassy was sent to Moscow, to be reciprocated by a Muscovite embassy that carried gifts and was greeted with much fanfare in Prague in 1595.[80]

Rudolf's diplomatic initiatives towards Saxony, Poland and Muscovy (which was Orthodox Christian) in the 1590s suggest that (as Grillparzer intimated) the Turkish War gave further impetus to repairing tears in the fabric of Christendom.[81] There are other signs that Rudolf's imperial strategy was to gain widespread support. As suggested, in order to gain support against the Turks, Rudolf called for meetings of the Reichstag in 1594, 1598, 1603 and 1608, and he personally attended the Diet of 1594. Much of the success that the imperial forces enjoyed, to the extent that they might claim them, may be attributed to material and personal support from other lands in the Holy Roman Empire.

In contrast, both hardline Protestant and Catholic leaders reacted negatively to imperial efforts. A cohort of Protestant

polities headed by the Palatinate opposed paying a tax to be used
to wage war against the Turks; one implication is that the Calvinist
camp opposed reconciliation among confessions even in the
face of what might have been a common enemy. The Catholic
camp also thwarted Rudolf II when in 1599–1600 Spanish,
papal and archducal pressure succeeded in removing his long-
term administrators and replacing them with a new team that
was more aligned to Catholic interests. The change in imperial
administrators probably lamed Rudolf's initiatives and certainly
disrupted attention to the war, which the emperor was tenaciously
pursuing. Archdukes Matthias, Maximilian III and Ferdinand
(of Styria, the future Emperor Ferdinand II) also conspired
against Rudolf, signing a pact at Schottwein in 1600 in which
they agreed to force Rudolf II to name one of them his successor
and to replace him.

It is approximately at this date that Rudolf II is supposed
to have had a mental or physical breakdown: some ambassadors
describe him as subject to outbursts of anger or bouts of melancholy, as discussed in the Introduction. But in the light of what
was actually happening at the time, Rudolf's anger, his feeling that
people were working against him, does not seem so unreasonable
– because people were. Reports that he was upset at this time,
moreover, say that he was bothered by changes made among his
administrators to put in people who did not enjoy his confidence,
the plotting of his brothers and cousin against him, and the covert
support the papacy and clergy lent to such plots – all of which
were legitimate complaints.

The conduct of diplomatic relations with Persia also casts
doubt on accusations that Rudolf was mentally ill and incapable of acting at this time. The Safavids and Ottomans had long
been foes, and, as noted above, the conclusion of a war between
them in 1590 freed the Ottomans to turn westwards. In 1601
the Safavids sent an embassy led by Robert Shirley to Prague, no

S. Cæs. Mᵗⁱˢ Sculptor Ægidius Sadeler ad viuum delineauit Cum Priuil. S: Cæ. Mᵗᵉ Anno . Pragæ . 1605.

doubt to discuss a two-front strategy against the Turks. In 1603 hostilities between Persians and Turks resumed, and another Persian embassy arrived in Prague in July 1604. Esaias Le Gillon portrayed two members of this mission that appear in engravings by Aegidius Sadeler (illus. 9). These embassies suggest that fruitful

9 Aegidius Sadeler II, *Mechti Kuli Beg, Persian Ambassador to Prague*, 1605, engraving.

conversations were taking place, and that a common strategy may have been contemplated.

The Persians were able to press their military ends successfully while the Turks were engaged with the imperial forces and thus had to fight on two fronts. The existence of what seems to have been a de facto alliance between the Habsburgs and the Safavids may provide part of the reason why Rudolf was opposed to making peace with the Ottomans in 1606. When combat stopped in Europe, the Turks were able to go on the counter-offensive against the Persians in Asia.

It is likely that it was in connection with seeking Rudolf's support to renew conflict with the Ottomans or support them otherwise that the Persians sent yet another embassy to Prague in 1609–10. In 1609 Safavid ambassadors gave Rudolf a painting depicting the shah feeding a gazelle that the ruler made himself; in 1610 they presented Rudolf with a painted casket, several jewels and jewelled weapons, and a topaz vase given in the name of the shah.[82] The Persians carried on the war after the Habsburgs stopped, and concluded it successfully: according to the terms of a treaty they signed with the Turks in 1612, the Safavid Empire regained what it had lost in 1590 and acquired still more territory.

In contrast, the Habsburgs' Long Turkish War, so-called because it lasted from 1593 until 1606 and in effect was the longest continued conflict to date between Turks and Habsburgs, did not end decisively. The imperial forces were occasionally victorious – at the Battle of Sissek in 1593, at the siege of Esztergom (Gran) in 1595 (illus. 10) and at Győr (Raab) in 1598. But they lost or drew several other battles. Habsburg forces took some cities, and Ottomans then retook some of them. As the war dragged on into the 1600s, neither side gained a definite advantage. The situation in Transylvania, over which Rudolf II was nominally suzerain and which both sides would have liked to have claimed as a fiefdom, remained unresolved.

While from 1603 the Persians may have reduced some pressure on the imperial forces, this advantage was offset by the increase in the number of adversaries that the Habsburg armies had to face in Transylvania. Sigismund Bathory succeeded his father, Stephen Bathory, King of Poland (d. 1586), as prince of Transylvania but committed treason to the Habsburgs: having abdicated in favour of the emperor in Transylvania, in 1598–9 and again in 1601–2, Bathory tried in vain to reassert his position as prince. The Hungarian Transylvanian prince Stefan Bocskai, who sided with the Turks and gained temporary control over Transylvania in 1605–6, and another sometime imperial ally, Michael of Wallachia (regarded as a Romanian hero because he was first to unite Moldavia, Wallachia and Transylvania), also countered the aims of Rudolf II. The Poles supported both Sigismund Bathory and Bocskai.

The conduct of war on all the Hungarian fronts including Transylvania was further complicated by the varied and largely

10 Hans von Aachen workshop, *The Conquest of Gran* (*Allegory of the Turkish Wars*), *c.* 1607, watercolour.

non-Catholic population (an estimated 75 per cent) of those areas of Hungary (and Croatia) that were not under Turkish control. Despite such difficulties, Rudolf continued the war until 1606. This may also be seen to be a sign of his personal sense of honour and dignity.

The war would have gone on longer still had it not been for the machinations of Archduke Matthias and the other Habsburg archdukes. Matthias finally achieved one of his ambitions to be a general when he assumed command of Habsburg forces in the area of historic Hungary. But he proved to be as incompetent as a commander as he had earlier been as an administrator in the Netherlands. A foretaste of what was to happen in Hungary occurred in the Low Counties in 1577 when, without Philip's approval or Rudolf's foreknowledge, Matthias took over as governor (*Staathalter*) of the Low Countries. By 1581 Matthias had made a mess of matters and fled. Although he did not demonstrate that he was an able commander in the war with the Turks, Matthias exploited opportunities to his own advantage and seized on an opening that seemed to ease his way to the crown.

In 1603 and 1604 Rudolf II made what seem to have been ill-considered attempts to suppress Protestant practices in the royal towns in Hungary that remained under his suzerainty, although again he may have seen it as the right of the ruler to determine the religious practices of realms under his control. The towns resisted, and Archdukes Matthias and Maximilian III, who had been even more militant in their support of Catholicism and suppression of Protestantism, cynically manipulated the situation. Matthias was outwardly a committed Catholic and had indeed prosecuted the Counter-Reformation in his own domains in Upper and Lower Austria, but when Rudolf II's actions seemed to threaten a compromise regarding religious practice he had made as King of Hungary he courted the Hungarian estates. Seeking to gain the support of Hungarian Protestants, a

vast majority of the population, Matthias granted religious freedom in Hungary in 1605. In 1606 he also granted Transylvanians
the right to select their monarch in contravention of what had
been imperial policy.

Matthias claimed that he was acting with plenipotentiary
authority. But in reality the archduke's actions resulted from the
protocol of the archdukes' meeting in Vienna that was signed on
25 April 1606, as discussed in the Introduction. There, to repeat,
they declared that Rudolf II was only interested in wizards, alchemists and cabbalists, the pursuit of magic and finding scandalous
ways to hurt his enemies. They insinuated that he had abandoned
God for another master. Hinting that he was insane (suffering
from melancholy and subject to angry outbursts) and incapable
of ruling, they used this as pretext to carry out their own policies
without consulting Rudolf.[83]

Although he lacked specific directives from Rudolf II and
also his approval, Matthias proceeded to negotiate a treaty with
the Turks, which was signed at Zsitvatorok on 11 November 1606.
The emperor firmly opposed what Matthias had done. However,
when the estates of Hungary, whose lands had been ravaged by
war and who Matthias had assiduously cultivated, did not support him, Rudolf reluctantly was forced to ratify the treaty on
9 December.

Although the treaty might to some extent be viewed to have
had a positive outcome – Turkish advances had been checked,
and the emperor gained recognition from the Ottomans as being
a ruler of equal rank – it spelled the beginning of the end for
Rudolf II. Around this time the emperor may have realized that
his position was in decline. Like Charles V, who abdicated in 1556
and retired to the monastery of Yuste in 1557, Rudolf seems to
have been thinking of retiring from Prague. In April 1606 the
archdukes mentioned that he had been thinking of retiring to
the Tyrol but had given up this idea.[84] This rumour may reflect

Rudolf's own intentions, because in January 1607 the emperor had it announced to the Upper Austrian estates that he intended to move to Linz to reside in the Schloss there.[85] Unlike Charles V, Rudolf could not, however, fulfil his wish because the Linz Schloss was not completed until two years after his death. And unlike Charles, Rudolf did not willingly abdicate any of his thrones.

In 1608 Matthias made open his opposition to Rudolf. He joined the rebellious Diet of Hungary who were meeting with the Lower and Upper Austrian estates in Bratislava. He then gained the support of the estates of Moravia, which was also home to many religious dissenters, and gained their tentative recognition as ruler of Moravia. With the aim of becoming King of Bohemia, Matthias marched on Prague and besieged it in April. Although the estates of Bohemia and most individual magnates did not take the side of Matthias, Rudolf wished to avoid armed conflict. In June he agreed to a compromise at Libeň near Prague by which he relinquished power to Matthias in Moravia and in Upper and Lower Austria and acknowledged the archduke's rule as king in Hungary: Matthias became King of Hungary on 26 June. Rudolf retained control over the Czech lands other than Moravia, including Bohemia proper, Upper and Lower Lusatia, and Silesia, and the imperial crown.

Historians who have believed the self-serving declarations of the archdukes and the reports of unfriendly ambassadors have claimed that Rudolf was mentally ill or even suffered a breakdown and became a recluse at this crucial time. They have taken at face value accounts like that of the Tuscan ambassador Daniel Eremita. Eremita wrote in 1609 that Rudolf was 'disturbed in ailment by some kind of melancholy . . . he has shut himself off in his Palace as if behind the bars of a prison.' But the first part of this comment should be balanced against Eremita's simultaneous emphasis on Rudolf's 'amazing knowledge of all things, wise judgment, and skill'.[86]

Eremita's assertion about Rudolf's self-isolation should also
be doubted in the light of another largely overlooked piece of
visual evidence. It suggests that even during troubled times, as
the years from 1606 would have been for him, Rudolf II did not
hide in the imperial palace, some of whose prominent spaces
were in fact open to the public. A well-known view of the Vladislav
Hall in Prague Castle by the imperial printmaker Aegidius Sadeler
dated 1607 gives a glimpse into life on the Hradčany at this time
(illus. 11). Sadeler's engraving depicts this famous vaulted hall,

11 Aegidius Sadeler II, *Interior of Vladislav Hall*, 1607, engraving.

which sports the first Renaissance windows in Bohemia. Completed in 1493 by Benedict Ried (Benedikt Rejt) for King Vladislav II Jagiełło, the hall was used for banquets, balls, receptions and coronation ceremonies, and possibly for tournaments. The central rooms of Bohemian administration, the Landrechtstube (Hall of Records) and Landtagssaal (Bohemia State Chamber), were adjacent to it; Maximilian II had had Bonifaz Wohlmut renew and restore the larger of these two halls. From circa 1570 the Vladislav Hall was transformed into an openly accessible space that contained fixed stalls for marketing objects; the imperial painter Arcimboldo was involved in designing the stalls. Sadeler's large engraving corresponds to documents that indicate a large assortment of wares was available for sale there during Rudolf's reign. It shows prints, goldsmiths' works, clocks and paintings among other items being sold at the stalls.

The inscription on the engraving also refers to the stalls and says that business went on in the room. Crowds of people identifiable by their costumes – including Hungarians, Bohemians and Persians in turbans – give an impression of the sorts of gathering that might have taken place in the hall, while other documents indicate that not only aristocrats but Prague citizens came into the palace to buy things. Although Sadeler's print is dated 1607, and the Persian ambassadors who had come in 1604 would probably have left Prague by then, there is no reason to doubt that the engraving shows the sort of encounters that may have frequently taken place there.[87]

A key detail appears in the background of the print. Although this detail has occasionally been noticed, its significance for the interpretation of Rudolf's activities and attitude has not yet been fully considered (illus. 12).[88] A group of men is shown doffing their hats and bowing in respect to a bearded man who holds a staff; they stand in a circle, keeping their distance from the person in the middle.[89] They have been called members of the court,

and the man in the middle has been identified as Rudolf II: this identification is correct, as he wears a stylized version of an imperial crown. Although Rudolf seems small because of his location in the print, Sadeler hints at his importance by portraying the emperor on the central axis of the image. This detail is credible, as it is tiny and not further emphasized. The depiction of the emperor appearing in public contradicts the rumours that Rudolf II was a recluse at this time.

Furthermore, even as he began to lose his power and his thrones, the emperor continued to defend his interests. In autumn

12 Rudolf II, detail of *Interior of Vladislav Hall* (illus. II).

1608 and at the turn of 1609 Rudolf sent agents to Lower Austria to try to exploit the problems that Matthias was having with the estates there, who were largely composed of Protestants, and to regain their allegiance. In order to solidify the support of the Bohemian estates, who had not supported Matthias previously, in 1609 Rudolf issued a Letter of Majesty that granted freedom of religion in Bohemia (as he later did in Silesia) to both Protestants as well as Catholics, albeit somewhat reluctantly. He also allowed the estates to establish their own state church – which encouraged the erection of Protestant churches in Prague and elsewhere in Bohemia.

In addition to the Persians, Rudolf II also continued to conduct diplomatic relations with other European polities during the last years of his reign. He sought to shore up support for his authority in the Holy Roman Empire by directing diplomatic efforts to the moderate Lutheran camp. In 1607 he welcomed Christian II of Saxony in Prague and is reported to have discussed matters of political concern with him. During the visit, a Lutheran minister was allowed to preach in the palace chapel, indicating that, like Maximilian II, Rudolf could be flexible in religious matters, especially when he needed political support. He gave several gifts to the duke elector that emphasize the Saxon–imperial alliance.[90]

In 1608 and 1609 diplomatic relations with Saxony and with other Protestant polities intensified as Rudolf sought support for his position at a Reichstag and a planned Kurfürstentag.[91] When Christian II of Saxony died in 1611, Rudolf quickly tried to ingratiate himself with his successor, Johann Georg I (r. 1611–1656). The courtier Maximilian von und zu Trautsmannsdorf brought presents to Dresden in 1611 to congratulate the newly installed elector.[92]

Although the exchange of gifts, often with a political message, seems to have been most significant with Saxony, the imperial court also exchanged them with other Protestant courts during these years. Another Lutheran ruler who received gifts (and also patronized the Prague artists) at this time was Heinrich Julius of Braunschweig-Wolfenbüttel. A friend of Rudolf, Heinrich Julius was named privy councilor in 1607 and began to reside largely in Prague. He rose to become the very top director of the imperial Privy Council (*Geheimrat*). Heinrich Julius died in Prague in 1613.[93]

The imperial court also maintained relations with several Italian courts. Even after 1606 other missions continued to come from Italy: a papal nuncio, Cardinal Caetani, came and resided in Prague from 1607, an embassy from Savoy came in 1608 and one from Tuscany in 1609 – this is the embassy to which Eremita belonged. They all failed to gain the emperor's ear or assent. The papal nuncio could, for instance, not dissuade Rudolf from being antagonistic to Matthias, nor convince him to settle the issue of imperial succession. Their lack of success should be weighed in the balance along with the failure of earlier ambassadors in assessing the validity of claims that Rudolf was unstable, neglected affairs of state for the arts and sciences, and retreated from public. Similar to Eremita, the papal nuncio recognized Rudolf's mental acuity (*ingegno*), saying it was superior to that of Matthias, as has also been noted in the Introduction to this book.

The carping critiques of Rudolf II made by ambassadors appear to be excuses for failure when one realizes that other envoys had ready access to his person during this later period while these critics did not. The emperor clearly acceded to the requests of some ambassadors but not to those of others, who then slandered him. In 1609 ambassadors from Lutheran Saxony and Brandenburg were received in Prague. (The former also brought a gift of jasper dishes).[94] It is, moreover, noteworthy that Rudolf II cultivated extensive diplomatic relations with rulers from the Catholic camp, including the prince archbishop electors of Mainz and Cologne and the Duke of Bavaria, who at the time was working to establish the Catholic League and was open about it with Rudolf. For example, the emperor gave the Bavarian ambassador an audience.[95]

Rudolf's intense and continuing diplomatic efforts should lead to a revised interpretation of his politics. It has recently been argued that the emperor conducted an independent policy almost to the end of life, that he was not politically inactive and that his policy seems to have been astute: the evidence seems to support this thesis. Rudolf clearly had reasons not to be pinned down by the papal nuncio, especially since letters from the nuncio were intercepted that indicate he was pushing for plans that had been resisted by Rudolf. The discovery of these letters understandably aroused the emperor's annoyance and increased his suspicions. Besides not committing himself for reasons of maintaining political balance, Rudolf II might also have been put off by those Italian courts whose eligible princesses, like Maria de' Medici, had been married to other rulers before he could announce his intentions even though they had been under consideration as possible spouses.[96] He also tried to keep a balance and support for his position amidst rival religious confessions.

Rudolf's penultimate initiative involved his participation in a *Kurfürstentag* that took place in Prague in May 1610, and for which, as noted, there had been much diplomatic planning. Electors and princes from different confessional camps came to the imperial residence; Rudolf received them lavishly and tried to win them over to his position in the struggle with his relatives. Although the rival archdukes were also in attendance, the meeting witnessed one of the last open assertions of imperial authority during Rudolf's reign. A statement was promulgated that tried to set limits on Matthias to exercise any interference in imperial politics through his position in the Austrian lands.[97]

Rudolf was, however, ultimately unsuccessful. Conditions seem to have been beyond his power to control, for reasons that do not have to do with his person. From circa 1600 an older generation of rulers who may have been more inclined to compromise was dying out. In the first decade of the seventeenth century the political and religious climate in Central Europe was becoming increasingly fraught. A Protestant Union and a Catholic League rivalling it were formed in 1608 and 1609, the years when Rudolf was making efforts to recoup his position.

A major crisis came to a head in 1609 when the Duke of Jülich-Cleves (in northwestern Germany) died. This duke was the last of his line: Protestant and Catholic rulers vied to succeed him and mobilized forces to seize his lands. Neither Rudolf II, even though he could also claim relationship with the last Duke of Jülich-Cleves, nor Christian II of Saxony, to whom the duchy had been assigned as director, openly asserted their rights. Presumably, they wished to maintain the peace and act as mediators among the interested parties. If so, their efforts were in vain: war broke out in 1610.[98]

Archduke Leopold V Habsburg, a cousin of Rudolf II who at the time was Bishop of Passau, intervened on the emperor's behalf but in the end sabotaged his cause. Rudolf had already utilized Leopold to intervene against Matthias in Austria in 1609. Leopold appeared to Rudolf to be the only acceptable successor to the imperial throne, since Rudolf's brothers as well as Leopold's older brother, Archduke Ferdinand of Styria (later Emperor Ferdinand II), had thoroughly antagonized him by repeatedly acting against him. The choice of Leopold moreover directly contradicts the archdukes' assertion, and the interpretation of historians who have believed their claim, that Rudolf had given no thought about how imperial succession should stay within the House of Habsburg. Rudolf was not going to choose Matthias, nor Archduke Maximilian III, nor Ferdinand, nor for that matter Archduke Albrecht, who had married Isabel and was serving as stateholder of the Spanish Netherlands. He preferred Leopold, again snubbing them.

Leopold assembled a mercenary force to represent imperial interests in the Jülich-Cleves conflict, likely with Rudolf's assent. These troops were, however, driven off from northern Germany. In December 1610 over 10,000 mercenaries commanded by Laurentius Ramée (known to history as the Passauer Kriegsvolk after the name of Leopold's episcopal see) moved into Upper Austria. They ravaged its land and sacked cities like Linz. In January 1611 the Passauer Kriegsvolk invaded Bohemia. They marched on Prague under the pretext of coming to the aid of Rudolf II, who might in fact have clandestinely encouraged them. The mercenaries went out of control: the Malá Strana (Small Side) was besieged, occupied and sacked. The Passauer Kriegsvolk were finally stopped at the Vltava (Moldau) River when they tried to cross over to the Old City (Staré Město). In March 1611 Matthias drove them out and occupied Prague.

Rudolf lost credibility with the Bohemian estates as a result of their actions. The estates finally recognized Matthias as king, and he was crowned on 23 May 1611. When Rudolf lost this penultimate dignity, he was indeed left with just the imperial crown. Only then was he truly isolated in the Hradčany. At this point the legend that Rudolf flew from politics into art and science may even have come true. One credible report says the emperor sought to be far away from the commotion surrounding the coronation of Matthias in Prague Cathedral, which was located near his private quarters in the palace. During these events Rudolf consoled himself by looking at jewels and at drawings by Albrecht Dürer.[99]

In November 1611 another meeting of the electors was called, probably with the aim of electing a new emperor, a decision which would have deprived Rudolf II of his last remaining title. If so, this action soon proved unnecessary, because he had only two months left to live. Rudolf II died in Prague on 20 January 1612, and Matthias succeeded him as emperor.

TWO

Rudolf II as Collector

Like much else concerning him, the collections of Rudolf II are the stuff of legend. Their size was truly remarkable, as was their quality, and they have been famous since their own time. The emperor invested a great deal of attention and resources in collecting. A biography must therefore deal with his activities as a collector, all the more so since a major issue of debate has been how to reconcile Rudolf as collector with his role as a ruler.

One feature of the black legend of Rudolf II has long provided an answer. Julius von Schlosser's pioneering book on the history of collections from the early twentieth century passed on the opinion that Rudolf II's *Kunstkammer* resembled the American impresario Phineas T. Barnum's museum of oddities, a nineteenth-century version of Ripley's Believe It or Not museums. Schlosser asserted that Rudolf's hodgepodge of art and curiosities characterized the mentality embodied in the Germanic *Kunstkammer*. According to Schlosser, this kind of collection corresponded to the 'witches' kitchens and spooky eccentricities of the North' that contrasted with the 'rational, scientific outlook of the Italian south', where the true origins of collecting were to be found.[1] Although several of Schlosser's arguments are no longer widely accepted – many works that once belonged to Rudolf II are, for instance, now displayed as masterpieces in the Kunsthistorisches Museum in Vienna – as suggested in the Introduction, the idea has persisted that the emperor's avid collecting is inconsistent with his activity as a ruler and even a sign of mental instability. It is still debated how effective the collections could have been in playing a role in statecraft.[2]

Since Schlosser wrote in 1908, many other interpretations have been advanced: the imperial collections have been regarded as a pastime, a form of entertainment, a place for investigations, a source of contemplation, a stockroom for ideas and materials, and a form of princely representation. While much may still be said about all these questions, this chapter concentrates primarily on how Rudolf's collecting relates to his responsibilities as a ruler. It reviews the origins, character, display, function, use and thinking involved in the emperor's collections. It connects them to his Burgundian and Habsburg predecessors. It summarizes the contents, housing and display of the collections in Prague, comparing them to developments in collecting on both sides of the Alps. It suggests that several Renaissance writings, including contemporary discussions of the virtues and occupations of a ruler, reflect and are expressed in Rudolf II's collecting practices. And it reconsiders the functions and uses of the imperial collections in diplomacy. In sum, it argues that Rudolf II's collecting was intrinsically related to his role as emperor. Finally, the chapter offers a preliminary evaluation of what – beyond epitomizing Renaissance rulership – Rudolf's collecting might reveal about his character. Discussion is continued in the following chapters, which address questions about the emperor's patronage of the arts and sciences.

RUDOLF II WAS HEIR to earlier Habsburg collectors in many ways. He inherited objects that his forerunners had acquired. As family traditions and expectations in general affected his actions and aspirations, his predecessors shaped much of his outlook as a collector. He thus adopted patterns of collecting that assumed earlier ideas and interests.

During the thirteenth and fourteenth centuries the Habsburgs possessed what may be described as a treasure. Fourteenth-century documents as well as some surviving items suggest that they owned collections containing a variety of objects including regalia (personal crowns and other crowns like the Archduke's Hat), jewellery, silver plate and unworked metals as well as finished goldsmiths' objects. In the fourteenth century a desire to retain some key objects was expressed, anticipating later tendencies in Habsburg dynastic collecting policies.[3] By the later fifteenth century the collection of Emperor Frederick III (r. 1452–1493) had obtained a definite location, a tower in the Vienna Hofburg, the city palace abutting the (no longer extant) city walls. While not entirely kept secret, it was, however, not open to the public. As far as can be determined, Frederick's collection contained, among other items, goldsmiths' works like those with his AEIOU emblem (illus. 13) and a valuable cross whose provenance his descendant Maximilian II discussed in 1550 with his grandmother Juana when he visited her in Castile.[4] Like church treasuries, early Habsburg collections contained objects that possessed both material (gold) and symbolic value: these are exemplified by emblematic artefacts and regalia.

From the later fifteenth century onwards, the dukes of Burgundy inspired Habsburg collecting. The dukes wore sumptuous clothing and carried along beautiful tapestries and luxurious gold objects on their frequent travels. These they displayed at entries, meetings, banquets and other ceremonies. Portraits and other masterworks by the leading Flemish artists of their time adorned their residences, while artists of the calibre of Rogier van der Weyden and Jan van Eyck portrayed the dukes and their courtiers. Charles the Bold (as he is usually known in English) provides a prime exemplar of the Burgundian love of splendour,

epitomizing their predilection for conspicuous consumption. They were following traditions that date back to antiquity, about which it may be observed that the 'use and display of visual material can continuously create, articulate and define an individual's social, economic, and political place'.[5] The Burgundian dukes put this into practice when they awed their rivals by their appearance and accoutrements, including the chain and medals of the knightly Order of the Golden Fleece, fine armour and elaborate horse trappings: these were on view at an important meeting

13 'Prunkbecher' (magnificent cup) of Emperor Frederick III, 1475–1500, silver, partially gold-plated, rock crystal, enamel.

held in 1473 at Trier where Charles the Bold dazzled Emperor
Frederick III.

One outcome of this meeting was the betrothal in 1476 of Mary,
Charles the Bold's daughter, to Frederick III's son Maximilian I
(r. 1493–1519). Both sides thought they might gain by this match,
but the Burgundians lost in the end. Indeed, Charles the Bold had
already lost many Burgundian treasures when he had to flee battle
in 1467.[6] But enough remained not only to bedazzle Frederick
but to leave Mary with a substantial dowry of artefacts, especially
beautiful manuscripts, when Charles died on the battlefield in
January 1477. Mary brought these with her when she married
Maximilian in August 1477.

Maximilian acquired the artefacts and claims to the Burgundians' lands when Mary fell from a horse and died in 1482. Along
with Mary's possessions, Maximilian inherited Burgundian ideas
of princely magnificence, the notion that appearances and collecting lend a ruler grandeur. Maximilian's second marriage (by proxy
in 1494) to Bianca Maria Sforza, daughter of the Duke of Milan,
reinforced notions of the importance of collecting (and patronage). In keeping with the customs of other contemporary Italian
rulers, the Sforzas were great collectors (and patrons of the arts):
for instance, Bianca Maria's uncle and protector Ludovico commissioned the painting of *The Last Supper* from Leonardo da Vinci.
After the French deposed Ludovico in 1498, Maximilian fought
wars in Italy against enemies of the Duchy of Milan in defence
of his claims. His frequent campaigns in Italy would have increased
his familiarity with the Milanese collections and with those of
other Italian princes.

Maximilian's thinly veiled autobiographical works and some
public pronouncements indicate that he believed collecting was
important for a ruler. Maximilian's well-known statement about
his goals articulates this belief. He asserted that deeds and possessions added to eternal fame and memory (*Ewiges Ruhm und*

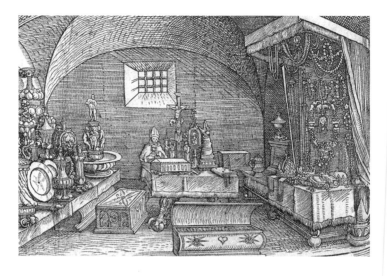

Gedechtnus), without which a ruler's name would be extinguished with the tolling of his funeral bell.[7]

A vignette on the Triumphal Arch (or Arch of Honour) for Maximilian I, a giant paper construction comprising prints by Albrecht Dürer, Albrecht Altdorfer and others, gives some idea of what this maxim meant for Maximilian's collections (illus. 14).[8] One image by Altdorfer shows Maximilian I's collection, which is described by a rhyme beneath it. The caption mentions silver, gold, pearls and jewels, while the illustration shows chalices, plates, ewers, reliquaries, the chain and badge of the Order of the Golden Fleece, unworked metal (presumably gold) bars and closed chests. While this depiction is no doubt idealized and displays objects in a sort of ascending order from secular treasures to relics to regalia set off against fabrics appropriate to their valuation,[9] it is not completely fantastic. Maximilian I did own items like those seen in the print, among them the paraphernalia of the Order of the Golden Fleece, an Archduke's Hat and a personal crown (that Rudolf II's resembles: see illus. 7): the crown

14 Albrecht Altdorfer (and others), detail of *Schatz,* from *Triumphal Arch (Ehrenpforte) of Maximilian I,* 1517, engraving.

is similar to others that appear in miniatures, paintings and prints of Maximilian I and in representations of Frederick III wearing his personal crown.[10] The inscription suggests that Maximilian's treasure (*Schatz*) was to promote princely prestige; the epigram calls it the greatest treasure (*grosten Schatz*), claiming that this was something not known by any other prince.

While the production of prints like those constituting the Triumphal Arch sprang from Maximilian's intention to disseminate images to a broad public, the vaulted space with barred windows in which Altdorfer sets the emperor's *Schatz* suggests that his collections would not usually have been seen by many people. It intimates that such a treasure would have been secured in a cellar-like room. It is also more likely that many objects would have been contained in chests like those shown on the floor in the print than exhibited on a canopied credenza like that seen on the viewer's right, or even exhibited like those works shown prominently in the centre. The display of sacralized objects, like relics, was reserved for special occasions, and some regalia, like that of the Holy Roman Empire kept in Nuremberg, were probably not seen except at coronations, as discussed in the previous chapter. Keeping a collection out of the sight of many people was most likely more than a matter of security: it relates to the concept of *arcana imperii* – as previously suggested, secrecy and viewing by a select few increased their and his aura. The print intimates that Maximilian's *Schatz* held objects with a quasi-sacral character, namely regalia as well as relics with sacred contents, just the sorts of artefacts that were regarded as *arcana imperii*.

In any case, collecting assumed greater importance in Habsburg propaganda during the reigns of Maximilian I's successors as emperor, Charles V and Ferdinand I. This development may be related to their deliberate appropriation of Burgundian traditions. Like Maximilian I, who had spent many years in the north, Charles V had been directly exposed to Burgundian culture: he was born in Ghent in Flanders, a centre of Flemish art-making (think of Jan van Eyck's *Adoration of the Mystic Lamb*), and raised in Brabant at the Mechelen (Malines) court of his aunt Margaret, the owner of an important collection herself. While Ferdinand was born and raised in Spain, he also lived for a while in the Low Countries and was familiar with Burgundian court ritual and customs.[11] As discussed in the preceding chapter, Charles and Ferdinand had Burgundian court ceremonial and attire adopted respectively in Spain and Central Europe.

While evincing continuity in some respects, Ferdinand I's collecting practices suggest that attitudes had changed about the sorts and significance of objects to be collected. On the one hand, Ferdinand echoed earlier instructions when he specifically expressed his wish that key objects in his collections should remain in Habsburg hands. In 1564 he declared that some items were never to be sold, given away or pawned. These were pieces that possessed a special aura which presumably was lent to the Habsburgs: a narwhal horn supposed to be that of a unicorn, and an agate dish thought to bear Christ's initials and once believed to be the Holy Grail. Ferdinand's successors heeded his demands, as both can still be seen in the *Schatzkammer*, the present treasury, in Vienna. Other bequests indicate that Ferdinand valued some collections per se. A last will drawn up in 1554 prescribed the separate bequest of a collection of coins and antiquities to Maximilian II, his son and immediate successor. Ferdinand said that the financial value of the coins was not small, but because of their age, variety and order they were not to be sold, as so many coins in such good order could not easily be found elsewhere.[12]

During Ferdinand's reign a change may be observed in the approach to the kinds of objects collected and consequently the names and types of collections. Ferdinand's remarks indicate what he liked: objects appealed to him because they were rare or artfully or wonderfully made. He was also interested in works that exhibited art or artifice in the sense of skill, one of the original meanings of *Kunst*. A commission for a bronze made for Ferdinand in 1525 called the *Ehrenpíld*, image of honour, reveals his predilections. He required a 'whole naked man, standing, in a clever pose, proportioned in the nicest and most diligent manner, with the elbow raised high [and it should be made] so that the casting

15 Stefan Godl and Leonhard Magt, *Ehrenpíld* (*Nackter Krieger*), 1525–6, bronze.

would come out well and no one would need to help with filing it or in any other way [and to be done] with all diligence, art [*Artlichkeit*] and appropriateness' (illus. 15).[13]

In 1564 Ferdinand also indicated that what he called rare and curious things (*raras, curiosas*) gave him pleasure.[14] A visitor to the emperor's collections at this time suggests what sorts of things they were. He mentions a unicorn horn (one used to make medicine), a mummy, a flute made from a crane's bones, a cow horn with 113 faces carved in it, and a painting made of peacock feathers (probably a Mexican feather painting), one of the sorts of works called *indianisch*, rare objects from the West and East 'Indies', that intrigued rulers like Ferdinand I and Charles V. Charles V put on display in his palace in Brussels Aztec works that the conquistador Cortés had sent back to Europe from Mexico (where, among others, Dürer saw them).[15] Ferdinand's correspondence also indicates that he was interested in fossils and rare antlers as well as coins, examples of all of which could be found in his collections. The collections may thus be said to have contained objects that conveyed a sense of wonder, reflecting Ferdinand's earlier comments.

A document of 1554 mentions Ferdinand I's *Kunstkammer*, the first reference to any such collection. In the context of Ferdinand's conception of *Kunst*, we may read the word *Kunstkammer* to mean, quite literally, a chamber of art, as the designation of *Kunst* here seems to correspond to the idea that *Kunst* is something that exhibits skill or artifice. Objects that Ferdinand is known to have possessed that fit this notion of art are goldsmiths' works and jewellery, manuscripts, portraits and paintings by Giuseppe Arcimboldo. Along with them, Ferdinand's collections, however, also contained objects that may be categorized as being rare or exhibiting wonder (as Arcimboldo's composite heads, which the artist made as royal painter to Maximilian II, to be discussed further below, also do).[16]

The combination of works of art and wonders of nature in Emperor Ferdinand's collection corresponds to the idea of a *Kunst- und Wunderkammer*, a chamber of art and wonder, a notion that Schlosser applied as a general term to these sorts of collections of what he called the Late Renaissance. Although the term has gained wide currency, it appears in only two documents from the sixteenth century, however. Both refer not to Emperor Ferdinand's collections, but to those of his second oldest son, Archduke Ferdinand II (1529–1595). While the conjunction of *Kunst* and *Wunder* might seem to be appropriate because the emperor's *Kunstkammer* and others comparable to it contained objects that produced a reaction of wonder as well as items that might be regarded as works of art, the use of *Kunst- und Wunderkammer* was never widely employed and is therefore not historically accurate as a comprehensive designation.[17] *Kunstkammer* was the more widely used term (as opposed to either *Wunderkammer* or *Kunst- und Wunderkammer*).

While the absence of a surviving inventory makes it difficult to reassemble Emperor Ferdinand's collections, a document of 1560 further establishes that his collection was called a *Kunstkammer*.[18] It has now been determined that in 1558 Ferdinand commissioned the construction of a building for his *Kunstkammer* in the *Hofburg* in Vienna. Built on a stretch of land 9 × 20 metres (30 × 66 ft) in dimensions, this building was finished and furnished by 1563. Despite doubts expressed by some scholars, it is thus likely that much of Ferdinand's collection was located in this *Kunstkammer*, although some objects, particularly paintings, were probably kept elsewhere.[19]

Ferdinand himself expressly stated that his possession of rare and curious objects (which may be associated with the idea of freaks of nature and other natural objects) would cause him to be remembered (*dejar memoria*).[20] This reference seems to embody a purpose for collecting similar to that of Maximilian I when he said that his goal was to ensure that his fame and memory be preserved. The role of art in representing princely power may, moreover, be further associated with Ferdinand and his possessions: Arcimboldo's paintings were imperial allegories, and a visitor described them as what may be read as being placed where we know that tapestries, which also conveyed such allusions to rulers, could also have been hung.[21]

Emperor Ferdinand's son Archduke Ferdinand II may be credited not only with the term *Kunst- und Wunderkammer* but with a fuller conception of what a Habsburg collector of the following generation could have obtained. The archduke resided in Prague during the years 1547–63 when he served as stateholder (viceroy) of Bohemia. During this time he had work continued on additions and reconstructions that Emperor Ferdinand had begun on the Hradčany (the Belvedere Villa). Archduke Ferdinand also inherited some of Ferdinand I's belongings. It is now known that the archduke had already established the kernel of his important collection of armour and weapons while he was in Prague: after he left Prague, 347 pounds of his armour and weapons were shipped to Innsbruck. What was described as his 'bella, & rara armaria' was located adjacent to the White Tower in Prague Castle.[22] During his Prague stay, Archduke Ferdinand also commissioned work from a woodcarver. However, it is not known (though likely) whether he had already begun to assemble collections in addition to those of armour and weapons while he was still living in Bohemia.[23] Because of his lengthy residence in Prague, his building projects there and his collections, Ferdinand may be considered an important forerunner of Rudolf II. Yet little trace of his collections remained in Prague after his departure.

Archduke Ferdinand's collections are much better known from the time in the mid-1560s when he took over governing the Tyrol and the Austrian forelands that Ferdinand I bequeathed to him. (He is consequently often referred to as Ferdinand of the

Tyrol, to distinguish him from his nephew, Emperor Ferdinand II, as well as from his father.) Before this time he had been dependent on Ferdinand I for the financial means to acquire armour and other objects. But during his Tyrolean period, when he could directly dispose of funds, the archduke collected on a wider scale. In the Tyrol he had his collections placed in separate buildings with rooms built and decorated for them at his Schloss at Ambras outside Innsbruck. The main components of the Ambras collections were an extensive library with a couple of thousand books and many manuscripts, a large armoury and the *Kunst- und Wunderkammer*, also called *Kunstkammer* in documents. At Ambras there were also stables, probably a small antiquarium (in whose niches small bronzes and possibly antiquities were placed) and collections of portraits. Ferdinand II seems to have been most intensely involved with his armour collection, which consisted of suits and weapons that had belonged to famous men. It has been called a theatre of memory and of virtue, and the first illustrated catalogue of any printed European collection was made of it.[24] Drawings and a print suggest where the collections were displayed (illus. 16).

A posthumous inventory of Archduke Ferdinand II's *Kunstkammer* lists 2,500 items, and they were organized in a unique manner. The Ambras *Kunstkammer* consisted of a room on whose walls paintings of unusual subjects (a giant, a man with a lance through his eye, the original Dracula, Vlad Tepes, monstrous animal births) were hung: the centre of the room contained eighteen cabinets placed side to side and in two rows set back to back that contained objects (illus. 17). The cabinets were painted in various colours, probably for aesthetic effect, although possibly with some symbolic associations. Some cabinets held what may be called *scientifica* or scientific objects, and other objects from afar called *Indianisch*, among them the first documented Chinese paintings on silk that survive in a European collection

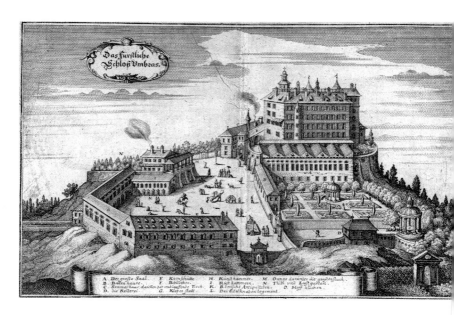

16 Matthäus Merian, *Schloss Ambras*, etching in Martin Zeiller, *Topographia provinciarum Austriacarum* (1649) showing the location of the *Kunstkammer* (H).

and a feathered headdress traditionally associated with the Mexica king Moctezuma II. Some cabinets contained what are now regarded as typical *Kunstkammer* objects: namely, works of art that incorporated *naturalia* like bezoars (stomach stones of animals that were thought to have medicinal properties), shark teeth or other such objects.[25]

The main principle of arrangement at Ambras was by material: objects made of or containing gold were grouped together, as were those of silver, ivory, wood and so forth. This system resembles the organizing principle of the work known as the *Natural History*, an 'encyclopaedic' treatise by the ancient Roman writer Pliny the Elder, who discusses objects including works of sculpture, painting, ceramics, and their histories or makers, but does so according to materials. The term 'encyclopaedic' has accordingly often been applied to the *Kunstkammer*. At Ambras works like Cellini's famous salt cellar, perhaps the most prized object in

Vienna's Kunsthistorisches Museum, were thus not singled out
for individual display but placed with similar items in the cabinets,
in its case with other golden objects.

While visitors to Ambras could obtain access to the collections
(a record of them exists), the vast number of objects crowded
together in the cabinets did not make it possible visually to appreciate individual pieces, like Cellini's, as the current installation
in the former space of the *Kunstkammer* at Ambras depicting the
contents of the individual cabinets on banners has also suggested.
They would have had to be taken out of the cabinets to be
inspected or admired closely. Rather than the individual objects
themselves, it would thus have been the quantity and variety of
what was on view that would have seemed impressive. Current
notions of display and 'visuality' must therefore again be tempered
in interpreting the possible properties, significance and symbolism
of collections of the late sixteenth and seventeenth centuries, and
Rudolf II's must be seen in this context. While the term 'museum'

17 View of interior of *Kunstkammer* at Ambras as reconstructed in 1974.

was applied to Ferdinand's collections,[26] representation in his time did not depend on contemporary ideas of museum presentation.

Although he did not inherit them directly, Rudolf II definitely knew about the collections at Ambras: after Ferdinand's death he made efforts to acquire them and eventually succeeded. However, he left them intact in situ, except for a few pieces that were brought to Prague. Archduke Ferdinand II's collections remained at Ambras until the nineteenth century, when they were brought to Vienna (some have been returned to Ambras), explaining why the Ambras *Kunstkammer* is not only the best documented but the best preserved of any of the collections that belonged to any single Habsburg: they have thus been the subject of much scholarship.[27]

Nevertheless, the collections of Maximilian II and of Philip II of Spain would have been most directly pertinent for Rudolf II. Many parallels exist between the collections of the two cousins, and Rudolf would have been familiar with both of them.[28] From his stay in Spain he would have known about objects Philip II had collected. It is reasonable to hypothesize that Philip had an impact on aspects of Rudolf's taste, and we will discuss this issue in subsequent chapters. However, the palaces in which Philip's holdings would have been housed, the Alcázar in Madrid and El Escorial, would have been under reconstruction or actually being built while Rudolf was in Spain; relatively less is known about them during these years than from the time after Rudolf left Spain, so much remains speculative. On the other hand, Rudolf could easily have seen his father's collections in Vienna and surroundings. He could have observed the beginnings of Maximilian's collecting before he left Central Europe, and their fuller formation when he returned in 1571.

The 1568 inventories of Maximilian II's holdings list clothing, gold, crystal and glass vessels, jewellery, precious religious objects and other household goods. They indicate that Maximilian II would have inherited some items from the collections of Ferdinand I.[29] But this list by no means contains all that Maximilian II owned, nor does it indicate how, as may be determined, he had also inherited principles of collecting from Ferdinand I.

Maximilian II acquired by purchase and by gifts exchanged among the Habsburgs (and with other princes) many objects that have been regarded as exotic, which along with foreign animals would have topped the list of what was preferred.[30] In 1570 Philip II promised to share with Maximilian all the goods and flora that arrived from the Americas. A stream of luxuries and exotica (rare birds, animals, plants, tortoise shells) from both Indies came via Iberia to Central Europe. While under Maximilian II many such items do not appear in inventories, other sources (including paintings by Arcimboldo) indicate that he owned them.[31]

Maximilian II owned antiquities, both coins and statuary. He attempted to obtain coins, medals and bronze and stone sculptures. When the pope sold many of his antique sculptures, the emperor was said to have acquired the best of them.[32] Maximilian hired the scholar-merchant Jacopo Strada to be imperial *antiquarius* to help procure, organize and study the collections. This position was more or less equivalent to that of a curator as well as what is still called an antiquary.[33]

Maximilian was interested in many artistic media. He obtained by gift and purchase bronze reliefs and statuettes by Giambologna, whom he tried to bring into imperial service.[34] He commissioned a large gilded fountain that was modelled by Wenzel Jamnitzer and by cast by Johann Gregor van der Schardt (illus. 18). He owned several other pieces by Jamnitzer and works by other goldsmiths as well. And he possessed several important paintings. These included composite heads, nature studies and portraits by Arcimboldo, allegorical and mythological works by Titian, and other pictures by Tintoretto.[35]

18 Johann Gregor van der Schardt and Wenzel Jamnitzer, *Flora* (Spring), one of the *Allegories of the Four Seasons*, 1569–78, gilded bronze.

Maximilian II had housing built for many of the things he collected. Jacopo Strada designed the Vienna Stallburg, a stable with an arcaded courtyard which still stands opposite the Hofburg, suggesting the esteem with which his horses were prized (illus. 19).[36] He also designed the extensive Neugebäude, a large Palladian suburban villa east of Vienna.[37] Now in a ruinous state, this was probably where the emperor's New Garden was located in which some of his rare animals and birds wandered. (They were also present in his other gardens in and near Vienna.) Again, although paintings and other objects may have been held in the emperor's private quarters, or perhaps in the Neugebäude, since a *Kunstkammer* continued to exist in the Vienna Hofburg during Maximilian II's reign, many of the items that he collected, including prized works by Giambologna, were probably located there (illus. 20).

Under Maximilian II, if not before, the practice began of using the collections on the occasion of diplomatic visits. When Duke-Elector Augustus of Saxony visited Vienna in 1573, he was entertained with a hunt and by being taken to see 'paintings and

19 Stallburg, Vienna, designed by Jacopo Strada, 1558–65.

other things' *in camera*: the choice of this word, literally meaning chamber, may likely be identified with the *Kunstkammer*, or art chamber, which we now know was located in the Hofburg. There they saw a painting of a reversible composite head which was probably the work of Arcimboldo.[38]

Imperial diplomacy also employed artworks as strategic gifts. Maximilian II commissioned several flattering allegories from Arcimboldo, which were given to Duke-Elector Augustus in 1574. Many other works by Arcimboldo may also have been sent to Dresden, as Dresden inventories record them, and drawings by the artist have also been found there.[39] Maximilian was following a widespread contemporary practice: for example, in 1565 Cosimo de' Medici gave Maximilian II bronzes by Giambologna, and his successor Francesco sent works by the sculptor along with porcelains to Dresden in 1587.[40]

While Duke-Elector Augustus's visit to the imperial collections is described as being one of many *passatempi* or pastimes – and it was undoubtedly that too – the use of art in diplomacy switches focus to how the character and quality of the objects, and for that matter the creatures, might be seen in this regard. The possession of luxury goods, rare animals and birds and exotica, particularly those from the Americas to which only the Habsburgs had direct access, added to the perception that they ranked first in status among rulers.[41] The intricate content and complicated messages of works like Jamnitzer's fountain and Arcimboldo's paintings were no doubt visually and intellectually entertaining, but they conveyed a deeper meaning. Jamnitzer's fountain also placed the emperor literally at the top of a model of the universe. Arcimboldo's allegories symbolized the Habsburgs' dominion over the world, represented by its components, the elements, and its eternal control, suggested by the never-ending cycle of the seasons. These objects also emblematize one ultimate meaning of the collections: universal in their extent, they suggested in microcosm that the

20 Giambologna, *Mercury in Flight*, c. 1585, bronze.

macrocosm of the world, and the body politic, were under the emperor's sway.[42]

RUDOLF II'S COLLECTIONS WERE BUILT on the actual and ideological foundations of his predecessors but surpassed them in size and significance. He inherited Maximilian II's collections as a whole without having to divide them with his brothers, unlike the way in which Ferdinand I's possessions – his lands and much of his collections – had been parcelled out among Maximilian II and his siblings. While Maximilian II possessed some important paintings, and Philip II, Rudolf's other paragon, owned major works that also provided models for him, Rudolf II's collections exceeded them both in quantity. The number of paintings the emperor owned is impressive even according to present-day standards: at Rudolf's death the Venetian ambassador Soranzo said that Prague Castle was packed with over 3,000 paintings, and recent estimates suggest this may be very accurate.[43] Rudolf's *Kunstkammer* was also comparatively large, though harder to estimate: while Archduke Ferdinand II's inventory lists around 2,500 items, the imperial *Kunstkammer* contained well over 2,800 items according to the inventory compiled by the imperial antiquary Daniel Fröschl during the years 1607–11, and this inventory lists the contents of only one space in the suite of rooms in which the *Kunstkammer* was located. The entire *Kunstkammer* must have been much larger and had many more objects with separate inventories, and much that the emperor owned was probably held elsewhere.[44]

While many entries in the Rudolfine inventory refer to books, it may be inferred that many other tomes were kept in another location, likely in a separate library, as other Habsburg (and contemporary) rulers are known to have had them. Some suits of armour and other weapons are listed as being in the *Kunstkammer*, but they do not amount to all that Rudolf II owned. It has been suggested that a separate armoury, to which later inventories refer, was also located elsewhere in Prague Castle.

The quality of the works that Rudolf owned was astounding. According to a list drawn up in 1621 for the imperial viceroy Prince Karl of Liechtenstein by artists who had worked for Rudolf II, the Prague collections contained paintings by Netherlandish artists of a slightly older as well as the current generation: these eventually included most of the painted oeuvre of Pieter Brueghel the Elder, much of which is still in Vienna. Many paintings by Quentin Metsys and his sons as well as by Jan Gossaert (Mabuse) were found in Prague. Among works by Netherlandish artists who were contemporary with Rudolf II were paintings by Joachim Beuckelaer, Pieter Aertsen and Karel van Mander. 'Old German masters' were represented by Matthias Grünewald and Dürer, whose works in various media Rudolf particularly admired. Rudolf owned several altarpieces by Dürer: when in 1606 Rudolf acquired Dürer's *Feast of the Rosary*, according to the painter/historian Joachim von Sandrart, porters carried it over the Alps from Venice to Prague, where it still resides. Among the pictures by Italian artists in the imperial collection were important paintings ranging from works by Leonardo da Vinci such as the *Lady with an Ermine* (now in Kraków) to pictures by Rudolf's contemporaries, including the Carracci and Michelangelo Merisi da Caravaggio (a now lost depiction of Joseph and Potiphar's wife). After a lengthy pursuit, Rudolf succeeded in buying the famed series of the loves of the gods by Correggio. In addition to works by Titian, Tintoretto and Veronese that he had inherited, the emperor acquired Titian's *Laura de Dianti*, commissioned Veronese's four allegories of love (now in London), and four pictures with stories of Hercules by Tintoretto. He owned many pictures by his own court painters, as well as some of the first paintings by Goltzius, who also created works specially for him.

Among works by Goltzius in Rudolf's hands were *Federkunst-stücke*, drawings as big as large paintings but executed in pen and ink on canvas that are done in a style that laboriously imitates the way in which engravings are made with a burin using swelling parallel lines, hatching and cross-hatching. Some had oil and chalk added; these true marvels of art (as they were called) were puzzled over by connoisseurs who wondered how they could

21 Hendrick Goltzius, *Sine Cerere et Libero friget Venus* (*Without Ceres and Bacchus, Venus Would Freeze*), c. 1600–1603, ink and oil on canvas.

have been done (illus. 21).[45] They complemented a large collection of drawings and prints by many artists including Arcimboldo
and Hoefnagel that were kept in books in the *Kunstkammer* along
with the actual copper plates (sometimes silvered), which were
used for engravings (by Sadeler and Goltzius). Many of the most
famous drawings by Albrecht Dürer, including the bulk of the
artist's drawings that are now in the collections of the Albertina
in Vienna, belonged to Rudolf II (illus. 22).

Although not as numerous as his paintings or drawings, Rudolf
also owned some important works of sculpture. Bronze reliefs
and statuettes by the noted sculptor Giambologna and many

22 Albrecht Dürer, *Hare*, 1502, watercolour and bodycolour.

other works of sculpture were placed on tables and other stands in the *Kunstkammer*. Giambologna's pupil Hans Mont produced works in bronze, terracotta and probably a form of stucco that the emperor owned. Rudolf also possessed sculpture by another, more renowned pupil of Giambologna, Adriaen de Vries, who supplied both large (illus. 23) and small bronzes for him both

23 Adriaen de Vries, *Mercury and Psyche*, 1593, bronze.

before and after he was lured to Prague (after Maximilian II and Rudolf II had both tried to attract Giambologna into imperial service), where he established a foundry.

The most famous antiquity in the imperial collection was the so-called *Ilioneus*, a version of a Hellenistic marble that had been owned by a series of well-known collectors, starting with the artist and theorist Lorenzo Ghiberti, and passing through the hands of Duke Alfonso II d'Este, from whose successors the emperor acquired it in 1604. Other antiquities included a version of the so-called *Bed of Polykleitos* and famous cameos such as the *Gemma Augustea*.[46] Copies and busts of emperors and empresses were displayed in several places in Prague, including picture galleries, the New Hall and the Spanish Hall in the castle and in the Belvedere, as well as the *Kunstkammer* (where from 1607 the *Ilioneus* seems to have been packed away, however).

Examples of the arts of design Rudolf II possessed count among the treasures now seen in Vienna and in other European and American museums. Particularly noteworthy for their novelty as well as quality are ivories, rhinoceros horns (illus. 24) and Seychelles coco de mer carved by Nikolaus Pfaff with mounts by Anton Schweinberger. Rock crystal vessels by Milanese artisans, including the workshop of the Miseroni that Rudolf brought to Prague, initiated a long-lasting tradition in the Czech lands. Other works that were to be found in the *Kunstkammer* were reliefs incised into glass by Caspar Lehmann, who began the production of this important medium in Central Europe. Creations of what are called *commessi in pietre dure*, mosaics made from semi-precious hard stones, an invention of the Florentine Castrucci family, were another feature of the Prague *Kunstkammer*: Rudolf II also attracted the Castrucci to Prague, where this sort of art endured. These items mentioned may be considered to be *artificialia*, works made with artifice or art, in the sense of *Kunst*, appropriate for a *Kunstkammer*.

The 1607–11 inventory also indicates the presence of objects for investigation of nature that are now categorized as *scientifica*, which, however, is a modern notion.[47] These were items such as terrestrial and celestial globes, armillary spheres, measuring devices, astrolabes, quadrants, sextants and telescopes for making astronomical observations, and scales. But visitors to Prague also saw other large instruments for astronomical observation in other places on the Hradčany, such as in the Belvedere (illus. 25).[48]

24 Nikolaus Pfaff, drinking cup, 1611, African rhinoceros horn, African warthog tusks and gilt silver.

25 Erasmus Habermel, *Sextant*, 1600.

As previously suggested, a *Kunstkammer* like Rudolf's also would have contained *naturalia* or specimens of nature: the Prague inventory indicates that Rudolf's collection had them in abundance. Dried plants, flowers and other flora, skeletons, antlers, stuffed animals and sea creatures, birds, parts of their bodies, bones and the like are all mentioned. Books with images of fauna and flora were also present in the *Kunstkammer*. All of these were far more numerous than comparable holdings of earlier Habsburg collections.

Many such *naturalia* were left unworked, but many were mounted, cut or otherwise made into artefacts. Such are the baskets, carved ivories, feather paintings, carved stones and other sorts of items that came from both 'Indies'. These are what have more recently been called 'exotica'. Although they are not designated as such in the *Kunstkammer* inventory, there is some recognition of their separate character, as they are grouped together at the beginning of the inventory.

Less attention has been given to the way in which the many living species, fruits and flowers that Rudolf collected complemented the *Kunstkammer*, as they did those of his predecessors. Like Ferdinand I and Maximilian II, Rudolf II had an orangery for the cultivation of citrus fruits, which were regarded as exotic north of the Alps.[49] He also had extensive gardens laid out in the precinct of the Hradčany. It is known that his ambassadors and other servants sent rare plants and flowers back to Prague. Emanuel Sweerts, a contemporary artist, writer and merchant, called the emperor the greatest lover of flowers in the world, which is not to be interpreted as simple flattery.[50] New fountains and ponds adorned the gardens.[51]

The moat of Prague Castle was stocked with deer and still bears this name (Stag Moat in English). The cultivation of deer does not seem to have been just for hunting: they often served as subjects for paintings (by Roelant Savery and others). Rudolf's lions, leopards and other wild beasts were not hunted, but given housing in a separate structure near the castle probably built from circa 1581 by Ulrich Aostalli known as the Lion Courtyard. These creatures were rare in Central Europe, as were other animals in the imperial collections. Exotic species of birds and aquarian beings were also sent to Prague, where they were kept in an aviary and fishpond made especially for them not far from the palace on the Hradčany. Many such creatures appear in paintings by the imperial court artists (illus. 26).[52]

Like Ferdinand of the Tyrol and Maximilian II, Rudolf also had many structures made or decorated for his collections. Soon after settling in Prague, he had the so-called 'Summer House' attached to the south wing of the palace reconstructed and decorated; work went on there simultaneously with the reconstruction of a similar space in Vienna, which, however, along with the Amalienburg inside the Hofburg, was probably being put up under the supervision of Archduke Ernst, who had been made governor of Lower Austria.[53] It was in the Summer House that Hans Krafft saw parts of the imperial collections in 1584.[54] From 1583 stately stables were built opposite them on the other side of what is now the second courtyard in Prague Castle: a corridor above the stables had already been built by the imperial *Baumeister* (mason-architect) Ulrich Aostalli in 1576, and it was now extended to connect the two wings of the courtyard. Corridors on the first and second floors were designed anew and completed circa 1601: they contained rooms for the *Kunstkammer* on the first floor above ground and a gallery for paintings on the second.

This extension was a consequence of the growth of the emperor's collections during the 1580s, when existing spaces proved insufficient to contain them. A gallery for paintings was commissioned in 1586 to be erected above the north wing containing the stables; it was completed in 1596–7. Its placement above stables suggests that creatures and art were both valued objects (and the

26 Dirck de Quade van Ravesteyn (?), *Dodo*, miniature from Rudolf II's bestiary, vol. II, 1590–1610.

simultaneous gifts of horses and works of art by princes to the emperor suggest the same). A 'New Hall' for sculpture was built adjacent to this so-called 'Spanish Hall': both were probably designed by Giovanni Gargiolli. However, a preparatory drawing of the elevation of a formal room with images of sculpture drawn by Bartholomeus Spranger dateable circa 1590 (illus. 27) indicates that designs for the display of sculpture were already being envisioned around the time of the initial construction of the paintings' gallery. Illustrations and descriptions of the finished rooms suggest in any case that the spaces being designed for Rudolf's collections were hardly jumbles, but majestically designed rooms.

The placement of objects in Rudolf's *Kunstkammer* can also be demonstrated to have incorporated a concern with display. While many artefacts were kept in containers or closed cabinets, some were placed on them, and many more stood on tables. Their display accords with a principle similar to that which might also be applied to the paintings' collections, which overflowed the rooms where they stood or were hung. These suggest ideas of abundance and variety, which underlie general conceptions of the collection.[55] While the placement of objects in containers suggests that the rooms for the collections no doubt served as repositories, objects could still be taken out to be studied or contemplated (and ambassadors describe how the emperor delighted in looking at his acquisitions).[56] In any case, the abundance of objects as well as their display suggests why the rooms might have been seen as suitably representative for diplomatic purposes.

All this again must be placed in contemporary context. By the later sixteenth century *Kunstkammern* and other collections were to be found at many courts in Central Europe. The dukes of Saxony and Bavaria, the Landgrave of Hesse-Kassel, the Margrave of Brandenburg (in Berlin), the Duke of Württemberg, the Duke of Saxe-Coburg, the Duke of Saxe-Gotha, the Duke of Saxe-Weimar and many lesser potentates and prelates had *Kunstkammern*.

Several of these were quite large and contained important works, as the inventories of the Munich, Stuttgart, Dresden and Kassel collections attest.[57]

Numerous documents also state that owning rare and precious objects was an expression of their owner's worth and made an impression. Founding documents of the Munich *Schatzkammer*

27 Bartholomeus Spranger, design for New Room, Prague Castle, *c.* 1590, drawing.

from 1565 say it was intended to express and increase the reputation of the Wittelsbachs.[58] A 1587 proposal by Gabriel Kaltemarckt
to establish (or reform) a *Kunstkammer* in Dresden states similarly that such a collection added to a prince's reputation.[59] Jakob
Bornitz, in a treatise of circa 1600, stated this as a matter of fact:
the Saxon electors had established *Kunstkammern* to increase, in
his words, their august magnificence.[60]

Bornitz's comment gives voice to a theory that had originated
in antiquity and was revived in Renaissance Italy: magnificence.
In Plato's *Republic* magnificence is treated as a virtue of the
philosopher-king, and in Aristotle's *Ethics* (1122) it is described as
a proper form of expenditure. Magnificence thus became a trait
of the ideal ruler. In fifteenth-century treatises such as Giovanni
Pontano's *De Magnificentia*, these and other ancient ideas were reformulated to provide an additional socio-political reason for the
usefulness of the arts. The arts offered a means by which a ruler
could demonstrate his magnificence through civic expenditure
and express his splendour.[61]

Several tracts on *Kunstkammern* rephrased the terms of this
discussion, beginning with Samuel Quiccheberg's *Inscriptiones*
of 1565. Quiccheberg was associated with the Munich court, and
while his treatise may be regarded as a proposal for reform (the
Munich *Kunstkammer* seems already to have been in existence), his
proposal mentions many of the kinds of things that were in collections, beyond the *Kunstkammer*. He refers to the *Kunstkammer* as
a theatre of the world. This notion has many connotations: it was
a place where all parts of the world could be seen, representing
the idea of much in little, *multum in parvo*; it was accordingly a
microcosm that reflected the greater world, the macrocosm. And,
as Quiccheberg states, he meant it in the sense of Giulio Camillo's
memory theatre, a mnemonic device that could be used to contain
concepts about the entire world, which was also realized in an
actual structure, as the *Kunstkammer* was.[62]

Bornitz's discussion of collections like the *Kunstkammer* brings us close to Rudolf II. Bornitz was in imperial service, knew several of the Prague court artists personally, described objects that were in the Prague collections and seems to have had wide knowledge of them and of other collections. Bornitz said that Rudolf 'exhibited the greatest understanding of the art of painting' and that the emperor 'brought together from everywhere the most excellent paintings at great price'. According to Bonitz, Rudolf also appreciated works of the mechanical arts, expanding his argument further. Bornitz treated *Kunstkammern* as being of such importance that he devoted a separate chapter to princely *Kunstkammern* in a book on the polity in which he outlined what a *Kunstkammer* should contain. Bornitz's description encompasses much of what was actually in the Prague *Kunstkammer*: books, works by goldsmiths, jewellers, clocks, automata, paintings and sculpture, along with rare works, including those from the 'New World', as well as extraordinary natural statues, antiquities, coins and antique devices. He uses the words *artificialia, technica* (where others would have *scientifica*) and the equivalent of exotica to describe them. He explicitly states that a prince should establish a *Kunstkammer* because it is a way to declare his magnificence by presenting rare and unusual works for view. Bornitz also planned to write a separate treatise on *Kunstkammern* that he suggests would be about the growth of the state and the augmentation of the polity, and would show the ways in which *Kunstkammern* might demonstrate princes' public magnificence.[63]

Similar ideas were openly expressed in princely circles during the era of Rudolf II. For example, aristocrats at the knightly academy in Tübingen heard them discussed in an oration Franz Karl of Sachsen-Lauingen delivered (or had delivered for him) before 1613. Franz Karl argued for the representational role of *Kunstkammern*, saying that princes should own them, and cites as evidence for the superiority of Germany the unequalled quality of German artisans who supplied works for such collections.

In a world in which rulers were interested in art-making and art collecting, and possessing objects was thought to represent the magnificence of the prince, collecting served as an implement of statecraft, as we have seen in its utilization as a tool of diplomacy. Rudolf II himself was explicit about integrating gift giving and collecting into diplomacy. He wrote a letter to Duke-Elector Christian II of Saxony that accompanied some gifts he was sending, saying that he had learned that the elector delighted in paintings and other works of art, and hoped the gifts expressed his wish to maintain good relations between the Houses of Austria and Saxony.

28 Adriaen de Vries, *Christian II*, 1603, bronze.

Several gifts directly appealed to a Saxon–Habsburg alliance. They include a bust of Christian II wearing a medallion of the emperor and modelled on Rudolf's bust, with allegorical figures representing Concord supporting it (illus. 28); an allegory on the Saxon–Habsburg alliance painted on the recto of a *commesso in pietre dure* depicting the Saxon coat of arms; and a set of allegories on the war with the Turks. Conversely, several ambassadors noted that giving works of art was a way to gain the emperor's favour: the inventory of the imperial *Kunstkammer* contains many references to such gifts.

While artefacts and other items in the *Kunstkammer* itself, the painting galleries and the emperor's quarters were not easily accessible as they were located in the more secluded parts of the palace, and many objects may have been contained in cabinets, this does not mean that they were invisible. The very seclusion of the imperial collections in private quarters would have made a visit to them something special. The practice known during Maximilian II's reign of taking important visitors to see collections was continued under Rudolf II. As mentioned in the preceding chapter, Rudolf took princely visitors such as Maximilian of Bavaria and Christian II of Saxony to see his collections. One envoy reported that it was also customary for the collections to be shown to ambassadors when they were about to leave Prague, a sign of recognition and to stress their importance. Granting ambassadors such a visit at other times (as when they brought gifts) was also seen as a sign of special favour.[64]

Other people who gained entry to the palace could have seen works of art. The hall in which ambassadors and other supplicants gathered was adorned with tapestries. Tapestries were the most labour intensive, expensive and therefore in some ways impressive of works of art, although they are not now often regarded as such, because they can be neither easily nor lengthily displayed in most museums.[65]

Even though access to Rudolf II's collections was limited, some people who were of lesser estate were also able to see them. Visitors including Krafft and several others are known to have been escorted by court artists. Rudolf II accorded one visiting artist a similar favour by allowing him repeatedly to see the collections.[66] The court artists themselves obviously had entry, since they both copied and emulated works in the collections. So evidently did other artists: drawn copies exist of paintings Rudolf owned for which no earlier reproductions were made.[67]

It is also mistaken to believe that collections like Rudolf's lacked a representative function because many people did not see them. During the era before the foundation of public museums, imperial and other princely collections were regarded as belonging to the ruler, to be disposed of as he (or in some cases, she) wished, except for those few objects that were understood to be inalienable possessions of the Habsburg or other dynasties, like the English crown jewels. The chief audience for the imperial collections beyond the ruler himself would have been other members of the court, similar circles of rulers beyond it, and their representatives, all of whom shared similar attitudes. Public opinion did not necessarily count for much in this world, in which important ideas were communicated to those of similar rank, and a general impression, or even rumour, of wealth and grandeur were enough for the masses. The relative inaccessibility of the imperial collections in fact added to their aura, suggesting that they were among Rudolf's *arcana imperii*.

And even though relatively few people may have been able to see them in person, the fame of the imperial collections reached far. Karel van Mander, the Dutch painter and writer on art, wrote in 1604 that Rudolf II was the greatest art lover in the world, and that Prague was the place to go to see art (adding, if it were possible): there one could see 'a remarkable number of outstanding and precious, curious, unusual, and priceless works'.[68] For the

German artist-writer Joachim von Sandrart, Rudolf II's Prague was a Parnassus of the arts, attesting to their lasting impact.[69]

The *Kunstkammer* has been described as a mirror of creation, an archive of knowledge, a summary of what was known, a stimulus to artists and a fund for experiments. It was all of these, and we will return to several of these functions. Curiosity – and Rudolf was undoubtedly interested in art, nature and science, to be discussed further in the next chapters – entertainment, reputation, memory and fame all went into establishing a *Kunstkammer*. But if one wishes ultimately to understand the fundamental reason why so many rulers of Rudolf's time made large collections and invested so much time and expense in them, the answer is that they were fitting, indeed in some respects necessary, for the status of a prince.[70] Whatever other roles they may have had, representation remained a chief, even major function for collections: collections provided visual proof of a prince's resources and power. In Rudolf's case, both key objects in the collections and the collections themselves would, moreover, have symbolically conveyed the message that the world was under the emperor's dominion. In a world of collectors, patrons and princely practitioners, the emperor owned the largest painting collection and the biggest and most impressive *Kunstkammer* of his time. One visitor described them as making a loud impression, another said (without irony) that they were worthy of their owner.[71]

Still, there remains a personal aspect to Rudolf's passion for collecting. He was more than merely involved: he wanted to possess all he could that interested him. Archduchess Maria Anna of Styria (Rudolf's aunt by marriage) is reported to have remarked that 'what the emperor knows about he thinks he must have' (*Wovon der Kaiser weiss, meint er musst's haben*).[72] Hans Khevenhuller, imperial ambassador in Spain, said that the emperor had to have the most rare and strange things. Khevenhuller also exemplifies how ambassadors were engaged not just in diplomatic activities, but in scouting out potential acquisitions and making them.[73] Beside using merchants, agents, artists and even princes as intermediaries, the emperor sent court painters such as Arcimboldo and von Aachen to make acquisitions.

Though it remains more speculative, another reason may be proposed for Rudolf's intense interest in collecting. This again may be related to the Habsburg tradition. While he had acquired objects and ideas from his predecessors, they may have served as more than examples. He may have wished not only to imitate them, but to surpass them as he did contemporary princes. This may also be seen in the kinds of works that his artists made for him (illus. 23 and 29). Collecting – and patronage related to it – were fields in which he could obtain primacy. Ultimately, Rudolf II did amass the biggest, best and most important collection of his time, one that surpassed even his, and his artists', models.

But when Rudolf II died, all that he had assembled began to dissipate. Works were sold to pay debts, moved to Vienna along with the imperial court and divided among his brothers. In 1619 the rebel estates made an inventory of the collections with the intention of selling them. Although after the Battle of White Mountain in 1620 Frederick of the Palatinate could not make off with works when he fled from Prague, during the course of the Thirty Years War Bavarian troops under Maximilian took objects with them. At that time Prince Karl of Liechtenstein had several court artists draw up another, more precise, inventory, probably as a means of stock taking, but works continued to be removed to Vienna. Saxon troops who occupied Prague in 1631 and 1632 took away fifty wagons full of booty. In 1648 while treaties were being signed in Westphalia that ended the war, Swedish troops were deliberately sent to Prague to seize what they could. They sacked Prague Castle and gardens as well as residences in the Malá Strana and made off with much of what remained of the

29 Adriaen de Vries, *Rudolf II*, 1603, bronze.

imperial collections.[74] This decisive blow spelled the end to the story of the bulk of Rudolf's collections in Prague, though not the end of the history of collections in Prague Castle, nor of the place of Rudolf as collector in history writing. The collections remained renowned, even as their interpretation contributed to the making of the black legend around Rudolf.

In the reinstallation and renaming of the collections of sculpture and applied arts as the *Kunstkammer* in the Kunsthistorisches Museum in Vienna in the early twenty-first century, Rudolf II seems, nevertheless, to have been vindicated. Objects from his *Kunstkammer* have literally been given a central place. Rudolf II seems to look proudly over them, as his bust now stands on the central north–south axis of the museum. In the end his collection and his status as a collector have gained him the renown that he deserves, if not in the way he might have imagined (illus. 29).

THREE

Rudolf II as Patron of Art and Architecture

udolf II has long been acknowledged as a great patron of the arts as well as a great collector.[1] His collecting and patronage are interrelated: Rudolf commissioned many works that entered the imperial painting gallery, including pictures from Italian artists like Jacopo Tintoretto, Federico Barroci and Paolo Veronese as well as from Netherlanders like Hendrick Goltzius.[2] Rudolf II also brought to Prague or maintained in imperial employ scores of Italian, German and Netherlandish painters, sculptors, goldsmiths and masters of stone and ivory carving, who made works for him. He acquired objects from other goldsmiths, carvers, clockmakers and masters of other arts of design from German centres like Augsburg and Nuremberg and elsewhere that were kept in the *Kunstkammer*. In turn, the imperial collections inspired artists in Prague.[3]

Like his collecting, Rudolf II's artistic patronage has also often been taken as an idiosyncratic aberration, but again much more was involved than simply personal interest. Like collecting, imperial patronage of the arts necessitated large outlays of energy, time and money. Patronage must also be considered in relation to matters of rulership, but not as Rudolf's approach has been understood heretofore.

This chapter focuses on the relation of Rudolf II's patronage of the arts to his role as a ruler. It adduces several different

30 Matthias Gateway, Prague Castle, built during the time of Rudolf II, with a later inscription to Matthias dated 1614.

contexts for interpretation. These include patronage as a princely pursuit, the influence of earlier models as well as contemporary court taste, rulers' concern with public welfare, and representation. It then assesses the character of Rudolfine art, and how the emperor may have helped shape some of its distinctive features.

RUDOLF II CLEARLY HELD the visual arts – and particularly painting – in high esteem. He provided artists active at his court with stipends and bonuses, and he freed them from local restrictions to practise their professions. He ennobled several of his favourite court painters.[4] In general, he raised the social status of artists, notably by issuing a *Letter of Majesty* for the Prague painters' guild that had a great impact on the local scene. It decreed that painting should no longer be referred to as a craft but as the 'art of painting' and exempted painters from standard guild rules.[5]

The emperor also implicitly raised the status of artists when he engaged directly with his court artists or worked as an artist himself. An incident involving Bartholomeus Spranger, the longest serving court artist, is illuminating. Soon after Rudolf II established his permanent residence in Prague circa 1583, he installed Spranger in the palace inside Hradčany Castle. On 24 June 1584, the German merchant Hans Ulrich Krafft dined with the painter in the imperial palace and witnessed Spranger being called to work by the emperor. Spranger told Krafft that Rudolf watched him paint and corrected things he did not like.[6]

Spranger's case is not unique: in 1588 Curzio Picchena, Florentine ambassador to the imperial court, reported that Rudolf sent daily for the wax sculptor and medal-maker Antonio Abondio to prompt him and to have him show all his models. Picchena added that in the workshops of Spranger, Arcimboldo and Abondio, he saw all that the emperor had had made. Picchena said that Rudolf greatly delighted not only in sculpture, painting, stucco and wax objects, but also in stonework, probably meaning *commessi in pietre dure*, originally a Florentine specialty that was introduced to Prague and produced in workshops about which Picchena could have known. The emperor is otherwise known to have made frequent visits to his artists' ateliers: Roderigo Alidosi, Florentine ambassador to Prague 1605–7, stated that on afternoons Rudolf did not hold audiences (again an indication that he was by no means a recluse) he went 'to see his artists paint, painting himself at times, and going to see his goldsmiths, clockmakers, and stone-cutters work'.[7] Rudolf directed the restoration of works of art and designed his own inventions for tapestries, paintings and sculpture, to be discussed presently.

A credible account published by Balthasar Exner a few years after the emperor's death suggests that Rudolf participated in a wider range of artistic activity. The emperor made a table out of gems, suggesting it was like *commessi in pietre dure*; Rudolf was a most ingenious painter and a goldsmith who made a crown himself, but mainly a clockmaker; in addition, he delighted in inspecting bronze casting. A reliable eighteenth-century source reports that Rudolf turned ivory in the workshop of Hans Wecker and Peter Zick.[8] A turned rhinoceros horn cup made by the emperor survives in the Royal Danish Collections displayed in Rosenborg Castle, Copenhagen, where it probably came as a gift to King Christian IV (illus. 32).[9]

Rudolf II's personal engagement in the visual and plastic arts was by no means singular. Writers starting with Leon Battista Alberti in the fifteenth century (for example, *On Painting*) picked up traces from antiquity (found, for example, in Pliny, *Natural History*, 35) that well-born youths had been taught painting: they argued sculpture and architecture were liberal arts, suitable activities for free-born people, not simply banausic or mechanical

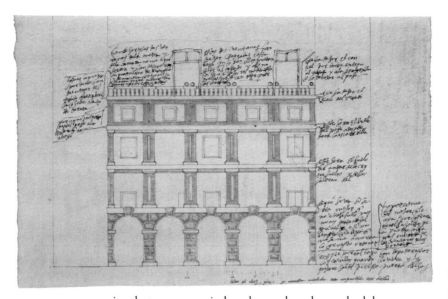

pursuits that were carried on by enslaved people, labourers or low-born artisans.[10] In his 1528 treatise on the ideal courtier (*Il cortegiano*), Baldassare Castiglione maintained that courtiers and princes should not spurn painting, but should both appreciate and speak knowledgeably about it, and that they should regard drawing as a worthy practice – an argument anticipated by Aristotle (*Politics*, 8), who had argued for drawing as a part of education and for its importance as a part of life. Castiglione's book became an international bestseller: it was translated or adopted in many languages, and his advice was followed in many places in Europe.[11] Many princes learned drawing as a matter of education as well as taking it up as a pastime. Among several other rulers, Emperor Maximilian II is reported to have been a competent draughtsman.[12]

Like Rudolf, during the sixteenth century other rulers determined subjects to be executed by artists, visited their workshops, corrected their works and concerned themselves with having

31 Philip's corrections on the architects' plans for the Alcázar, Madrid, 1561–2.

paintings restored. Among Habsburg precedents for Rudolf II are Charles V and Philip II commissioning portraits and mythological works (*poesie*) from Titian; Charles V visiting the Venetian painter's atelier (Giorgio Vasari tells a story of how Charles V picked up Titian's brush); Philip II writing corrections on architectural elevations for the palace of the Alcázar in Madrid (illus. 31); Charles ordering the restoration of Titian's portrait of the emperor's deceased spouse; and Emperor Ferdinand I having Arcimboldo copy Habsburg portraits.[13] One more noteworthy example from another contemporary court may suffice. In a painting of circa 1570 made for the *studiolo* in the Palazzo Vecchio, Florence, Giovanni Maria Butteri shows Grand Duke Francesco visiting the ducal glass works (considered further in the next chapter).

Many of Rudolf's contemporaries were also directly involved in the production of artworks. Archdukes Matthias and Leopold, Duke (later Elector) Maximilian I of Bavaria and Augustus, Christian I and Christian II, duke-electors of Saxony, all turned ivory on the lathe: works by Augustus were held in the Prague *Kunstkammer*.[14] King Sigismund, Duke Heinrich Julius of Braunschweig-Wolfenbüttel and Count Simon VI of Lippe-Detmold were painters. Like Archduke Ferdinand II (of the Tyrol), Landgrave Moritz of Hesse-Kassel designed buildings. Archduke Karl (Charles), ruler of Inner Austria, is said to have been a joiner.[15] When Rudolf II worked as an artist, he was thus participating in what was a common princely pursuit.

Princes participated in the arts for many reasons. Exner adduced several examples of such involvement as characteristics of the ideal ruler.[16] Princely patronage was praiseworthy for other reasons as well. According to several humanists, a ruler was supposed to demonstrate magnificence or liberality in his expenditures, among other things on buildings and objects.[17] Patronage of art and architecture was believed to have a broader social purpose. In his treatise on fortifications, which presented ideal plans for cities as well as forts, Albrecht Dürer suggested that spending money on building was a way for a ruler to supply employment and payment to poor subjects, and thus alleviate their need to beg or to have an excuse to rebel.[18] Rudolf was a great admirer of Dürer, and a copy of this book was in his *Kunstkammer*.[19] Giovanni Botero, whose treatise on reason of state (*ragion di stato*, 1589) was soon available in German in 1596, also argued that expenditure on building provided a ruler with a means not only to display his authority but to put people to

32 Rudolf II, covered cup, *c.* 1600 (?), East African rhinoceros horn with mahogany and gold.

work.[20] Bornitz, an imperial official who has been discussed in the previous chapter, indicates that similar ideas drawn from Botero were current in imperial court circles.[21] In Bornitz's eyes, painting, sculpture and other kinds of artefactual production functioned as did surgery, physics, medicine, anatomy, the building of fortifications and all the other arts that had previously been considered mechanical. They and all the liberal arts with which they were connected and that they utilized were necessary because they promoted the public good. Hence, Bornitz says that Rudolf II spared neither time nor expense on the arts because, as he says, they served for public utility and greatness (*amplitudinem*).

An emblematic device (*impresa*) that Rudolf II adopted suggests he was long associated with the ideal that a ruler supports the public weal. A portrait medal of the emperor made circa 1576 by Antonio Abondio bears the inscription *saluti publicae* on its obverse (illus. 33). This is the motto of a device in which the accompanying image depicts an eagle flying aloft into the sky where a laurel wreath crowns it. As the eagle often symbolizes the emperor, this device suggests that Rudolf II would gain glory and immortality through his devotion to the welfare of the public.

33 Antonio Abondio, medal of Rudolf II, with the reverse showing *saluti publicae* as an inscription, *c.* 1577, silver.

The medal exists in copper, silver (seen here) and gold versions, and may have circulated widely.[22]

Amplitudinem, the word in Bornitz's text, brings up another reason princes patronized the arts: representation. *Amplitudo* is translated here as greatness, but in Cicero, Pliny and other Roman writers, and in the works of Renaissance authors who were familiar with them, the term conveys connotations of dignity, grandeur and prestige. All these concepts relate to the notion of representation.

Princely representation is most easily visualized in buildings. The importance of building for princes was articulated later in seventeenth-century Central Europe, but the language in which it was expressed suggests that this ideal had become broadly familiar over the years. Prince Karl Eusebius von Liechtenstein (1611–1684), Karl von Liechtenstein's successor, wrote that building brought undying name and fame and eternal memory for the builder, and that this desire drove the ancient Romans and all nations to create majestic buildings.[23] In seventeenth-century discussions of architecture, large palaces were believed to embody the idea of *grandezza*, meaning grandeur. The château of Versailles offers the best-known example, but many large palaces were also built in Central Europe and earlier.[24] Whether or not princes primarily intended what they built to serve the public good, representation in the form of buildings was certainly an aim of their patronage, as even those scholars agree who have criticized the idea that collections were a form of representation, discussed in the previous chapter.[25]

While the expression of grandeur through large palaces was an idea that was openly discussed in the seventeenth century, earlier Habsburg palaces could also be large, made a similar impression and were probably also meant to do so. In Spain Charles V's and Philip's reconstruction and extension of the Madrid Alcázar provides one example, Philip II's building of the palace-monastery of El Escorial another and the expansion of the palace at Aranjuez a third. In contrast with Karl Eusebius von Liechtenstein's appeal to use ornament (*Zier*), by which he meant the application of the five orders of columns or pilasters to buildings, royal palaces in Philip's Spain had long expanses of unarticulated mural surfaces. Their external walls were punctuated only by windows, horizontal stringcourses and largely flat vertical elements. These features appear prominently on the lateral facades of the Escorial (illus. 35), and were originally also to be seen on the Alcázar and in Aranjuez. These Spanish palaces have been described as epitomizing an *estilo desornmentado*, a 'disornamented' style in architecture, which differed from architecture ornamented by the use of the traditional orders.[26]

Rudolf II would have been very familiar with royal palaces in Spain. During Rudolf's Spanish sojourn, Philip II was moving his court to Madrid, where the principal royal residence was the Alcázar. The construction and decoration of the palace-monastery of the Escorial commenced the year Rudolf arrived. Philip frequently consulted with his architects and workers on site, and Rudolf must have often accompanied him on these travels, as the king kept him close. Rudolf's experience of Spanish architecture evidently made a long-lasting impression. The emperor repeatedly tried to obtain drawings of Spanish palaces.[27]

Spanish architecture, especially the Escorial, provided a model for several of Rudolf's building projects in Austria and in Bohemia. A key example is the relatively little known Schloss in Linz (Upper Austria) that was the emperor's largest long-lasting construction project. From the beginning of Rudolf's reign, he expressed interest in this castle, had an earlier building on the site torn down in 1599, and after several years of planning had a new one erected from 1604. Rudolf II was personally concerned with examining and approving projects for this building as well as with overseeing the progress being made on it: he is

documented as having received, sent or ordered models and drawings of the Schloss.[28] An appeal for funding made in 1600 on the emperor's behalf to the Landtag (Estates) of Upper Austria says that the Schloss would be an ornament of the Land (*ein zier und wolstadt des Landes*), as well as a comfortable residence (*bequeme Residenz und hofflager*), hence representational as well as functional.[29] As noted earlier, in 1607 Rudolf II thought of retiring to the Linz Schloss.[30]

Both the appearance and intended function of the Linz Schloss as an imperial retreat suggest that it may be regarded as a response to the Escorial. The castle at Linz (illus. 34) is a symmetrical, quadrangular four-storeyed structure with plastered granite facades which remain unadorned except for stringcourses, quoins at their corners and occasional visual strips. These all resemble aspects of the Escorial's disornamented style. Other

34 Linz Castle.

imperial Habsburg residences of the late sixteenth century with which Rudolf was concerned, including the Amalienburg in Vienna and, as far as earlier illustrations indicate, the Schloss at (Kaiser-) Ebersdorf, were built in a similar style.[31] The Rudolfine version of this 'Hispanic' style is found in important imperial building projects in and near Prague, notably parts of the castle.[32]

Florentine influences probably reinforced the impact of Spanish models. Eleonora of Toledo, Duke Cosimo's spouse, provided a major conduit for the translation of Spanish taste to Florence.[33] The Pitti Palace constituted one of the most important Medici projects during Rudolf's as during his predecessors' reigns and is to be seen as a possible example. Eleonora had purchased the palace in 1549, and from 1550 it was expanded to nearly twice its original size; under Cosimo's successor Francesco it came to house the Medici collections. The facades of the Pitti's wings facing the Boboli Gardens have limestone rusticated pilaster strips on otherwise unadorned expanses of brick. They thus resemble some Spanish buildings, in which these materials were also traditionally used. The wings are also only two stories tall, like Philip II's contemporaneous construction at his garden palace at Aranjuez, whose facade details the Pitti wings also resemble. Architectural planning connected Florence to Rudolf's Prague. In 1578 Rudolf II had designs and models prepared by the Florentine architect Antonio Lupicini for the rebuilding of Prague Castle.[34] In the mid-1580s the Florentines Giovanni Gargiolli and Bernardo Buontalenti, who obviously would have known about the Pitti (Buontalenti designed the grotto in the Boboli Gardens behind the palace), submitted ideas for the new gallery in Prague Castle.[35] In 1604–5 another Florentine painter-architect, Constantino de' Servi, had direct and close contact with Rudolf II.[36]

A large imperial coat of arms over the main entrance to the Schloss in Linz announces its imperial associations, and similar motifs are found on the castle in Prague. Two griffins support an imperial coat of arms in the upper field of what is usually known as the Matthias Gateway (illus. 30), the main entryway from the west to Prague Castle on the Hradčany. Though linked to Matthias by the inscription in a cartouche in the upper register, this inscription was added in 1614 after Rudolf's death: scholars now date the gateway to Rudolf's reign. The arms of Austria, Brabant, Bohemia (the kingdom of Germany), Hungary, Moravia, Silesia and Transylvania, over all of which the emperor could claim to rule, appear in the metopes of the architrave. The triumphal arch type also conveys imperial power.[37]

Buildings like these palaces represented princely grandeur and authority, while they and other similar structures also supplied backdrops for further uses of the arts to stage displays of power. Such were the banquets and other celebrations, especially tournaments which, as mentioned in the first chapter, were frequently held during the first decade of Rudolf's reign. Imperial artists like Giuseppe Arcimboldo and Jacopo Strada designed them, as noted. Princes played the role of heroes, conquerors, countries, seasons and gods in them. For those who could not understand their programmes, opulent costumes, elaborate settings, magnificent conveyances and paraphernalia, and free wine and food would have communicated an impression of majestic splendour.[38]

Representation in another sense, meaning artistic imitation of reality, was a fundamental aim of European Renaissance painting. Portraiture provides an obvious example. An artistic portrait provided depiction of an individual's physical features, and was, as was said at the time, a counterfeit. Court artists executed portraits as one of their primary tasks and are accordingly listed in the imperial payment records from the time as *conterfetter* and *maller*, meaning portraitists and painters.[39]

Portraits could also possess a definite political purpose, representing the ruler in another way. They stood for an absent individual. A current usage suggests how such images continue to

serve a political function: portraits of a head of state or sovereign are still hung in governmental buildings, where they symbolize state authority. In Rudolf's time portraits circulated among courts, and even could, like von Aachen's portraits of princesses, be used as photographs might now be to give the appearance of a possible match.

Portraits might improve on physical features, idealize personal accomplishments, and by doing so present an ideal image of a prince or princess. In this way they could represent the status, position and relations of a ruler. It has already been mentioned (see illus. 3 and 5) how Charles V and Philip II utilized such

35 El Escorial, exterior, side view.

portraiture, and how Rudolf II emulated portraits of Charles, as he also did of his grandfather and father, Ferdinand I and Maximilian II. Rudolf would have seen both painted and sculpted portraits of Charles and Philip in Spain. One such work was a half-length bust of Charles V made by Leone Leoni in 1555 (illus. 36): its use demonstrates how Rudolf emulated his Habsburg predecessors and the sources from which they drew. Leoni's

36 Leone Leoni, *Charles V, c.* 1555, bronze.

portrait is based on ancient Roman busts, including those of
emperors, which are truncated at the waist; it is raised on an
allegorical base, as some of its prototypes also were, while a novel
twist is that Charles is presented in the same armour he wore at
the Battle of Mühlberg, as in Titian's equestrian portrait. In 1566
even while he was in Spain, Rudolf II had ordered his own bust
in silver from Leoni's son and collaborator in Spain, Pompeo Leoni.
In 1600 he acquired Leone's bust of Charles V for his *Kunstkammer*,
and this then served as the model for the even more elaborately
allegorical bronze bust of Rudolf II made by Adriaen de Vries in
1603 (illus. 29) – suggesting the link between collecting and
patronage.[40]

Reproductions of bronzes like that of Charles V exist, as do
copies of painted portraits of him and other rulers. Replicas like
these and those made in more easily reproducible media like prints,
medals and coins spread rulers' images. When given additional
allegorical trappings, as they often were in prints and in coins or
medals with an emblem or allegory on their verso, these images
glorified the ruler. Many portraits of Rudolf II made by von Aachen
and his workshop and numerous copies after them survive;
Abondio made medals and coins of the emperor; and Aegidius
Sadeler was called to Prague, among other things, to provide portraits. Sadeler's appointment as imperial printmaker in 1597 is the
first such position known: it suggests that Rudolf was aware of
the power of printmaking. Portraits of the emperor with allegorical
surrounds that alluded to his power, virtues and dignity disseminated this sort of imperial propaganda (illus. 37). The high quality
of engraving associated with the Prague court has also been recognized, and its visual attractiveness no doubt helped it gain
audiences.[41]

Rudolf II was not the first member of the Habsburg dynasty
to recognize that the new media could spread imperial imagery.
Maximilian I utilized prints for propaganda, as in his Triumphal

37 Aegidius Sadeler II, after Hans von Aachen, *Rudolf II*, 1603, engraving.

Arch (see illus. 14). Hans Burgkmaier's woodcut of Maximilian I in armour on horseback is a forerunner of Titian's equestrian image of Charles V. Printed portraits like these, along with art in other media and architecture, projected what has been called 'soft power' that spread imperial propaganda beyond the use of the hard power of military force. Charles V deployed both types of power in tandem. Charles had the Netherlandish painter Jan Cornelisz Vermeyen accompany his 'crusade' to Tunis, where he made many drawings on the spot; these later served to provide the sources for the design of cartoons for tapestries of the emperor's campaign in North Africa.[42] These tapestries also provided a model for Rudolf.

When in 1609 Rudolf II asked his brother Archduke Albrecht (whose residence was in Brussels, a centre of tapestry manufacture) to have tapestries made that celebrated his victories, he was again emulating Charles V. In the course of the execution of the project, the emperor intervened directly in the process of artistic creation. Rudolf requested that these tapestries incorporate *imprese* that were his own inventions, and von Aachen is said to have used these inventions in designs he drew for the tapestries.[43] Von Aachen's designs are probably related to a series of oil paintings on parchment described in the 1607–11 inventory of Rudolf II's collection as comprising the emperor's *impresa* book.[44] Although the book has subsequently been unbound and the pictures scattered in several collections, they may be identified with several small easel paintings dateable to 1603–4 that depict events from the 'Long Turkish War' which they embellish with allegorical details. The existence of drawings in Dresden that copy the surviving paintings indicate the original oils were probably the *imprese*, as they have epigrams on their versos commenting on the battles, as an *impresa* or device would do (see illus. 10). The Dresden drawings were given to Duke-Elector Christian II of Saxony when he visited Rudolf II in Prague in 1607, further suggesting how not only large objects like tapestries but smaller images like drawings could communicate imperial propaganda.

Von Aachen's designs for Turkish allegories served several more purposes. They provided a source for medals by Paulus van Vianen that showed battles of the Turkish war. They were combined into a larger, complex bronze relief by Adriaen de Vries (illus. 38). De Vries's relief also indicates how the emperor was involved in the creation of allegorical imagery, particularly that related to the war with the Ottomans: the 1621 inventory of the Prague collections describes this relief as the emperor's invention.[45] In this way the emperor's ideas spread across media.

Imagery related to the Turkish war appears in much Rudolfine art, reflecting Rudolf's desire to pursue the conflict to a successful conclusion. Beginning in the 1590s, many works by Spranger and von Aachen deploy mythological figures allegorically to allude to the triumph of the emperor or the imperial cause over the Turks.[46] Many were done on a small, intimate scale probably intended for contemplation or enjoyment by the imperial patron or his closest associates. But some are quite large, such as a painting by the court artist Dirck de Quade van Ravesteyn that allegorizes Rudolf's reign. It combines personifications of Justice, Peace, Abundance

38 Adriaen de Vries, *Allegory on the Turkish War in Hungary*, c. 1603, bronze.

and probably Wisdom, heraldic elements (the Archduke's Hat atop an unusual tricolour shield) and an imperial device, while a figure of Mars (signifying war), behind whom a Turk lurks, is pushed away. The message is that peace and prosperity return with the victorious peace that Rudolf's reign will establish (illus. 39). While the smaller images were made for a select audience, even just the emperor himself, larger allegories, of which in some cases several versions exist, were probably intended to circulate such messages as a form of pictorial propaganda.[47]

Rudolfine allegories on the Turkish war contain complicated, often abstruse content, and may in this way be compared to earlier but equally if not even more elusive imperial allegories created by Arcimboldo. Arcimboldo's original series of the seasons and elements were presented to Maximilian II: they foretell the harmony of the world under the Habsburgs, their universal power and undying rule. The series culminated with the portrait of Rudolf II in the guise of the emperor Vertumnus that Arcimboldo painted circa 1591, just when allegories on Rudolf by Spranger and other artists alluding to conflicts with the Turks also began to proliferate (illus. 40). Arcimboldo's disguised portrait of the emperor suggests that the Golden Age of eternal spring, one undifferentiated season, has returned: hence fruits or flowers of all the seasons are shown together. With Rudolf II a golden age of peace and prosperity, like that of Augustus, will return, and his reign will last forever, as was prophesied by presence of a herm of Vertumnus in the Roman Forum.[48] Composite pictures by Arcimboldo were sent to other courts, including those of Saxony and Spain, where they complimented their rulers.[49] But this conception of Rudolf II as Vertumnus remains unique – no similar painting of another ruler in the guise of Vertumnus exists.

Allegories related to conflict with the Ottomans made for Philip II differ greatly from those made for Maximilian II and

39 Dirck de Quade van Ravesteyn, *Allegory on the Reign of Rudolf II*, 1603, oil on canvas.

Rudolf II. Take paintings related to the victory at Lepanto. Arcimboldo's collaborator Fonteo related his designs for a festival held in 1571 incorporating figures dressed like his paintings of the seasons and elements to the victory at Lepanto (see illus. 6).[50] A painting of approximately the same date by El Greco that was possibly painted for Philip II contrasts greatly with the imagery of the Vienna festival. Celebrating the Holy Alliance against the Turks, El Greco shows King Philip in martial garb as he adores the

40 Arcimboldo, *Rudolf II as Vertumnus*, c. 1590, oil on canvas.

Holy Name of Jesus alongside the pope and the Doge of Venice: a heavenly host appears on their side, while the jaws of hell open to swallow the Turks.[51] An allegory of circa 1573–5 that Titian painted for Philip II to celebrate Lepanto strikes a similar note (illus. 41). The Venetian artist shows a sea battle raging in the background with its outcome clear, as in the foreground a Turk is shown bound before a pile of arms piled up like a trophy, a sign of triumph. A winged personification of Victory flies down carrying a wreath and palm of victory, which Philip's short-lived infant son Ferdinand takes in his hand. A Latin banderole inscribed *maiora tibi* (may greater things come to Thee) is emblematic of this elusive promise. Philip holds his son over a table that recalls an altar, seeming to offer him to Victory – and this picture has been described as a votive offering. Reference to religion is also direct in a painting of approximately similar date that Philip commissioned from Titian. In this picture a personification of Spain armed with a breastplate, holding a banner and sustaining a shield with the arms of Philip II, succours a nude personification of Spain, shown with a chalice and cross, who is beset by snakes. In the background galleys seem to retreat, while a turbanned figure identifiable as a Turk is pulled along by sea horses, suggesting further identification with Neptune/Poseidon.[52]

Allegories on Rudolf II never make the kinds of direct religious references seen in these paintings for Philip II. Only one of the *imprese* depicted in von Aachen's inventions contains any directly religious reference. This is an allegory on the reconquest of Esztergom (Gran) by the imperial forces that presents a figure of a Roman emperor, probably standing for Rudolf, who offers a mitre to a bound figure of Hungary, while a personification of Victory removes a crescent, a symbol of Turkish domination, from her head (illus. 10). The mitre alludes to the fact that Esztergom was the traditional seat of the primate of Hungary, which had just been retaken from the Turks.[53] No such overt Christian symbols appear in other Rudolfine imperial allegories: even though Rudolf was fighting for a purportedly Christian cause, it is not religion, but the imperial virtues, that works made for him emphasize.

The differences between the allegories on wars with the Turks made for Rudolf II and for Philip II point to some of the distinctive features of Rudolfine art. Like Arcimboldo's allegories, von Aachen's, van Ravesteyn's, Spranger's and de Vries's imagery is still more complicated than the works by El Greco and Titian.

41 Titian, *Allegory of the Battle of Lepanto* (*Philip II Offering the Infante Fernando to Victory*), c. 1573–5, oil on canvas.

Even when they were made in a larger format, Rudolfine compositions seem to be restricted to an audience that consisted of those who could comprehend them. Works by the Rudolfine artists connote another meaning of *arcana* as secrets of rule: they suggest the more common usage of the word arcane, meaning understood by the few. But in a world of rulers aspiring to absolute status, this was enough.

A comparison of portraits of Philip II and Rudolf II (illus. 1 and 5) suggests how they nevertheless project different kinds of imagery. In the seated portrait of Philip II from which the often-copied portrait of Rudolf depends, the Spanish king (though initially depicted holding a sword) holds a rosary in his hand. The rosary indicates Philip's religious devotion (praying the rosary was and still is a widespread practice), and its appearance in the portrait has a deeper resonance. The rosary was a devotional practice the Dominicans promoted. In Spain as elsewhere, Dominicans conducted the Inquisition, which had Philip's backing: the substitution of rosary for sword is not inappropriate, as force was used to carry out these policies. Rudolf's attitude to religious tolerance was radically different. No such overt religious reference is found in depictions of Rudolf II when he was alive, aside from his quasi-sacral coronation rite.

The portrait of Philip II also relates to another aspect of propaganda favoured by many Habsburgs: namely, their promotion of a specifically Austriac piety. Austriac piety was expressed by the Habsburgs' veneration of the Virgin and saints, especially those associated with their dynasty (like St Leopold).[54] Many Habsburgs believed combating Turks and Protestants were also pious acts. They expressed their piety in public devotions (such as pilgrimage) and in patronage of pilgrimage and religious sites related to them. But other than his role as opponent of the Turks, Rudolf II did not emphasize Austriac piety, either in his personal actions or in his artistic patronage.

Imperial patronage of religious art and architecture is noticeably sparse. Rudolf II did pay for the foundation of the chapel dedicated to a plague saint, Roch, at Strahov west of the Hradčany in Prague to fulfil a vow the emperor had made for the ending of an outbreak of the plague in 1606. Beyond this and alterations to private chapels, Rudolf is not, however, recorded to have commissioned the construction of other churches.

Yet religious architecture designed by the imperial artists is not lacking. The architect Ulrico Aostalli provided the design for the chapel of St Barbara attached to the Augustinian church of St Thomas in the Malá Strana in Prague, probably because it was the burial chapel of Italians in court service. Giovanni Maria Filippi designed the original plan of the Lutheran church of Trinity that after the Battle of White Mountain was converted into the church of Santa Maria della Vittoria. Joseph Heintz also planned the court church for Wolfgang Wilhelm in Neuburg an der Donau.[55] But these were not imperial commissions.

The works of the Prague court sculptors also suggest a different orientation than that of sculptors in Spain. For example, some of the most important sculptures done in the Escorial were of the Spanish royal family in prayer. While Adriaen de Vries contributed works for the Escorial and executed several bronzes with religious content while he was in imperial service, he made none of these for the emperor himself.[56] The one partial exception seems to prove the rule: this is an *Adoration of the Three Kings* probably made for the chapel in Brandýs nad Labem primarily by Giovanni Baptista Quadri, for which de Vries claimed payment for making some subsidiary figures.[57]

The Prague court painters also made religious works for patrons other than the emperor himself. Spranger painted several epitaphs and altarpieces earlier in his career, including works for Maximilian II, but these were done before he started work for Rudolf II. His paintings of female and male saints from the 1580s

42 Hans Vredeman de Vries and Hans von Aachen, *The Annunciation*, exterior of the wings of the altarpiece for the All Saints Chapel, Prague Castle, 1598, oil on panel.

were probably made for patrons from ecclesiastical orders such as the Benedictines.[58] A brief survey of von Aachen's religious works leads to a similar conclusion. Tellingly, an altarpiece on which von Aachen collaborated with Spranger, Heintz and Vredeman de Vries that has been thought to have stood on the altar of Prague Cathedral originated as a commission from Archduchess Maria of Bavaria to von Aachen (illus. 42).[59] During his period of imperial service, Heintz made several epitaphs for patrons from Augsburg, including creating a large altarpiece for the Fugger family, and also dedicated a *Lamentation* to the courtier Wolfgang von Rumpf, but the religious works Heintz did for Prague patrons were again not painted for the emperor.[60] The story of a 1607 commission to Heintz from Ernst von Schaumburg-Lippe is instructive. This painting of the *Last Judgement* was intended for Ernst's castle chapel in Bückeburg, but never delivered.[61] Found in the painter's estate, the picture was absorbed into the imperial picture gallery, where it would have been regarded as a work of art rather than one for devotion (illus. 43).

Rudolf II explicitly said that this was what he wanted. Rudolf did not collect objects with a sacred aura unless, like regalia, they pertained to imperial majesty. Unlike the Bavarian dukes or many of his Habsburg relatives, especially the Spanish, including his own mother, or his sister, Rudolf did not intentionally

43 Joseph Heintz the Elder, *The Last Judgement*, 1607, oil on canvas.

collect relics or reliquaries, even if some were in the *Kunstkammer*, where they most likely related to other qualities they exhibited, such as the materials used. It is thus reasonable to assume that it was the style or execution of paintings with religious subject matter in his collection that he appreciated, not their content. He demonstrably did not want artists to make works with religious subject matter for him. His commission to Federico Barroci led to the creation of the only secular narrative in the artist's oeuvre, a painting of Aeneas fleeing from Troy. In discussing the commission Rudolf made a telling comment: he specifically demanded a work not of devotional character, but of another taste (*non di devotione ma di altro gusto*). Because of Habsburg claims to be the last descendants of Aeneas,[62] this painting probably also has imperial overtones. Rudolf's own artists may well have known about his predilections when they dedicated prints that contained religious subjects to courtiers like Rumpf and Trautson rather than to the emperor himself, to whom they instead usually dedicated compositions with mythological, allegorical or classical references.[63]

On the other hand, it is debatable if Rudolf had especially lubricious taste, as has long been claimed. Nudes are conspicuous in many works by Rudolf's court painters, and they are relatively numerous in the total of paintings done in Prague. Many by Spranger, von Aachen and other court artists with intertwined nude figures exist from the 1580s onward; von Aachen, Spranger, Heintz and van Ravesteyn also painted single nude figures (illus. 44). Paintings like these and other works from the imperial collections may have provoked the reaction of a Mantuan ambassador who in 1587 said that Rudolf liked paintings that were lascivious (*lasciva*),[64] the first of many such comments about his supposedly lubricious taste.

But observations like the ambassador's must also be set in context. Nudes appear in allegorical compositions because

personifications were depicted as nude females. Like personifications, the gods were shown unclothed because they represented
an ideal of beauty. Rudolfine paintings with seemingly erotic
content must also be related to a common princely taste. When
one considers that Giulio Romano, who was a court artist for
the dukes of Mantua, designed a series of pornographic prints,
and that paintings of Mars and Venus by him are even more
suggestive than Spranger's, the Mantuan ambassador's remarks
may be regarded as more than a little disingenuous. In fact, many
of the sorts of paintings that Rudolf collected had been cherished
or sought after by Renaissance princes including the Gonzaga
rulers of Mantua. This is the case of the four loves of Jupiter by
Correggio that had belonged to Federigo II Gonzaga of Mantua
and which Rudolf pursued until he finally acquired them. Many
allegories and mythologies with prominent nudes were made for
earlier (and contemporary) rulers.[65]

The erotic is only one of the features of such works by Spranger
and other Rudolfine artists, which often contain a strong dash
of wit or humour. This is most obvious in the gestures of a cuckold

44 Dirck de Quade van Ravesteyn, *Sleeping Venus*, c. 1608 (?), oil on wood.

being made at Hercules in *Hercules, Nessus and Deanira* or his smaller *Hercules and Omphale*.[66] These features may also be related to the literary sources for Rudolfine paintings in Apuleius (for Cupid and Psyche), in the witty dialogues of Lucian, and in the Roman comedian Terence. Terence was, for instance, the source of the adage 'Without Bacchus and Ceres Love Freezes' (Love needs nourishment), which for example von Aachen and Spranger painted in several variants. Lucian was the source for the *Dialogue of Reason and Lust* painted by von Aachen.[67]

While paintings by Dirck de Quade van Ravesteyn of reclining nudes (see illus. 44) have also been regarded as depictions of courtesans, seeming to reflect Barclay's observations cited in the Introduction, they also have antecedents in earlier masterworks by Giorgione and Titian. Titian's recumbent nude is now known as the Venus of Urbino. However, an earlier owner, the Duke of Urbino, who was anxious to acquire it, referred to it simply as the 'naked woman'. It should, moreover, be noted that the Mantuan ambassador coupled his observation about Rudolf's taste for the lascivious in a larger context, noting he delighted in painting but that, particularly in small works and especially lascivious ones, they had to exhibit mastery.[68] Many small paintings (and other works of art) were present in the imperial collections – again suggesting the idea of much in little, while the quality of paintings, whatever their subject, was obviously important, indeed that they be masterworks: Rudolf's collections over and over again indicate his eye for quality, and contain what today are regarded as masterpieces.

Furthermore, Philip II of Spain probably informed Rudolf II's taste for 'lascivious' works – as well as for the artistic mastery that created them. Despite his religiosity, Philip owned many works with overt erotic content, among them the famous erotic mythologies known as *poesie* that he commissioned from Titian, and clearly was interested in their lubricious content. When he received one

of the series from Titian, he asked the Venetian master to provide
another painting of a nude to complement what he had been sent,
wherein the nude could be seen from another angle. Rudolf could
have seen the initial set of *poesie* Titian painted just when they were
arriving in Spain, and he may also have been familiar with a subsequent series of *poesie*, from which several pictures exist in the
Vienna collections. The later set was probably initially intended
for Maximilian II.[69]

The series of mythologies of the 1580s by Spranger, and by
extension his later works, must be understood in relation to Titian's
poesie, and not solely for their supposedly erotic content. A reference in an imperial inventory of paintings explicitly described
them as middle-sized *poesie* (*poetische Mittelstuckh*). This can be con-
strued to mean not simply that they were nudes. On the basis of
the old analogy between poetry and painting, they were to be
regarded as comparable to pictorial poetry, as were Titian's paintings. Like poems, they used myths to suggest poetic content: they
are related to the tradition of Ovid's *Metamorphoses*, which along
with Virgil and Homer provide sources from which paintings by
Spranger and the other Rudolfine masters draw.[70]

Comparison with some of the sources for Rudolf's court
artists suggests that they responded to the works of their predecessors by directly copying them. Part of the reason for this is
that invention rather than execution was what was valued. The
imperial artists – Spranger, von Aachen and notably Heintz – all
frequently repeated their own successful compositions. Rudolf
also encouraged making copies: for example, he requested copies of
Correggio's works be made if the originals could not be acquired.
This accounts for the presence of many works noted as copies in
the 1621 inventory of works in Prague Castle. One such example
of a work with obvious erotic content that also suggests its source
of inspiration is Heintz's imitation of Parmigianino's *Cupid Cutting
His Bow*, a painting that Rudolf acquired in 1605. Heintz made at

least three versions of this work, one of which must have been owned by the emperor (illus. 45).[71]

The court artists also responded to earlier works, including those in the imperial collection, by emulating them. Emulation is a form of imitation that involves an attempt to compete with

45 Joseph Heintz the Elder, after Parmigianino, *Cupid Cutting His Bow*, after 1603 (?), oil on wood.
46 Bartholomeus Spranger, *Salmacis and Hermaphroditus*, 1580–82, oil on canvas.

and even surpass precedents. Several good examples are supplied by Spranger. In his *Salamacis and Hermaphroditus*, the figure of Hermaphroditus is based on an ancient sculpture of a boy drawing a thorn from his foot, known as the *Spinario*, which was frequently copied by Renaissance artists. Spranger sets this ancient prototype against the female figure of Salmacis, which resembles bronzes by Giambologna (illus. 46). In Spranger's *Glaucus and Scylla* he derives the figure of Scylla from another bronze by Giambologna, which presents a bending female in contrapposto, but is seen from a different angle.[72] Spranger's slightly later *Bacchus and Venus* plays upon a similar contrast of Renaissance and ancient sculptures.[73]

By showing pairs seen from both front and back, and ancient and 'modern' figures in the same work or a complementary work, Spranger also seems to be engaging in the *paragone*, a Renaissance debate whether painting or sculpture was the superior form of art. This debate was certainly familiar to de Vries and Giambologna, with both of whom Spranger worked. In this case figures of Mercury by Spranger may be compared to those of de Vries and Giambologna, and his embracing couples to those of Hubert Gerhard (see illus. 47).[74]

The notion that they were visual *poesie* suggests there is a further aspect to Spranger's paintings. Like Titian's, several of Spranger's works – for example, *Glaucus and Scylla* and *Salmacis and Hermaphroditus* – suggest complementary pairings. In both one figure faces towards the front, while one is turned to the background; one shows a seascape, another a landscape; one an open setting, the other a darker forest scene. One work shows a male pursuing a female, the other a female pursuing a male. These and other details like their contrasting body colours may be regarded as the visual equivalents of poetic or rhetorical antitheses: contrapposto itself has been regarded as a form of antithesis. The x-shaped patterning in these and other paintings may be regarded the equivalents of rhetorical and poetic chiasmus. Other pairings, like Spranger's versions of *Odysseus and Circe* and *Hercules, Nessus and Deianeira*, also show intertwining figures in complementary postures.

Imperial patronage set up some of these sorts of competition across media as well as within the same medium. In commissioning works of the same subject by different sculptors or goldsmiths, Rudolf may have initiated such contests or stimulated artists to see them. Examples of such 'rivalry' have been found in the making of ewers and basins by Christoph Jamnitzer versus Anton Schweinberger and Nicolaus Pfaff together with Christoph Lencker, and possibly by Paulus van Vianen, again responding to Jamnitzer.[75]

In another of his few recorded comments about art, Rudolf II contrasted bronzes by de Vries and Hubert Gerhard, probably rival versions of *Hercules and Deianeira* that the sculptors executed around the same time. Rudolf reacted to the work by Gerhard (illus. 47) saying it was subtle and clean (*sauber*), but somewhat lacking in its depiction (or presentation, *Darstellung*), and that the imperial bronze caster, de Vries, made something that was good even better. While providing a notion of the aesthetic criteria that Rudolf II used, this comment suggests that he may have set up such competitions.[76]

On the other hand, by bringing artists to Prague and commissioning works, Rudolf's patronage clearly made collaboration possible, even when he did not himself commission the works they made. Some examples: an epitaph by Spranger with frame by de Vries; an altarpiece for St Veit's by von Aachen, Vredeman de Vries, Spranger and Heintz (see illus. 42); the medal executed by van Vianen that von Aachen designed; de Vries's use of von Aachen designs for a relief; the likely collaboration of Pfaff and Anton Schweinberger on a mounted Seychelles coco de mer; or the rhinoceros horn goblet on whose manufacture they probably also collaborated (illus. 24). Many more examples may be mentioned. Besides von Aachen, van Ravesteyn painted the staffage (figures) in architectural fantasies by Vredeman de Vries; van Vianen supplied the mounts for cut stone works by Miseroni, as did Vermeyen; de Vries made several bases for tables that were *commessi in pietre dure*; Vermeyen made the settings for clocks by Jobst Burgi.[77]

Whether they were competing or collaborating, artists clearly also picked up motifs and even stylistic forms from each other, again across media. The jewellery that the women in paintings by van Ravesteyn wear resembles the cabochon mounts of the Rudolfine goldsmiths. The facial types seen in von Aachen, Spranger and sculpture by de Vries after 1600 are also close. And a similar darkening of palette also appears in the work of all the painters around the same time.

Ongoing study of Rudolf's painting collection allows for further insights.[78] Perhaps contrary to expectations, the greatest number of pictures in Rudolf's collections came from the northern and southern Netherlands. These far surpass the number of Italian (or Italian inspired) works. Here again Philip II may be considered to have been a source of inspiration for Rudolf II. He owned pictures by Brueghel, Bosch, van der Weyden and many other Netherlandish artists. And none of these were paintings of erotica. While some Netherlandish paintings like those by Jan Massys were of nudes, most were of other genres.

Van Ravesteyn, a Netherlandish painter in Rudolf II's service, supplies a good case study. His nudes, including what have been regarded as paintings of courtesans as well as mythologies and allegories, have attracted much attention. But he also painted religious works, and scenes of everyday life, including staffage in pictures by Hans and Paul Vredeman de Vries, which would later be called genre subjects. Finally, it is known that van Ravesteyn made studies of animals and of birds. The number of such oil paintings of creatures by Ravesteyn is far greater than that of

47 Hubert Gerhard, *Hercules, Nessus and Deianeira*, 1605, bronze.

paintings with human figures — far more than his supposed erotica.[79]

Painting in Rudolfine Prague thus ranged over many subjects and styles which reflect its universal aspect: this feature again may be related to a ruler who had all-encompassing aspirations. While artists such as Daniel Fröschel executed miniatures with erotic content, as did Joris and Jacob Hoefnagel, and perhaps Hans Hoffmann, the overwhelming majority of their work consisted of nature studies. Artists such as Roelandt Savery and Pieter Stevens executed many landscape paintings, drawings and prints, with few human figures in them. Savery also represented many animals.

Paintings like these point to an important aspect of Rudolf's collecting and patronage: interest in the world of nature. The imperial artists made studies of plants, flowers and animals, and created landscapes, still lifes and scenes of everyday life (later called genre paintings) that were based on them. The *Kunstkammer* contained artefacts along with technical devices, automata, clocks and objects with a more occult significance, many made in Prague, as well as all kinds of natural specimens. In the end, a consideration of imperial patronage of the arts is inseparable from that of the sciences: this leads to the subject of the next chapter, the role of imperial patronage in the sciences and the interrelationship of art and science.

FOUR

Rudolf II as
Patron of Science

udolf II is notorious as a patron of the 'Hermetic' sciences, the so-called 'occult' sciences of alchemy, magic and astrology named after a corpus of writings attributed to Hermes Trismegistos, thrice great king, god and priest of ancient Egypt.[1] Alchemists seeking Rudolf's support called him the new Hermes, the Hermes Trismegistos of Germany.[2] But soon after Rudolf II's death, Isaac Casaubon in 1614 demonstrated that the Hermetic Corpus, which had had an impact on European culture from late antiquity to the Renaissance, was written by neither the Egyptian god Thoth, nor his counterpart the Greek god Hermes, nor the legendary Hermes Trismegistos, and that it was not as ancient as had earlier been believed. (The texts are now thought to have originated circa 100–300 CE.)[3] Once it was revealed that the Hermetic writings lacked divinity, royalty or great antiquity, and could even be forgeries, Hermeticism began to lose its lustre, and it has continued to do so. At present, the Hermetic tradition survives largely either as a subject for scholarship or as a fringe cult interest. Yet the image of Rudolf II as the Hermetic emperor persists.[4]

This is another consequence of the criticism and calumniation of Rudolf's intellectual interests. Rumours like the following were spread by Rudolf's brothers, cousin and their allies:

His Majesty is interested only in wizards, alchemists, cabbalists and the like, sparing no expense to find all kinds
of treasures, to learn secrets and use scandalous ways of
harming his enemies . . . He also has a whole library of
magic books. He strives all the time to eliminate God completely so that he may in future serve a different master.[5]

Many stories about magic and science in Rudolfine Prague
derived from slanders like this one. They have formed the basis
for another outgrowth of the legend of Rudolf II. This is the
legend of golden Prague that originated in the nineteenth century and became widespread in the twentieth, when tales like
that of the Golem of Prague (a clay creature magically brought
to life by Rabbi Loew that ran amok) became popular.[6] While
there is a kernel of truth to such tales – Rudolf was interested
in the occult, as in other sciences, and probably did meet Rabbi
Loew – they are misleading.

R. J. W. Evans, who emphasized 'Rudolf and the Occult Arts'
and coined the notion of 'Prague Mannerism and the Magic
Universe', said himself that Rudolf's occultism was difficult to
study.[7] For instance, one of the major accusations the archdukes
made when they met to plot against the emperor cannot be easily
supported: hardly any evidence for books or manuscripts related
to magic, astrology or alchemy exists in the inventory of Rudolf's
Kunstkammer, although such books may have been kept elsewhere.
Nor is there much material evidence for the existence of alchemical
laboratories or distilleries in or near Prague Castle, even though
stories are still told to tourists about the swarms of alchemists
who lived on the Hradčany. Their houses and laboratories are
said to have been located in what has accordingly been named the
Golden Lane (Zlatá ulička) within the castle precinct. However,
the small shops on the castle wall side of this alley were probably
dwellings of lesser court attendants and guards. While some

48 Georg Roll and Johannes Reinhold, celestial globe clock, 1584,
copper alloy, cast, engraved, punched and gilt.

mentions may be found of Rudolf's laboratory, the few fragments that indicate the existence of laboratories on the Hradčany also document locations in a street alongside the cathedral (*Vikarská*) and adjacent to the wing with the Spanish Hall of Rudolf's palace, not within the imperial palace itself.[8]

Significantly, recent studies of Rudolf II and alchemy suggest that the division between empirical, observational and practical sciences, on the one hand, and occult sciences such as alchemy, astrology and magic, on the other, is schematic and anachronistic. The practice of alchemy could entail empirical procedures related to its roles in assaying metals and metallurgy, and in medicine and pharmaceutics as well. Assaying, metallurgy, medicine and pharmaceutics were based on the study of and interaction with the natural world, as was alchemy, which like many other scientific activities involved observational and experimental procedures.[9]

Astrology, another of the 'occult' sciences, entailed observations of the stars and planetary motions. The court astrologers/ astronomers were appropriately designated as *mathematici*, as their studies involved mathematics as well as observations.[10] Induction *a posteriori* from observations and the use of mathematical calculations like those associated with the present-day natural sciences were essential to the formulation or testing of theses about the stars and planets. Astrology was furthermore inseparable from many tasks that engaged Tycho Brahe (who was also an alchemist)[11] and Johannes Kepler, Brahe's successor at the Prague court, as astronomers.

To judge from the rewards they obtained (in addition to the patents of nobility they received or were promised), the court *mathematici* were valued more highly than even alchemists or practitioners of the other 'occult' sciences in Prague. Brahe was promised 3,000 florins (gulden) a year to become imperial *mathematicus*, and he received a down payment of 2,000.[12] This amount surpassed what the most important court functionary, the

Obersthofmeister, was paid at any time during Rudolf's reign, and far exceeded what any alchemist or other occultist ever obtained from the imperial court.[13] At the imperial court Kepler was supposed to be paid the not inconsiderable salary of 500 florins a year beyond the gifts or bonuses he received, an indication of the relative appreciation of his work.

Other scholars in Prague clearly engaged in what could be called empirical and observational sciences. These include the humanists and especially physicians at the imperial court who investigated what may be regarded as forerunners of botany, zoology and geology. In addition, the work of such scientists relates to the activity of the court artists. As noted at the end of the last chapter, many imperial artists made nature studies that could aid investigations of natural history, while they may also have been utilized for works of art. Drawings, miniatures and paintings by artists active in Prague and elsewhere complemented the specimens, technical objects, automata and books in the imperial collections.

The imperial collections also housed some of the many instruments that were needed for measurement and location in the study of astronomy and chorography. Rudolf II bought or commissioned such tools from artisans in Prague and Germany, as well as having them fashioned by Erasmus Habermel, the imperial instrument maker (see illus. 25). Along with clocks, terrestrial and celestial globes, and other sorts of automata, many of these objects were kept in the *Kunstkammer*. From a present-day viewpoint these objects may be regarded as splendid specimens of technology (illus. 48). But from an early modern perspective they may be interpreted as 'works of wonder' whose manufacture exemplifies application of natural magic (a notion that covers technology and aspects of engineering).[14]

The following pages explicate the relation of 'occult' to other 'scientific' pursuits. Relating Rudolf II's interests in the 'occult' and other sciences and technology to those of his predecessors and contemporaries, this chapter reconsiders the emperor's role as a stimulus for practitioners at the imperial court. It recounts the connection of the sciences to the visual arts in Rudolfine Prague. Re-examination of Rudolf II's role as patron of the sciences leads, however, to a different conclusion than that reached by early critics and most subsequent historians. The emperor did have personal reasons to be interested in the sciences, including what is now regarded as the occult, but these resulted from and expressed his role as ruler.

IT HAS RECENTLY BEEN REMARKED that Rudolf's interest in alchemy, much like his promotion of Hebraic and cabbalistic studies, is by no means to be regarded as a psychological anomaly, but as representative of continuing dynastic concerns. The same may be said for his interest in other occult (and natural) sciences. The emperor's support for alchemy, like that of other rulers in Central Europe, rose out of pragmatic motivations among others. The importation of massive amounts of ore from the Americas brought wealth to Spain, but drastically reduced the value of silver in Europe, where the mines were being depleted. A crisis occurred.[15] The improvement and increase in production of local ores consequently became an economic priority: alchemy grew in importance, and not only because it was purported to be a means to transmute baser metals into gold (or silver). For the princely entrepreneur in early modern Central Europe, alchemical methods were entangled with mining, and as this was related to financial considerations, alchemy became fundamental to political economy.[16]

Astrology also had broad applications, as it was believed to be a predictive science. Rulers had their horoscopes drawn up and also commissioned horoscopes for projects with which they were involved. They often relied on astrological prognostications for guidance before making important decisions.[17]

Other products of the natural world could be exploited to bring wealth. Hence interests in other aspects of nature could also have directly practical bases. Perhaps needless to say, many parts of the population shared these interests, particularly in astrology and to a degree alchemy.[18]

For various reasons rulers had long been interested in a diverse range of sciences. Among them were many of Rudolf's Habsburg forebears, and Rudolf continued patterns of patronage they had established. Maximilian I was keenly interested in astrology and natural magic.[19] Ferdinand I brought Paulus Fabritius into imperial service as his personal physician. Fabritius was examined by the linguist and Christian cabbalist Guillaume Postel, to whom the emperor gave a chair at the University of Vienna and funds to support publication of his works; Fabritius was then appointed imperial *mathematicus*, preceding Brahe and Kepler in this position.[20] The emperor ennobled the Czech astronomer Tadeáš Hájek z Hájek, who wrote that Ferdinand often conversed with him about hidden things of nature, especially astronomy.[21] Furthermore, a description of topics of conversation at Ferdinand's dining table from the time indicates that natural history, including talk about freaks of nature, was a major topic of conversation there.[22] In this domain Ferdinand I also laid out gardens and had an orangery made for what were regarded as rare fruits north of the Alps.[23]

Maximilian II shared Ferdinand I's interests in the rare or strange in nature as in art. He instructed his ambassador in Spain to procure for him things described as 'the rarer the better'.[24] In 1572 Maximilian wrote to his cousin (and sister-in-law) Infanta Juana, a daughter of Charles V, to express his desire to acquire rare things (*fremde Sachen*). Maximilian owned many fine horses; to house them suitably he had Jacopo Strada design the Stallburg, a structure with an arcaded courtyard in the area of the Hofburg in Vienna. Like Ferdinand I before him, Maximilian II paid much attention to gardens and garden buildings, including those in

Prague.[25] Among the flowers and plants in the imperial gardens were probably some of the first tulips known to have come to Europe, which had been acquired by one of the imperial ambassadors in Constantinople.[26] Maximilian II appointed Charles de l'Écluse (Carolus Clusius) prefect of the imperial garden: Clusius was perhaps the most famous botanist of the time.[27] The renowned botanists Pietro Andrea Matthioli and Rembert Dodoens also counted among the emperor's personal physicians.

Maximilian II retained Fabritius as imperial *mathematicus*, and Dodoens published several tracts on astronomy while he was serving as Maximilian's physician.[28] During Maximilian's reign, Hájek also continued to circulate in court circles and published both prognostications and a treatise on the nova of 1572. Hájek wrote a tract on metoposcopy, a form of divination in which the lines on a person's forehead predict personality, character and destiny. Hájek has most often been treated as an astronomer/astrologer, but his involvement with alchemy and related interests, and the extensive circle that shared them, have also recently been brought to light.[29]

Other spiritualists and occultists entered Maximilian's milieu. In 1563 the mathematician, astrologer and spiritualist John Dee came to Maximilian's coronation as King of Hungary in Bratislava (Poszony, Pressburg) to present him with a copy of his *Monas Hieroglyphica*. This was a treatise on a glyph Dee invented that incorporated symbols of the planets and the zodiac; he hoped it would magically provide a key to the universe and to control over it.[30] Followers of Paracelsus also dedicated books to Maximilian II.[31] The connection with Paracelsans is noteworthy. Paracelsus was, among other things, an astrologer; his work had a strong Hermetic component; and he argued for alchemical medicine, otherwise known as chemiatry, what would now be called chemical medicine. Several physicians and scientists at the imperial court, like Hájek and later Brahe, were interested in a Paracelsan approach.

On a more mundane level, Maximilian II was very interested in what may be called problems of physics, hydrostatics and mechanics.[32] Some of these concerns are embodied in the fountains made for him, among them the large silver fountain designed by Wenzel Jamnitzer that represented the cosmos (see illus. 18). Other works that Jamnitzer made for patrons like Maximilian's brother Archduke Ferdinand II 'of the Tyrol' literally incorporated aspects of nature, among them a silver writing box on which are placed casts of insects and other small creatures: the practice of making such casts of creatures implies interest in generation and reproduction that relate to natural history.[33]

Archduke Ferdinand II provided other Habsburg precedents for his nephew Rudolf's involvement with the sciences as well as with collecting that pertain directly to Prague.[34] During his residence in Prague (1547–67) as stateholder of Bohemia, the archduke had a new garden laid out at Prague Castle,[35] inserted the 'singing fountain' in front of the Belvedere there, and began collecting natural rarities. Czech and German translations of an important herbal by Ferdinand's personal physician Pietro Andrea Mattioli, a noted botanist, were then published in Prague. Giorgio Liberale, Mattioli's illustrator, made numerous depictions of sea creatures for Ferdinand. The archduke acquired all the publications of Paracelsus; the contents of Ferdinand's library further indicate that he devoted attention to alchemy, probably in connection with his interest in mining.[36] Archduke Ferdinand was also interested in astrology: it is likely that the design and decoration of Villa Hvězda on White Mountain near Prague had astrological associations.[37]

Philip II of Spain, another uncle of Rudolf as well as his cousin, also probably had an important influence on the future emperor's interests in the sciences as in the arts. Rudolf may even have been introduced to alchemy and astrology in Spain while he was under Philip's tutelage. One sign of Philip's keen interest in astrology/

astronomy is that Fabritius worked in his employ as astrologer/
astronomer before coming to Vienna.[38] The Spanish king was
furthermore fervently interested in alchemy.[39] Juan de Herrera,
the architect who brought the Escorial to completion, was close
to Philip, and it has been generally accepted that Herrera's plan
for the Escorial may have had magical overtones. Herrera's library
contained a preponderance of books on the occult, Hermeticism
and magic, and Hermetic content has been discerned in some of
the frescoes in the Escorial.[40] Philip shared some of Herrera's
interests in the occult and magic.[41] In any case, one of the few
spiritualist or occultist tracts that is identifiable as having been in
Rudolf II's possession is a copy of a book (*Mathematica*) by Herrera's
pupil, J. B. Vilalpandi, that is listed in the 1607–11 inventory of
the imperial *Kunstkammer*.[42] Vilalpandi penned the most comprehensive occultist interpretation of the Temple of Solomon, which
supports the interpretation that the Escorial embodied it.[43] (Rudolf
is also occasionally called the new Solomon.)[44] Considering Philip
II's extreme orthodox Catholicism in relation to his probable
interest in magic and known involvement with alchemy, one
scholar has said that in the sixteenth century, 'magic was not only
a diabolical activity, but could also mean a wise use of the secret
forces of nature.'[45] The archdukes' slanderous comments about
Rudolf II's interests should be reconsidered in this light.

Grand Duke Francesco I of Tuscany, Rudolf's uncle by marriage
(he had wed his aunt Johanna in 1565), was yet another relative
who was passionate about alchemy. Francesco frequented alchemical workshops; we have already referred to his glass manufacture.
Glass was produced in the Casino di San Marco: it has been related
to alchemy, laboratories for which were also housed in the casino,
and regarded as one aspect of the leading role given to support
of alchemy in Francesco's patronage and that of his successors.[46]
Francesco also collected and studied magical objects in his *studiolo*
in the Palazzo Vecchio.[47]

Many other important monarchs in Europe shared these sorts of interests. In France Catherine de' Medici and Henri III were noted for their concerns with astrology. In England Elizabeth I called John Dee 'my philosopher' and used him as her astronomer/astrologer and advisor.[48] She was also very interested in alchemy.[49] Her successor James Stuart was obsessed with witches and magic.[50]

Several contemporaneous German princes were immersed in alchemy and related pursuits. Friedrich of Württemberg was a great patron of the occult arts.[51] Heinrich Julius of Braunschweig-Wolfenbüttel had alchemical tracts illustrated by his court artists.[52] Landgrave Moritz of Hesse-Cassel, son of and successor to Wilhelm IV, was an avid alchemist in addition to being a musician, composer, promoter of theatre (and builder of the oldest surviving theatre in Germany) and collector who established an important *Kunstkammer*, even though he was a Calvinist iconoclast. He designed laboratories and ultimately abdicated in order to devote time to alchemy. Besides the material or exoteric side to alchemy, Moritz was a proponent of what has been called spiritual alchemy. By this is meant that he sought for the redemption of the world through alchemical and related procedures. Rosicrucianism involved alchemy as one element in its movement to reform religion, politics and knowledge; Rosicrucianism's origins have been traced to Moritz's Hesse and directly to Moritz himself.[53]

Besides the Habsburgs, several other contemporary German princes were extremely interested in technology and astronomy. Among them was Moritz's predecessor Wilhelm IV of Hesse-Kassel. Wilhelm had clocks, mechanical and celestial globes, and measuring devices made for him by, among others, the Swiss clockmaker Jost Bürgi, whom he employed from 1579, and the architect and clockmaker Ebert Baldewein. Clocks and measuring devices were useful for more than making measurements. These devices had a high political value, as the power of geometry also expressed the geometry of power. They suggested that rulers had access to hidden knowledge.[54]

Duke-Elector Augustus of Saxony offers the clearest connection to Rudolf with his interests in various sciences, the practical consequences to which their application might lead, and their symbolic significance. Augustus and his consort, Anna, Princess of Denmark, had a large library and a *Kunstkammer* that contained many books on agriculture, husbandry, geography and mining. The Dresden *Kunstkammer* was conspicuous for its holdings of tools, scientific instruments and clocks.[55] Augustus also had devices made for him by Baldewein, while he worked on several instruments himself. Instruments could be used for practical economic purposes: as Augustus turned ivory on a lathe, he turned the fortunes of Saxony around, creating a surplus through his entrepreneurial policies in mining and agriculture.[56]

Another ruler who had fountains made and was fascinated by astronomy was Frederick II of Denmark. Frederick merits mention here, because the kings of Denmark as dukes of Schleswig were heads of the north German circle of the Holy Roman Empire. Frederick gave the island of Hven to Tycho Brahe, and had an observatory, what became Uraniborg, constructed for him to carry out his work there.[57] Furthermore, the imagery of the Danish fountains symbolically projected Danish power over the sea at a time when Denmark was contesting Sweden for dominion over the Baltic Sea.[58]

Rudolf II took into his service many of the physicians, botanists, and astronomers who had served his Habsburg predecessors, including Fabritius, Dodoens, Clusius and Hájek (who became one of his personal physicians). He shared interests and personnel with many of the rulers just mentioned, to several of whom he gave employment. In 1601 Rudolf called Daniel Fröschl to Prague from Florence, where he had been miniaturist to Grand Duke Ferdinand I, whom he continued to serve for a few years.[59] Bürgi

worked for Rudolf II after his service in Hesse. Brahe came to
Prague from Denmark – Hájek helped to mediate this transition.
Conversely, after having served Rudolf II as court physician, the
alchemist Michael Maier, who rose high in Rudolf's esteem (he
was made an imperial count palatine), became physician to Moritz
some years after Rudolf's death.

Rudolf II thus belonged to a community of rulers comprising
patrons and practitioners of many of the sciences, including those
now called occult, as well as the visual arts and architecture. In
such a community, having scientists as well as artists and collectors
at one's court was a matter of prestige. Employing notable scholars,
whose renown and achievements enhanced one's own, provided
another demonstration of one's power and prestige. Patronage of
the 'occult' among other sciences could consequently have a representative function, as did support of the arts. Since the emperor
was the leading sovereign in Europe in view of both protocol and
tradition, he should have had the best and most important scientists in his service that he could obtain, just as he had the biggest
and best art collection and the largest number of court artists.
And so he did: in both the number of scientific practitioners and
the significance of what they accomplished, the imperial court
in Prague surpassed other contemporary courts in Germany, and
indeed in most of Europe.

IN COMPARISON WITH OTHER important centres of its time
and slightly later, Prague was, however, distinctive in several
respects. The imperial court held some of the purse strings, but
control of the sciences as of the arts was much looser in Prague
than it was in contemporary Florence or later in Louis XIV's France.
Although they may have collaborated with each other, scholars
did not form a regular association in Prague like the academy
founded by Giovanni Battista della Porta in Naples (1603) or

the Academia dei Lincei in Rome (1603), nor were they placed under the direct control of the crown as was Louis XIV's later academy.

The interests of scientific practitioners (including occultists) at the imperial court were, however, clearly intertwined. Many of Rudolf II's court physicians were interested in or practised alchemy, as did many other physicians or scholars in other fields with whom they communicated or consulted. These approaches and the ideas supporting them often coincided with those around the court whose concerns encompassed Hermeticism, cabbalism, Pythagoreanism and magic, among occult interests, as well as those who did not share such ideas.

Some characteristic individuals may be briefly reviewed. Michael Maier, court physician, alchemist, emblematist and musician, has already been mentioned. Maier presented his ideas about alchemical transformation in a way that combined the visual, the verbal and the musical. They were embodied in his *Atalanta Fugiens* (Oppenheim, 1617), a book on the 'secrets of alchemy' (according to its title page) that combines emblems with motets (illus. 49).

Others who engaged in alchemy include Martin Ruland the Younger, who in 1607 was made court physician. Ruland may have followed his father (Ruland the Elder) in this position: Ruland the Elder was an alchemist and Paracelsan physician. The younger Ruland compiled an important lexicon of alchemy, which he dedicated to Heinrich Julius of Braunschweig-Wolfenbüttel.[60]

Oswald Croll, a physician and Paracelsan, lived in Prague from 1597 to 1599 and from 1602 to 1609. Croll was in close contact with the imperial court, where he served as agent for Christian of Anhalt: when Croll died in 1609, Rudolf expropriated his effects. Croll published a major treatise on alchemical medicine (*Basílica chymica*) in 1608, and in 1609 a work on the signatures of things (*De Signatura Rerum*). The inscriptions on the title page of the *Basílica chymica* (illus. 50) suggests that he combined Kabbalah,

astronomical/astrological magic (*magia astronomica*) and medical alchemy (*halchemia medicea*).[61] The treatise *De Signatura Rerum* explicates Croll's version of the theory of signatures, one of the ideas that underlies his (and many contemporaries') thinking. This is the notion that all things and phenomena in nature have their

49 Michael Maier, *Atalanta Fugiens* (1618), with engraving by Matthäus Merian the Elder.

own sign: signs reveal their essence, which may be related to other aspects of the universe. The doctrine of signatures underlies metoposcopy; physiognomy, in which human features are related to those of animals; astrology, whereby parts of humans are related to the stars or signs of the zodiac that influence them;[62] and phytotomy, the relation of plants to human features.

Heinrich Khunrath visited Prague in the 1580s and then became physician to Rudolf's High Treasurer and the High

50 Title page of Oswald Croll, *Basilica chymica* (1609).

Burgrave of Bohemia, the important Bohemian nobleman Wilhelm von Rosenberg. Khunrath was another adept of spiritual alchemy. The inscription on the title page of his mystical work of incantation suggests his aim: it translates as the amphitheatre of Christian cabbalistic wisdom. Khunrath's symbolic illustrations again encapsulate its essence, for instance an idealized image of an adept in his study (illus. 51).[63]

Several other important magicians and occultists were invited to or came to the imperial court. Among the most famous and most read was Giovanni Battista della Porta, who wrote treatises on physiognomy and phytotomy and an important compendium

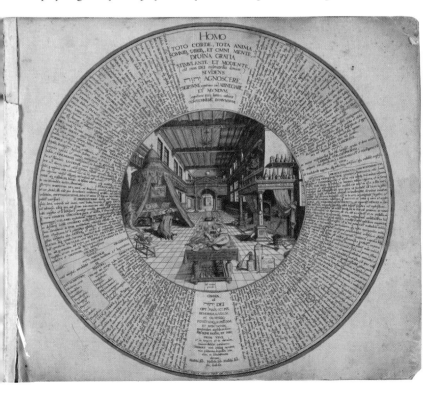

51 Alchemist's laboratory with text, engraving by Hans Vredeman de Vries from Heinrich Khunrath, *Amphitheatrum sapientiae aeternae* (1595).

on natural magic. Although Della Porta never visited Prague, where his books and ideas on natural magic had a great impact, the emperor invited him to come or send a disciple there, and Della Porta dedicated a treatise on magic to Rudolf II.[64] Giordano Bruno, the leading Hermeticist in Europe, did visit Prague and dedicated two treatises to the emperor. One of these alluded to a major theme in his work: namely, the spiritual reformation of the world through universal monarchy.[65]

Best known in the English-speaking world are perhaps John Dee and his accomplice Edward Kelly (Kelley). Dee and Kelly resided in Hájek's house in Prague in 1584 at the beginning of a stay in Bohemia that for Dee lasted until 1589, and for Kelly until his death in 1597. Dee was a man of several faces: he was a mathematician and astrologer to Queen Elizabeth I as well as being a visionary and spiritualist. He believed that world reform was to be achieved by harnessing ancient spiritual powers and working through occult and magical forces.[66] Dee professed to use spiritual and angelic magic, but was deceived by Kelly, a charlatan who pretended to communicate with angels through a crystal ball by which he predicted the future. After serving for a time as the emperor's alchemist, Kelly was repeatedly imprisoned in Bohemia because of his fraudulent claims, among others to predict the future and to transmute base metals into gold. At one point he was punished by having his ears cut off; he died as a result of an attempt to escape.[67]

Two frequently illustrated objects that evoke the emperor's interests in the occult epitomize his congeries of interests. One is a bell made by Hans de Bull (illus. 52). Its exterior is adorned with images of the zodiac, the planets related to them, symbols of the metals and pseudo-Arabic inscriptions. Three rows of meaningless Greek characters spiral inside, while the clapper of the bell has indecipherable Hebraic characters, which may be pseudo-Aramaic. Analysis of the metallic content of the bell indicates that it combines the seven traditional metals: it is thus an electrum, an alloy that is associated with the 'philosopher's stone' in alchemy. Someone with sophisticated knowledge of alchemical (metallurgical) practices must have made it. Along with its alchemical connotations, the use of an electrum and the signs, sigils, symbols and letters on the bell suggest references to astral, spiritual and angelic magic. Bells exemplify one way in which music relates to magic: they were commonly used in magical practices because their ringing evokes the harmony of the cosmos. This bell, which was found in the imperial *Kunstkammer*, condenses many contemporary beliefs associated with Rudolf II.[68]

Another object whose decoration combines references to astrology, theology, minerology, the Kabbalah and angelic or spiritual magic is a medallion previously known as the *chosen* of Rudolf II. (A *chosen* was the emblematic device of the High Priest of Israel.) This interpretation derives from details that seem to relate to the Kabbalah: a group of beliefs based on the idea that the supreme being had imparted to Moses a secret revelation along with the Law, and that this had been passed on at first through the High Priests. These details include the seven-armed candle-stick (menorah) with an imperial crown above it that decorates the central onyx on the obverse, and the placement of these symbols within a Hebrew blessing for Rudolf that invokes angels and the deity (illus. 53). A circular inscription around this inscription contains the names of the twelve angels in Hebrew, while the twelve signs of the zodiac are inscribed in a white layer around them. The names of the twelve tribes of Israel surround them in the black layer. Embedded in the lid are twelve gemstones. The use of Hebrew, the letters and the inscription seem to support a cabbalistic interpretation and the idea that it was a *chosen*, as does the six-pointed star and Hebrew letters on the outside of the gilt cover on the reverse. But the name of Jesus may be read in the centre of the hexagram, and an image of Christ at the Last Judgement appears on the inside of this cover. The object is thus probably a token of Christian Kabbalah. It may have been made with the aid of a Jewish scholar, but it was probably not a gift to the ruler from the Jewish community in Prague, as has previously been assumed. It contains notable astrological (magical writings ascribe the planets to the seven arms of the menorah) and mineralogical, possibly alchemical (the gemstones), components as well cabbalistic ones. Many different fields of knowledge went into its manufacture: it most likely functioned as an amulet, a talisman used magically to invoke spiritual influences or to ward off evil ones.[69]

In their combinations of signs, symbols, inscriptions, writing and materials, these two objects incorporate what is often taken to be the aim of magical or occult undertakings and in some interpretations all scientific endeavours at Rudolf's court. They have been described as aiming at pansophy, the desire for universal knowledge, in which everything is related to everything else.[70] Forms of magic, including astrological magic, which works

52 Hans de Bull, alchemical table bell of Rudolf II, c. 1600, gilded metal alloy (electrum), iron.

through the signs of the stars and planets, spiritual magic, which works through angels and is related to the Kabbalah, musical magic (music also played an important role at court), which works through tones, and ceremonial magic, which uses letters and signs, all converge with astrology, alchemy and the Kabbalah in this view.

But if the endeavours at Rudolf's court described so far involved a pansophic search for knowledge or wisdom, they also may be called esoteric. They utilized modes of communication that were deliberately occluded. They proceeded from the premise that knowledge is powerful and therefore dangerous, that only those who knew how to handle it could be initiated into its use. Important knowledge was in particular to be withheld from the masses: hence the use of symbols, emblems, signs and obscure means of expression that could not be immediately understood.

These pursuits may be called esoteric or arcane sciences (arcane in that they contained secrets), and they may also be called occultist

53 Amulet (*chosen*) of Rudolf II, *c*. 1600, gold, enamel, gemstones.

for another important reason. They may be considered to be occult because they investigated nature in order to reveal its hidden secrets.[71] For physicians of a traditional Hippocratic or Galenic bent, the secrets of nature were inherent in the combinations of the four elements or humours, and for Paracelsan physicians in salt, sulphur and mercury. For alchemists, the secrets of nature resided in how metals were to be purified (or combined into an alloy) that would lead to the making of the philosopher's stone or alchemical gold. For cabbalists, the secrets were those that Moses had received in a hidden revelation that was to be interpreted from the Hebrew letters in which he had written the Books of the Law. (Hebrew letters – like Greek and Latin – have a numerical as well as alphabetical connotation, as may be suggested by the inscriptions on Rudolf's bell.) The divine message and the power the text imparted might be revealed through deciphering numerical computations based on readings of the letters. For Pythagoreans, and for other thinkers of related Platonic traditions, geometrical forms and the numerical relations underlying them revealed basic, hidden harmonies of the universe, as communicated by music. For those like della Porta, for whom the doctrine of signatures applied to physiognomy, phytionomy and natural magic, as it did to Hájek's metoposcopy, understanding the signs that were visible in nature led to deeper knowledge. For astrologers, knowledge of the position and conjunction of the stars and planets revealed how their influences affected people and events. And for magicians, whose work relates to all of these previously mentioned traditions, secrets of nature were the basis of natural, spiritual, astrological and ceremonial magic.

THE COUPLING OF ASTROLOGY with astronomy nevertheless suggests how seemingly esoteric or occult concerns could be conjoined with exoteric pursuits and lead to important advances and discoveries at Rudolf II's court, which moreover were not kept secret but communicated to a broader audience. Paulus Fabritius, who continued as imperial mathematician during the first part of Rudolf's reign, published both astrological prognostications and calendars (ephemerides) and astronomical works with an observational character on comets among other phenomena. He also provided a calendar for the University of Vienna based on the Gregorian reform, and was consulted on the adaptation of its calendar. Fabritius also was aware of and incorporated a Copernican model together with one of the Ptolemaic geocentric system in his designs for Rudolf's entry into Vienna in 1577, which furthermore employed a technological demonstration.[72]

After the death of Fabritius in 1588, Rudolf would initially have been able to consult with Hájek for astronomical/astrological matters: as mentioned, Hájek became one of his personal physicians. When Hájek died in 1600, the presence of astronomers/astrologers at court remained seamless, because Brahe had arrived in Prague in 1599. When Brahe then suddenly died in 1601, Kepler quickly assumed his legacy and his post as imperial *mathematicus* and occupied it until the emperor's death in 1612.

During his stay in Prague, Kepler was extremely prolific in his publishing activity: he published thirty works during this time, some of revolutionary importance, while working on the catalogue of stars and planetary motions based on Brahe's observations that he published in 1627 and named – in honour of his patron – the Rudolphine Tables. Kepler provides a key demonstration of how in Prague what have been presented as occult interests and approaches developed into those that at present are called scientific.

As seen in a work Kepler titled the 'Cosmographic Mystery' that was published a few years before he came to Prague (1596), Kepler at first sought to find the hidden order of the universe. Kepler thought that the structure of the cosmos reflected God's plan through its geometry. Basing his cosmological theory on the

Copernican system in which the sun is located at the centre of the universe, he proposed that this plan was revealed through the relation of the distances between the orbits of the planets that circled the sun to the imagined interposition within them of the five geometrical solids (the tetrahedron or pyramid, cube, octahedron, dodecahedron and icosahedron). These solids are often called the Platonic solids, because Plato discussed them in his dialogue *Timaeus*: Plato treated the solids as related to the elements of nature.[73] Kepler wrote that the revelation of the mystery of the cosmos he had found was comparable to Kabbalah, invoking the Platonic notion of ideas when he said that he planned a little work, Geometric Kabbalah, which is about the ideas of natural things in geometry. However, Kepler believed that such matters should be demonstrated not merely by their symbolism but by descriptions of the ways things are connected and their causes.[74] Ultimately, this led Kepler from astronomical observations via their quantification and calculation using mathematics to the promulgation of scientific theories on the movement of the planets.

The use of astronomical mapping for astrological purposes started Kepler on this path. The charting and observation of the location of planets and stars and their relation to the constellations of the zodiac were essential for the casting of horoscopes and the construction of prognostications. But the faintness of stars and discrepancies in their apparent position as well as that of planets led Kepler to consider the nature of light itself. This development may have begun when Brahe and Kepler made observations during a solar eclipse in 1600, in which the moon appeared smaller to observers.

Kepler realized that astronomical observation therefore depended on the propagation of light and its perception by an observer. He understood that a knowledge of visual theory was accordingly indispensable to astronomy. But rather than treating light as mystics or philosophers in the tradition called Neoplatonic had done, Kepler took up the study of optics. This led him to compose a treatise on optics that he published in 1604. In it he described the reversal of an image on the retina of an eye, and compared this to the way an image is seen in a *camera obscura*.[75]

Kepler's involvement with observational astronomy in Prague expressed itself not only in the composition of the Rudolphine Tables based on Brahe's observations, but in his own observations of a new star, or nova, and later in his confirmation of Galileo's observation of the moons of Jupiter. From other problems affecting observational astronomy that came from astrology, Kepler took up a question that Brahe posed to him. Why does Mars seem to an observer to move backwards at a certain point in time during its path in the night sky? As a firm believer in the Copernican model, rather than the mixed system in which Brahe believed, Kepler derived a solution that involved hypothesizing that planets move in ellipses rather than in perfect circles around the sun; he thus further contradicted assumptions that had been fundamental in previous astronomical models. Kepler expressed this idea in what is known as his first law of planetary motion, published in his *New Astronomy* of 1609. The insight articulated in the first law led to the formulation of his second law, published at the same time. Kepler's second law holds that an imaginary line joining a planet and the sun sweeps equal areas of space during equal intervals of time as the planet orbits around the sun. Kepler based his insights, and subsequently his third law, published after he left Prague, on a conception of celestial physics in which he applied to heavenly or celestial bodies principles of terrestrial mechanics.[76]

In trying to solve the problem of the motion of Mars, Kepler had to make increasingly complicated mathematical calculations (as ultimately used in formulating his third law). This effort relates to the development of logarithms, whose calculations were implied by Kepler, but were explicitly developed by Jost Bürgi. Bürgi created clocks and automata for Prague during the 1590s while he was collaborating with Brahe in Kassel (see illus. 48). He also visited the imperial residence on several occasions starting in 1588. In 1604 Bürgi was appointed imperial clockmaker (*Uhrmacher*) with a monthly salary of 60 florins, a large amount (even larger than what Kepler was originally promised), and moved to Prague.[77] Bürgi served as an assistant to Kepler in Prague. He helped him directly with mathematics, while his measuring devices and time-pieces also would no doubt have been helpful for making calculations and observations. Although John Napier published his idea of logarithms before Bürgi did, Bürgi conceived of them first, and probably worked them out during the time he was collaborating with Kepler.

Kepler's attempt to use the telescope as a device to aid astronomical observations also led him from magic to optical science. Kepler was at first sceptical about della Porta's description of the telescope as an object that makes things that are far away seem as if they are near, because della Porta had presented this object as an example of natural magic.[78] Stimulated nevertheless to use telescopes in order to confirm Galileo's astronomical discoveries, Kepler became frustrated with the inadequacies of the instruments available in Prague. Hence he investigated how telescopes work, leading to the composition of a treatise on dioptrics that he published in 1611. Although he did not quite solve all the problems involved, Kepler did describe how the use of convex and concave lenses together allowed for the construction of a telescope, and he also developed his own double convex-lensed telescope. Kepler further explained how images are inverted.[79]

Kepler's observation of a snowflake that fell on him as he was crossing the Charles Bridge led to the writing of the last treatise he published in Prague, also in 1611. Kepler noticed that whatever their form snowflakes always have six corners. He argued that the geometric shapes of crystals like the snowflake can be explained in terms of the packing of their constituent particles. This involved another approach to the issues which developed into crystallography and ultimately molecular biology and chemistry than that offered by alchemy, which is also one of their antecedents. It has been well said that Kepler's thinking represents a transition from geometry to mechanics in which an older, Neoplatonic idea of a geometrically ordered universe that reflects God's design merged into the newly emerging mechanistic philosophy, in which natural phenomena are explained by proximate causes that may be hidden, or 'occult' (like gravity), but are not mystical.[80]

THE WAYS IN WHICH PRACTITIONERS of the visual arts in Prague developed new approaches to nature may be compared to the scientists. Indeed, some individuals may be regarded as both scientists and artists. One good example is Cornelis Drebbel, who was interested in mechanics, optics and alchemy as well as in the visual arts. Rudolf invited him to Prague in 1610. While there Drebbel presented his inventions, including most famously a clock that supposedly was also a perpetual motion machine. Drebbel was also a printmaker: his teacher was his brother-in-law, the famous engraver and painter Goltzius, whose style his own resembles. Drebbel was living with Goltzius around the time the latter was making works for Rudolf II, and both were said to have dabbled in alchemy, with results that included the distillation of gin.[81]

Anselm Boethius de Boodt, another of Rudolf II's private physicians, demonstrates the conjunction of spiritual and occult tendencies with an empirical approach in his involvement with both the sciences and visual arts. De Boodt was demonstrably interested in alchemy, in large part probably because of his work as a medical doctor. But he became sceptical because alchemy failed to demonstrate what it purported to do for his purposes – namely, create a philosopher's stone that might have curative or restorative powers – as well as failing to help make gold. A related set of interests, however, is evident in Boodt's best-known contribution to natural history, a treatise on gems that studied and catalogued all the gems, rocks and minerals of which he knew.[82] While his book mentions the mystical, magical and alchemical properties of gems, it is the most important early contribution to gemology; it offers much information on where stones may be found, the hardness of rocks and the medical qualities of certain minerals.

De Boodt's discussion of paints and colour theory in his treatise on gems suggests how his interests approached those of visual arts.[83] So do his illustrations of tools and devices utilized to cut, carve or polish gems, which may have been made after de Boodt's own drawings. Earlier, de Boodt had issued an edition of a print by Martino Rota, and more importantly he had worked with Aegidius Sadeler and Ottavio Strada in supplying explanations of emblems of Italian princes for the third volume of their emblematic compendium.[84]

De Boodt's compilation of illustrations of animals, birds, insects, plants and animals that are now bound into twelve volumes represents his greatest artistic accomplishment that is at the same time an important contribution to natural history. Elias Verhulst and de Boodt himself (and possibly other artists) painted the watercolours (illus. 54). Like other natural history illustrations, they descend from an earlier tradition and are in part derived from images by Netherlandish predecessors and Dürer. Yet some of the illustrations, especially images of birds like the cassowary that came from tropical regions of the South Pacific, were probably based on studies from life and could only have been made in Prague, where such creatures could be seen. And even those images that were based on earlier models were no doubt thought to represent creatures faithfully. By presenting such images and inscribing the names of animals on many pages, de Boodt's compendium represents a phase of natural history that consisted of compilation, description (here visual) and incipient classification.[85]

By inscribing the names in several languages, de Boodt anticipated a development that ultimately led into Linnaean nomenclature. This parallels de Boodt's discussion in his book on gems, which he organizes according to genera and then specific types employing various descriptive categories.[86]

De Boodt's compilation of nature studies may furthermore be related to many other such watercolours and drawings that were

54 Anselm Boethius de Boodt, brown bear (*Ursus arctos arctos*), *c.* 1596–1610, watercolour.

collected or created at the imperial court.[87] In addition to Dürer's watercolours and gouaches, the imperial collections contained studies of animals, birds, insects and fruits by such Netherlandish artists as Simon Marmion, Hieronymus Wierix and Ludger Tom Ring. Rudolf II was also given studies of avian and aquatic creatures by Jacopo Ligozzi. Artists in imperial service who made studies of birds, animals, fish and insects in watercolour and gouache include Joris (Georg) and Jacob Hoefnagel, Giuseppe Arcimboldo, Daniel Fröschel, Esaie Le Gillon, Hans Hoffmann and Dirck de Quade van Ravesteyn. Like de Boodt, the works of the court artists could, however, also be based on sources from earlier artists, notably Dürer. Rudolf II owned Dürer's famous gouaches of a *Hare* (see illus. 22), *Great Piece of Turf, Stag Beetle* and *Jay*, and Hoffmann, Fröschel and Hoefnagel among others emulated them.[88]

Joris Hoefnagel exemplifies how, on the one hand, nature studies could be presented in traditional formats while, on the other, they suggested deeper meanings. In calling himself a *pictor hieroglyphicus*, Hoefnagel implied there was spiritual or philosophical basis to his images, which also may contain allegorical content. Corresponding to other contemporary works that used *naturalia* as the source for emblems, he combined a motto and a poem with a central image of fauna, flora or insects in many of his miniatures. Van Mander describes four such volumes of animal, sea creatures, birds and insects that grouped creatures according to the traditional four elements.

At the same time, these volumes may be seen as offering a compendium of natural history as it was known at the time. Numbers on many of the sheets may suggest that a separate volume of explanations accompanied those of the *Four Elements*, like one that accompanied another book by him listed in the *Kunstkammer*. Hoefnagel probably actually observed many of the creatures for which no models exist, including many of the insects he painted. The wings pasted on the pages with flies and other creatures indicate that they were probably done directly from ocular inspection, and that they were intended to give the appearance of creatures as they once lived (illus. 55).[89]

This approach corresponds to an attitude towards the imitation of nature that, according to inscriptions on many sheets, is known as 'after life'. Van Mander contrasts works done after the life (*naer het leven*) from those done out of the imagination (*uyt den geest*). 'After the life' or 'after life' may be interpreted as meaning 'made from life', but it does not necessarily mean that a study was made from a living creature, although some studies may have been. The term and its variants seem to signify something more like 'from direct ocular inspection'. Arcimboldo, for instance, probably made studies directly from living creatures (illus. 56). But he also made drawings of antlers, claws and other such details: many such skeletons, skins and stuffed birds and animals were found in the *Kunstkammer*, where they could have been studied. Arcimboldo then combined these studies of parts or enlarged them to complete his representations of creatures. Paintings like Arcimboldo's and those of other court artists could serve to suggest how the

55 Joris (Georg) Hoefnagel, *Ignis*, plate 54: Hairy Dragonfly and Two Darters, *c.* 1575–80, watercolour and gouache (with insect wings pasted on page).

embalmed, desiccated or skeletal specimens found in the *Kunst-kammer* looked when they were alive. The visual representation of creatures that were not present in Prague complemented the holdings of the gardens and the actual creatures there. Illustrations, especially of creatures that were hard to see or obtain, provided a kind of surrogate.[90]

Nature studies in Prague served more purposes. Much as they complemented the *Kunstkammer*, gardens and other imperial collections, they could be useful for scholars of natural history. From Prague Arcimboldo sent the renowned Bolognese naturalist Ulisse Aldrovandi versions of many of his animal studies, and another Italian natural historian requested a representation of a rare Persian lily from him. The subsequent use of Arcimboldo's gouaches for illustrations in Aldrovandi's publications suggest their function in this context.[91] Likewise, Le Gillon made watercolours of mushrooms, including drawings in Hungary, that were utilized by Clusius for the first serious mycological publication.[92]

Nature studies could also be used in paintings by the artists who had made them and by other artists. Arcimboldo utilized studies

56 Giuseppe Arcimboldo, coati (*Nasuella olivacea*), 1577, watercolour.

of animals, fish, birds, flowers, fruits and vegetables in his own composite heads. But van Ravesteyn copied Arcimboldo's studies in the oils now contained in the so-called bestiary of Rudolf II, and probably in his easel paintings, while Spranger used Arcimbolo's studies of a cheetah and duiker in a painting of *Venus and Bacchus*.

Arcimboldo and other artists who served the emperor or whose works were owned by him also made studies of flowers, fruits and vegetables. These not only served study purposes, but appeared in still-life paintings. As noted above, Arcimboldo's own fruit and vegetable studies entered his composite heads: the artist made several of these, which, when turned upside down, may be read as still lifes. Van Mander reports that Rudolf owned watercolours of flowers and small creatures by Jacques De Gheyn, and these were probably utilized for oils on panels of independent still lifes, one of which van Mander says Rudolf also owned.[93] Arcimboldo's are among the earliest independent still life paintings by an Italian born painter, much as De Gheyn's and the Prague court painter Savery's easel paintings are some of the first independent still lifes by a Netherlandish artist.

With its holdings of pictures by Pieter Brueghel the Elder and Jan Brueghel (who also visited and made drawings of Prague – Prague monuments appear in his paintings), Frederik, Lucas and Marten van Valckenborch and other artists, the imperial collections were rich in landscape paintings. The imperial artists Savery, Pieter Stevens, Filip van den Bossche and van Vianen also created many works in this genre. These Prague painters also followed the example of their distinguished Netherlandish predecessor, Pieter Brueghel.

Van Mander suggests that on his travels Brueghel drew so many views from life that it is said when he was in the Alps, 'he swallowed all those mountains and rocks which, upon returning home, he spat out again [regurgitated] on to canvas and panels, so faithfully was he able, in this respect and others, to follow Nature.'[94] While no such drawings by Brueghel himself survive, this description does apply to many works by Savery (illus. 57), Stevens and van Vianen, all of whom made studies of rocks, trees, houses and towns, including views of Prague. Comparable details appear in paintings by Savery: even though he executed them in the studio, they were based on studies like those he labelled 'from life' (*naer het leven*).[95]

Savery also populated his landscapes with birds and animals. Some of these were derived from other Rudolfine artists, but some also utilized the sorts of studies that the artist often inscribed 'naer het leven'. Savery employed such studies for some of the first independent pictures of animals, which initiate yet another pictorial genre.[96]

WHAT WAS RUDOLF'S ROLE in all of this? The preceding chapter discussed how the emperor invented themes and subjects for his artists, besides participating alongside them in making objects such as clocks. The emperor also promoted the study of the natural

57 Roelandt Savery, *Study of a Tree*, c. 1606–7, grey watercolour wash, red chalk wash, charcoal dipped in oil and graphite on off-white laid paper.

world, as Sandrart, who probably learned about such matters from
Sadeler, from whom he went to study in Prague (Sadeler was also
a collaborator of Savery), and the eighteenth-century art historian
Arnold van Houbraken inform us.

According to Sandrart, Savery gained experience (presumably
because of drawing in the environs of Prague) in representing
rocks, cliffs, mountains and waterfalls. Hence Rudolf was moved
to send him to the Tyrol to draw, as Sandrart says, 'rare wonders
of nature'. Houbraken adds that Savery was 'to draw all fair views
of landscapes and waterfalls from life, and impress himself with
the character and nature of things through steady observation'.
Sandrart also writes that Savery made watercolours of mountains
and valleys of this land and large trees with chalk (illus. 57) that
served him for his landscape paintings – and as noted some of
these drawings survive.[97] In this way Rudolf helped to catalyse
the development of naturalistic landscapes.

Because of his interests in flowers and gardens, Rudolf may
also have played an important role in the stimulation of new developments in the study and representation of flora and fauna,
including still-life painting. In the preface to his compendium of
engravings of flowers, Emanuel Sweerts reports that he showed
Rudolf most of the depictions of flowers engraved in his *Florilegium*.
He calls Rudolf a 'lover and admirer of these things', but adds (in
the German and French versions of the preface), 'as of rare oddities
of nature and art'.[98] Kepler's wife Barbara corroborates Sweerts's
comments. She describes a visit that she and her daughter made
to the imperial garden, where among other things they saw three
lions and other strange animals. She says that the gardener reported
that Rudolf went to this garden around three o'clock every day.[99]

Besides the natural sciences, it may be assumed that the emperor
directly participated in alchemical procedures – he is mentioned
as being in a laboratory – and he may also have participated in
magical activity, but no evidence exists for his direct engagement

as distinct from his observing magical demonstrations. However, there is direct proof of the emperor's involvement with astronomy. Rudolf was said to have understood mathematics, and so could perhaps have grasped the importance of what Kepler and Brahe were discovering. Giordano Bruno also mentions that he was competent to speak with scientists: Rudolf's interchanges with Kepler demonstrate that this was true. According to his own account, Kepler was pressed by Rudolf about the possibility of the existence of an instrument like that described by della Porta which worked like the telescope. While this suggests that the emperor read della Porta's book on natural magic, which describes something like a telescope in a chapter 'of strange glasses',[100] it also indicates that he read Galileo's *Starry Messenger* before Kepler did, indeed within two months of the book's appearance. Rudolf lent the astronomer a copy of Galileo's book and let him look at the moon through his own looking glass. This provided another stimulus for Kepler to verify Galileo's observations. Kepler summarized his opinion of the emperor by saying that Rudolf was comparable to Galileo in having an instinct of the same restless spirit that went about discovering nature.[101] Since the date of publication of Galileo's book is 1610, these interchanges moreover contradict the false but frequently repeated characterization of a demented ruler who was losing his faculties towards the end of his life.

WHAT, THEN, MAY BE INFERRED about Rudolf's interests in the 'occult' and natural sciences? First, he no doubt had personal concerns. The presence of so many physicians at imperial court attests to continuing problems with Rudolf's health, as has been discussed. Alchemical, magical and Paracelsan efforts could be aimed at finding a nostrum like the philosopher's stone that would have cured all ailments or, like the bezoars and rhinoceros horns the emperor collected, provided antidotes. Since Rudolf's ailments were not fully diagnosed (and are still debated), the more preventatives or possible cures the better.

As Kepler said, Rudolf was also genuinely curious. Some comments by Tommaso Contarini, the Venetian ambassador to the imperial court 1605–7, lend support to Kepler's observation and also underscore the acuity of Rudolf's faculties at a time when his opponents were accusing him of losing his grip. Contarini wrote that the emperor delighted 'to hear about the secrets of natural matters, as of artificial, and he who has the chance to treat of these things will always find the ears of the emperor ready . . . He is of good intelligence, as is proved by his understanding of mathematics.'[102]

For the emperor curiosity was, however, not simply a private matter. The study of the world of nature and the cosmos was for him, as for scientists, a search to reveal its underlying secrets or mysteries. Knowledge led to mastery of nature in an abstract or intellectual sense. Knowledge of nature could also be leveraged. Scientific studies and theories could have a political impact. Reaction to papal promulgation of the calendrical reform and related imperial decree in 1582 suggests how scientific or calendrical reforms in Rudolf's time were politicized, much as debates about pandemics and the environment in our own time have been. Many Protestant (and Orthodox) areas in Europe resisted adopting the Gregorian calendar, in some cases up to the twentieth century, and even regarded it as a popish plot.[103]

Gaining knowledge could therefore be not only a matter of prestige, but a means to strengthen one's rule and the polity over which one ruled. Description and observation of nature could provide a way to gain wealth, as could occultist and other means be used 'to find all kinds of treasures', as has been discussed above. In this sense, the path to knowledge could also be a path to power.

As has been seen in the authoritarian states of our own time, control of knowledge may strengthen political control. In Rudolf's time, mastery of nature or the natural world was believed to help establish mastery of the world of states. The symbolism of paintings by Arcimboldo is built on these parallels, which thus offer a key to one interpretation of the imperial *Kunstkammer*: the emperor controls the macrocosm as he controls the microcosm in his collection. And while not employed for 'scandalous ways of harming' his enemies, revelation of and symbolism of natural secrets could provide a kind of protective cover for such ideas. As intimated earlier, mysteries or secrets of nature thereby relate to mysteries of rule, the basis for claims to imperial majesty.

Many of the beliefs of the occultists around Rudolf II were predicated on the assumption that the emperor played a central role in the system of the world. Many promoted the idea that the emperor would establish a universal monarchy. This resonates with a major belief of spiritual alchemy: reformation of the world would be achieved ending in one ruler and one flock, to use an expression of Giordano Bruno. Dee also believed that the redemption of nature would be achieved around the ruler. Dee believed that the universal key his hieroglyphic monad provided would make the ruler supremely powerful: hence he presented it to Maximilian II, and later sought support from Rudolf II. The deliberately elusive and emblematic nature of Dee's and others' work was justified by the belief that the emperor was the only person who could or should understand the whole.

Whether or not their use of esoteric imagery withheld easy access to their ideas, thinkers around Rudolf II believed that knowledge is power. In the end, much more was involved in Rudolf's interests in the sciences than his individual inclinations. His efforts to maintain and assert authority likely reinforced the belief that knowledge of various kinds could bring real power.

FIVE

Rudolf II and the Wider World

ontrary to the myth of the isolated emperor, the imperial court maintained many connections with the world outside the castle. While Rudolf II resided on the Hradčany from 1583, he engaged with the wider world in numerous ways. Living creatures and specimens as well as artefacts made from them and from other faraway materials were visible in the imperial gardens and *Kunstkammer*. The inscription on Sadeler's depiction of the Vladislav Hall (see illus. 11) suggests that people from many different places, among them Persians who are shown in the print, could also be encountered in the imperial palace. Ambassadors like the Persians and numerous other visitors came to Prague, and presented gifts with diverse provenance to the emperor. The emperor reciprocated: through gifts and other conduits, artworks were disseminated from the imperial capital. Consequently, Rudolf II – and Rudolfine Prague in general – had an impact on many different places. This chapter discusses the involvement of Rudolf II with the wider world and some of its implications.

GOUACHES AND WATERCOLOURS made by Giuseppe Arcimboldo during the 1570s and '80s suggest that a wide variety of animals, birds and plants lived in the emperor's vicinity both in Prague and in Vienna where he had previously resided. Nature studies like these indicate that the imperial aviary, animal dens and gardens Rudolf established in Prague, like those in and around Vienna, contained creatures from many corners of the world. For example, Arcimboldo's works suggest that besides his famed lions, Rudolf owned African animals such as a hartebeest, a blackbuck antelope and a cheetah, a nigiri marten from India, a mountain coati from South America (illus. 56) and a striped squirrel from North America. Arcimboldo also made studies of animals from Scandinavia like the reindeer, which would have been regarded as exotic in Central (and Southern) Europe, as would an Asian elephant and a dromedary that he also depicted. Arcimboldo painted rare birds from many parts of the world, among others a helmeted curassow from South America, a blue-headed quail dove native to Cuba, a rock ptarmigan from northern (possibly Arctic) climes, a crested crane from Central Africa and a blue-capped lory from the Moluccas (Indonesia). Comments made by a scholar on the catalogue of animals and birds Arcimboldo sent to the natural historian Ulisse Aldrovandi in Bologna demonstrate that these creatures were actually painted in Prague. The comments also indicate that the gardens 'beyond the moat' (meaning the castle gardens) held many trees and plantings that were not domestic in Central Europe but from Italy, Spain (and probably its dominions in the Americas) and 'farther off regions'.[1] Other fabled creatures such as a bird of paradise and the dodo may also have been painted by Arcimboldo (a bird of paradise by him is recorded); they appear in paintings by Savery and van Ravesteyn, who also painted cassowaries from the Moluccas.[2]

Such creatures are otherwise documented in Prague. For instance, the folios at the beginning of the 1607–11 inventory of the imperial *Kunstkammer* indicate that the collections contained specimens of many creatures that did not live in the imperial capital. The inventory was probably comparatively accurate as far as its descriptions are concerned, even if the nomenclature does not correspond to current terminology; it was compiled by Daniel Fröschel, who was a knowledgeable student of animals and birds, since he not only painted them but collaborated with natural historians before he came to Prague.[3] Fröschel lists hartebeest, antelope and auroch horns; eland, stag and moose antlers as well as elephant, hippopotamus, walrus and narwhal tusks. He also lists skeletons or shells of armadillos, crocodiles, tortoises, sea horses, sea urchins, sea stars and crustaceans. The *Kunstkammer* also possessed preserved avians like birds of paradise along with animal skins and skeletons. Ostrich eggs, amber, bezoars, Maldive (beetle) nuts and coco de mer from the Seychelles were some of the unworked materials that are mentioned, including flora. Prague court artists beyond Arcimboldo – van Ravesteyn and others – illustrated these sorts of objects together with birds, animals and sea creatures in gouaches, oils and watercolours (illus. 58, 26).[4]

The inventory interposes listings of artefacts made from these specimens or parts of them amidst the creatures from which they were created. Among these are carved ivories, nuts, antlers and horns, woven baskets, Mexican feather paintings and objects made from tortoise shell or mother of pearl. Previous discussions of the *Kunstkammer*, including those in the present book, have called such objects *artificialia* in contrast with *naturalia*, the natural creatures or materials from which they were made. But the inventory often intermingles the two categories. The Prague *Kunstkammer* inventory should thus be reconsidered: it takes into account geographical as well as material provenance.[5]

Since specimens and other objects from all over the world were gathered in the *Kunstkammer*, it may rightly be called global. Some examples that attest to the global character of their provenance may be offered. The *Kunstkammer* contained pieces of what is explicitly called porcelain: it is likely that some of these items, especially those described as having been sent from Spain,[6] came from China. Ivory carved in Senegambia, fans from Southeast Asia, tortoiseshell works and boxes of mother-of-pearl made in India are all noted. In addition, baskets and other artefacts came from the Americas.

In the 1607–11 inventory the word *Indianisch* is applied to many such items that came from either the West or the East Indies: from the Americas as well as from India or from Asia in general. Because of the mention of colchas, mother-of-pearl dishes and other such objects which do have a provenance from Bengal or Gujarat, some such *Indianisch* objects may be so described because they were in fact Indian. But the term *Indianisch* is used very broadly and may just designate objects that are considered global goods whatever their place of origin, as seems to be the case in the Ambras *Kunstkammer*.[7] In any instance, the use of *Indianisch* to describe objects in Rudolf's *Kunstkammer* suggests it is a primarily employed as a geographical designation, albeit broad and ambiguous. Other objects are specifically listed as having come from points of

58 Dirck de Quade van Ravesteyn (attrib.), 'Rhinoceros Horn, Tooth, Piece of Hide, and Lathe-turned Rhinoceros Vessel', in *Museum of Emperor Rudolf II* (1601–10), gouache drawing.

different origin such as Siam, Persia and elsewhere. *Indianisch* objects are, moreover, followed by items that are specifically called Turkish, which in context may mean Arabic or from the Arab world – over which the Ottomans ruled. Many objects with a definite European provenance are then listed after them.

This approach to compiling an inventory seems to relate objects to their geographical origin. This system differs from the organization of other collections, such as that in Dresden, where the objects are listed in general according to type. Although there is a distinction between the organization of the inventory and that of the display of the Prague *Kunstkammer*, the thinking behind what happened in Prague also differs from that of the Ambras *Kunstkammer* in which objects were displayed in groupings of materials. It has been suggested that the Prague inventory follows a different approach towards the subdivision of objects in collections. It may represent an early stage in a process that would lead to the general use in museums of characterization and ordering according to place of origin (for example, divisions of Dutch versus Italian paintings, or northern Renaissance versus southern Renaissance sculpture).[8]

Fröschel's procedure, which likely embodied the ideas of the emperor or other court counsellors,[9] may be related to contemporary discussions of the arts and of collections in which geographical designations were important. This was an interest in Medicean Florence, as witnessed by Giorgio Vasari's *Lives of the Artists*; Fröschel, who was for many years a Medici servant, may have been familiar with these concepts.[10] Differentiation according to geographical origin may help to explain the relative importance given in the inventory to creatures and other objects that might be called exotica. As noted, they are listed at the beginning of the inventory and they take up over a hundred folios. This represents a quarter of the total number of folios in the document: approximately a third of these folios contain objects that are called *Indianisch*. The position of these objects at the beginning of the inventory and their quantity may even suggest that they are being given pride of place because they came from far away.

Regardless, it is clear that rare animals, artefacts and other luxurious objects like those found in Prague circulated in a system of exchanges that joined together like-minded collectors in much of Europe. The exchange of luxury goods between the Iberian courts and Central Europe has been well studied.[11] However, the use of the Spanish language to describe objects on several pages in the Prague inventory does not indicate that these items had an immediate Spanish source: the inventory index indicates that these particular folios refer to *Indianisch* items (*Sachen*) that Archduke Albrecht, Rudolf II's brother, sent to Prague.[12] As Albrecht was stateholder of the parts of Low Countries that remained under Spanish control (and nominally of the whole), Brussels or some other entrepôt probably served as their point of transfer or mediation, suggesting the existence of a wider web of exchange – Rudolf's order of tapestries in Brabant has already been mentioned.

The web of exchanges also interacted with places of manufacture. Artefacts made from exotic materials like coral (from the Caribbean or Indian Ocean, or possibly the Mediterranean) could, for example, be fashioned in Central Europe and become gifts for the emperor. One such object is a coral ship 'containing little children' that the Palatine elector (called the Elector of Heidelberg) gave to Rudolf. Northern exotica such as elend horns could also be fashioned into gifts, such as those presented to Rudolf by the Duchess of Prussia.[13]

Beyond personal or familial connections, the flow of gifts to Prague was channelled through diplomacy. Rudolf II stimulated cultural exchange by utilizing gift giving to express his aims through diplomatic means, as discussed in previous chapters. The Augsburg patrician collector-dealer Philipp Hainhofer summarizes the general situation: he quotes an opinion that whenever Rudolf learned that someone shared his interests, he sent gifts to him.[14] The emperor thus encouraged latent interests and brought them into focus. This approach is most evident in the conduct of imperial–Saxon relations, as previously discussed (see illus. 10 and 28).

Just as those who sought to gain the emperor's ear might mention secrets, those who sought Rudolf's support came with gifts as a consequence. An agent of Moritz of Hesse-Kassel remarked bitterly about this practice, which he implicitly regarded as a form of courtly bribery. He arrived in Prague bringing three wagons full of coins, gold and jewels to try to win the emperor over to his master's interests.[15] Other Protestant rulers than the Hessian landgraves, among them those of the Palatinate and Prussia, Brandenburg, Pomerania, Saxony and Braunschweig-Wolfenbüttel, and their agents acted similarly when they brought gifts to Prague. Diplomatic relations involving gift exchange spanned Europe, including, in addition to Protestants, Catholic rulers of Europe in polities in Portugal, Spain, France, Italy, Poland and parts of Germany, to whose camp Rudolf's relatives wished he would adhere. The interconnection of gifts and diplomacy, and their role in connecting networks, were discussed in Chapter One. One sign of how this works is the way that Rudolf expressed his gratitude in 1608, saying that he hoped the gift would indicate they would represent the imperial cause at a coming Reichstag.[16]

Whatever their efficacy may have been, circles of reciprocal exchanges not only encompassed Europe but reached far beyond it. Though the Habsburgs waged war with the Turks, spoils of war and diplomatic gift giving led in effect to cultural exchanges between them. The Prague (and the Ambras) inventory contains Turkish objects such as weapons and standards, many of them probably taken from the battlefield. Spolia were carried or otherwise displayed in triumphal and other ceremonies, such as triumphal processions celebrating victory over the Turks, or in tournaments.[17] Some such items arrived as diplomatic gifts.[18]

Many Turkish weapons became enmeshed in Habsburg networks of gift giving, for instance to the Saxon court, where they would have been regarded as prestige objects.[19] Conversely, besides the booty they carried off from Habsburg lands, the Ottomans received from Prague (and Vienna) what the Habsburgs regarded as gifts while the Turks thought of them as tribute. Such 'gifts' were proscribed by treaty until the end of the Long Turkish War in 1606: they often consisted of clocks or other automata, often ones with Turkish themes.[20] It has even been argued that changing and subtle relations between antagonistic powers were often negotiated through such objects (illus. 59).[21]

Because of their conflicts with the Ottomans, Safavid Persia carried on relations with Rudolfine Prague, as previously discussed. While Persian embassies brought many gifts to Prague, artists in Prague like Esaie Le Gillon portrayed Persian ambassadors and their ilk in portraits that Sadeler and others distributed in prints (see illus. 9). European works and artists also circulated in the Persianate world.

Many rulers were accordingly situated in a field of forces in which Rudolf II formed one of the main epicentres of contemporary culture.[22] Rudolfine Prague had a large impact on the making of art throughout Europe. Through its imagery of majesty, Rudolfine iconography influenced the conception of symbolic representations of rule. Court artists like Hans von Aachen and Joseph Heintz sent paintings to places like Dresden, Wolfenbüttel and Bückeburg, where rulers coveted their works. Artists who were active in Dresden and Wolfenbüttel conversely came to study with court artists in Prague. The King of Denmark and the Duke of Schaumburg-Holstein-Lippe (who owned Bückeburg and Stadthagen) both commissioned works from Adriaen de Vries, as the latter did from Heintz (see illus. 43). Through prints and drawn copies that were already being made of Rudolfine paintings in the 1580s, the court artists' compositions became

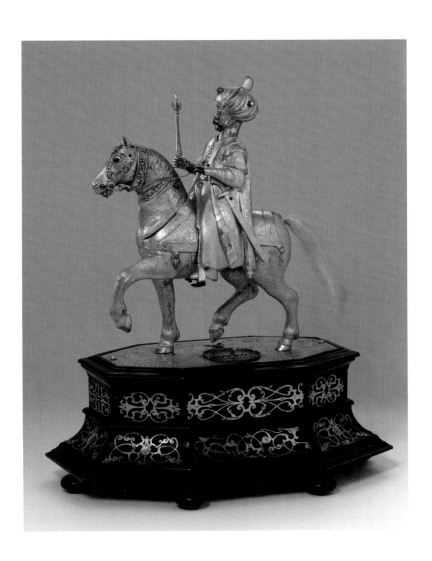

59 Mounted Turk automaton, probably Augsburg, *c.* 1595, brass, gold-plated, bronze, gemstones.

widely known. Netherlandish printmakers spread their inventions, and European artists copied them in epitaphs, altarpieces and independent canvases or panels from East Prussia to Apulia and from Lorraine to Latvia.[23]

Flows of images and objects also were transcultural. The prestige that adhered to the Holy Roman Emperor as the chief ruler of Europe, and the aura of the empire itself, meant that it had tremendous attraction for rulers around the world.[24] Habsburg –Ottoman relations demonstrate how this might work out as a process of rivalry and exchange, but this was not the only modality. Rudolfine art – and more generally the circulation of images from Northern and Central Europe – also had a generative impact in Safavid Persia. The Persian court attempted to recruit artists, and in one case was successful in luring one from Prague to Asia.[25] Paintings on the facade of the bazaar in Isfahan incorporate Western figures and may have been inspired in part by similar subjects depicted by van Ravesteyn and de Vries.[26] Similar subjects and portraits are found on the exterior of the Chihil Sutun, the shah's reception hall at his residence in Isfahan.

Western imperial imagery was also attractive to and readily recontextualized by the Mughal emperors in India.[27] Many European prints and miniatures were known at the Mughal courts in Fatehpur Sikri, Delhi and Agra, where direct use of Prague imagery may be found. It is, for example, seen in a miniature from an album dateable to 1600–5 that was painted by Mughal artist Abu'l Hasan Nadir al Zaman after a print by Jan Sadeler of a *Holy Family with St John the Baptist* by Spranger dateable before 1597.[28] Possible parallels exist between Rudolf II and Mughal rulers such as Jahangir and Shah Jahan, especially in the use of Orpheus as a paragon.[29] Hence Netherlandish landscapes may also have inspired Mughal painters:[30] Savery, who painted Orpheus imagery, may have provided one of their sources. In any case, the presence of automata at the Mughal court and appropriation of automata elsewhere in South Asia evince the spread of European imperial influence.[31] Inlays in *pietre dure*, a medium invented in Florence but practised in and spread from Prague and conveyed to Asia by Dutch envoys and traders, were avidly copied in India.[32]

This expansion of Rudolfine imagery no doubt extended beyond the Mughal court: Cornelis de Hem was active in Golconda after he had been seized on his way to Persia, even though we have no images by him. The net of influence was even wider: it reached Portuguese Goa.[33] Sadeler prints were copied by painters in Peru and probably in Japan, where paintings after Bloemaert and Goltzius are known; they were possibly imitated in China, though the presence of European artworks there before the mid-seventeenth century is difficult to determine.

In as much as they transcended any one source or polity, Rudolf II's holdings could have been regarded as both truly imperial and truly global.[34] In many ways Prague was of central importance for Europe while it had worldwide repercussions. Recently, the negative impact of European imperialism on people and the planet has been emphasized. But in this biography of the emperor, which seeks to understand its subject in the context of his own time, one may ask what this might have meant for and about him.

Although the contemporary inventories of Rudolf's collections are not always clear-cut about the origins of the objects in them, and there is no comprehensive account of all the fauna and flora that were to be found in Prague, it may nevertheless be established that artefacts and living creatures from all over the world were present there. They would have helped assuage what seems to have been Rudolf II's insatiable curiosity. Still, one may offer some more ideas about their significance in the light of Rudolf's acute consciousness of his status and position.

The broad geographical compass of what was present in Prague demonstrated the emperor's global reach to himself and to others who had seen, heard or read about it. The global dimension would have displayed Rudolf's ability to obtain precious objects and creatures through the connections of his dynasty, of which he was nominally the head. To reiterate, Rudolf II demonstrates the validity of an observation about the significance of acquired goods in antiquity: 'the act of acquisition in itself becomes a mark of exceptionality, exclusivity, ability to control, and allows the cultivation of a kingly image.'[35]

Again, this relates to a central theme of his reign: Rudolf's projection of an imperial image. Like the recurrent imperial imagery seen in many works like Arcimboldo's that were made for him and the tournaments in which he participated, the global character of his collections would have continued to imply that whatever might happen in the world of states, he might still be regarded as ruling over the world of nature, a microcosm of which he could have seen around him in actual creatures and objects, not only as symbolically expressed in his *Kunstkammer*.

Conclusion

Rudolf II was an extraordinary ruler. He was extraordinarily interested in the arts and sciences. He demonstrated extraordinary intelligence in his learning and comprehension and displayed extraordinary discernment in his choices of art and artists. He was extraordinarily curious about the world, its fauna, flora, minerals and metals, and things made from them.

He was not, however, extraordinary in the way that previous writings have portrayed him. Rudolf's interests in the arts and sciences did not distract him from attempting to carry out his responsibilities as a ruler. They may be understood in relation to the ideals and norms of Renaissance rulers. They follow from earlier models, accord with contemporary princely interests, participate in the conduct of diplomacy and were deployed to gain prestige through self-representation and by means of propaganda.

Rudolf II pursued a mediating course in a time when antagonisms were growing in Europe and many other people did not want to compromise or moderate their behaviour or point of view. Antagonists within his own family and others who were sceptical about his policies and openly opposed him created impediments and gradually brought about his downfall. The consequences of their actions became clear six years after the emperor's death, when the Thirty Years War broke out. Rudolf cannot be blamed for this conflagration: one can only imagine that this disaster would have come much sooner had Rudolf followed what his mother, uncle, cousins and brothers urged and openly sided with the Catholic camp in the empire, allied with Spain and the papacy, and forcefully suppressed Protestants. This supposition belongs to the world of what ifs. But does a reassessment of Philip II's reign suggest that his course led to great success? It is true that under Philip II the Spanish Empire might be thought to have reached its apex circa 1580 when it incorporated Portugal and its overseas dominions. But already in the 1580s the supposedly prudent king wasted many of his advantages. In 1588 the loss of the Spanish Armada epitomized the disastrous result to which his policies towards England led. Queen Elizabeth remained an implacable foe, English ships continued to interrupt Spanish commerce, and the growth of the British Empire in the Western Hemisphere soon followed. Spanish support for the Catholic League in France was also thwarted in 1589 when Henri IV, the Protestant king of neighbouring Navarre, became King of France. In 1593 Henri converted to Catholicism, and in 1598 compromise ended the French wars of religion. France remained an enemy of Spain until the eighteenth century, when a Bourbon king assumed the Spanish throne. In the Low Countries continuing religious repression, failure to offer concessions, and the brutal tactics of the Spanish armies provoked a revolt, stiffened Netherlandish resolve, and set the northern Netherlands on their way to independence, which they gained juridically in 1648. At the end of Philip's life, the economy of Spain was in shambles. A recent study suggests that the king left the world with many regrets. He would have had cause to do so, as he had set Spain on a downwards slope.[1]

On the other hand, a good argument may be (and has been) made that by not following his mother's and uncle's wishes and marrying, Rudolf avoided exacerbating differences between rival religious camps (something that not only Philip's anti-Protestant but Elizabeth's anti-Catholic policies aggravated). In contrast, the impolitic marriage of Elizabeth Stuart, daughter of James I, with the Protestant elector Frederick of the Palatinate provided the spark that kindled the Thirty Years War. Frederick was leader of the Calvinist camp in the empire, and in part because of his mistaken hope that James would support him he accepted the offer of the throne of Bohemia, precipitating the conflict.[2]

Rudolf II continued the temporizing policies of his predecessors instead. These policies accompanied and may well have enabled there to be the longest period of comparative peace in Western and Central Europe in modern times. Peace ruled during the reigns of Ferdinand I, Maximilian II and Rudolf II. So did the Bohemian-born Nuremberg poet Sigmund von Birken (1625–1681) describe Rudolf and his reign accordingly, and in so doing contradicted his black legend:

> Moderation is counted among the chief virtues of a ruler . . . This virtue also adorned the present Emperor Rudolf, second of this name, no less equally his praiseworthy predecessors, from which they were likewise propagated on him. He was of such a majestic appearance, as can be seen in part in his portrait, that foreign ambassadors were often astonished and struck dumb . . . The 37 years of his rule were nothing but golden years of peace, years of joy and of well-being in which the broken and emaciated Reich could again recuperate and rest. But he equally did not let his weapons rest and rust but moreover with them protected the borders of the Reich against the archenemy, against Mohammedan incursions and attacks . . .
>
> Meanwhile his court was a right archshrine of the Muses and a dwelling place for scholars and artists, but especially of painters and astronomers, who had in the emperor not

only a most generous patron, but a fundamentally informed companion in art.[3]

In the end, Rudolf II's life may therefore be read like the tragedy Grillparzer made of it, although not exactly in the way the playwright depicted. The difference between reality and illusion, between political circumstances and the illusions of power dear to the emperor, was real. Rudolf's sense of authority and self-importance may seem alien to us, but they were very much of his time, place and background. And the contrast between illusion and reality nourished the realm of imagination, providing sources for artistic and scientific creativity. Rudolfine Prague left many lasting monuments of art and science. About how many supposedly successful leaders may this be said?

CHRONOLOGY

1452 (−1493)	Frederick (Friedrich) III Habsburg Holy Roman Emperor; succeeded by Maximilian I
1500	Birth of future Emperor Charles V
1516	Death of King Ferdinand of Spain; Charles V succeeds him on the throne
1519	Death of Emperor Maximilian I; Charles V becomes Holy Roman Emperor
1526	Death of last Jagiellonian King of Hungary and Bohemia at Battle of Mohács; Ferdinand I Habsburg (b. 1503), brother of Charles V, becomes King of Hungary and Bohemia
1527 (31 July)	Birth of future Maximilian II, father of Rudolf II, in Vienna
1529	Turkish siege of Vienna
1546 (−1563)	Council of Trent
1547	Victory of Charles V over the Schmalkaldic League at the Battle of Mühlberg; Ferdinand I crushes uprising in Bohemia; his son, Archduke Ferdinand (later called 'of the Tyrol'), begins residence as stateholder (governor)
1552 (18 July)	Birth of Rudolf II, son of Maximilan II and Archduchess/Infanta Maria, in Vienna
1555	Treaty of Augsburg ends wars of religion in Germany
1556	Emperor Charles V retires from rule; Habsburg Empire divided as Philip II assumes rule as King of Spain
1558	Ferdinand I Holy Roman Emperor; Elizabeth I Queen of England
1562	Maximilian II King of Bohemia, elected and crowned King of Romans; beginning of wars of religion in France;

Giuseppe Arcimboldo called to Vienna, remains in
Habsburg service under three emperors until death in 1593

1563   Rudolf II and Archduke Ernst sent to court of Philip II in
Spain (arrive in 1564); Archduke Ferdinand leaves Prague for
the Tyrol

1564   Death of Ferdinand I; Maxmilian II emperor crowned

1565   Marriage of Archduchess Johanna, sister of Rudolf II, to Grand
Duke Francesco of Tuscany; beginning of revolt of Low
Countries against Spain

1570   Marriage of sisters of Rudolf II: Elizabeth to King Charles IX
of France, Anna to King Philip II of Spain

1571   Victory of Holy League over Ottomans at Battle of Lepanto;
return of Rudolf II from Spain and participation at
tournament to celebrate marriage of Archduke Karl (Charles)
in Vienna

1572   Rudolf II crowned King of Hungary in Bratislava

1575   Rudolf II crowned King of Bohemia in Prague, and King of
Romans (designated successor to imperial title) in Regensburg

1576   Death of Maximilian II in Regensburg; Rudolf II becomes
Holy Roman Emperor; Hans Mont and Bartholomeus
Spranger in Vienna; Spranger later serves Rudolf II, until the
artist's death in 1611

1577   Funeral ceremonies for Maximilian II in Prague; Rudolf
rendered homage in Vienna, Bautzen, Olomouc and Wrocław;
Polizeiordnung promulgated by Rudolf II; birth of future King
Philip III of Spain

1582   Rudolf II attends Reichstag in Augsburg

1583   Rudolf II takes up residence in Prague; conflict over succession
to bishopric of Strasbourg (ends in 1604)

1585   Rudolf II receives the Order of the Golden Fleece at
ceremonies in Innsbruck

1587   Renewal of testamentary contract between Habsburgs and
Saxony

1588   Defeat of the Spanish Armada

1589   Henri IV of Navarre becomes King of France

1593   Beginning of 'Long Turkish War' with the Ottomans

1594   Rudolf II attends Reichstag in Regensburg

1595   Death of Archduke Ferdinand II (of the Tyrol); Archduke
Ferdinand (of Styria, future Emperor Ferdinand II) takes over
government of 'Inner Austria'

1596	Publication of *Mysterium Cosmographicum* by Johannes Kepler; Hans von Aachen (appointed *Kammermaler* in 1592) begins residence in Prague
1597	Rudolf II attends tournament in Vienna; Tycho Brahe in Prague as imperial astronomer; Aegidius Sadeler appointed engraver to the imperial court
1598	Death of King Philip II of Spain; Philip III succeeds him (reigns until 1621); Reichstag called by Rudolf II; end of the French wars of religion with promulgation of the Edict of Nantes; Joseph Heintz (named imperial painter 1591) begins residence in Prague (d. 1609)
1600	Archdukes meet at Schottwein to plot against Rudolf II
1601	Death of Tycho Brahe in Prague; Kepler becomes imperial *mathematicus* (astronomer)
1602	Archduke Maximilian III becomes governor of Tyrol
1603	Reichstag called by Rudolf II; death of Elizabeth I; James I becomes King of England (and Scotland)
1604	Jost Bürgi (inventor of logarithms) imperial clockmaker in Prague
1606	(25 April) Protocol directed against Rudolf II signed by Archdukes in Vienna; (11 November) Archduke Matthias signs treaty with Turks without approval of Rudolf II
1607	Christian II of Saxony visits Prague, one of many such by ambassadors and princes to the imperial court in the early 1600s; Daniel Fröschl compiles inventory of Rudolf II's *Kunstkammer* (until 1611); Duke Heinrich Julius of Braunschweig-Wolfenbüttel becomes head of imperial Privy Council and resides in Prague
1608	Reichstag called by Rudolf II; Matthias crowned King of Hungary, besieges Prague and assumes power in Moravia, Upper and Lower Austria
1609	Letter of Majesty assuring toleration granted by Rudolf II to Protestants in Bohemia; Kepler publishes his first two laws of planetary motion in *New Astronomy*
1609–10	Jülich-Cleves succession crisis
1610	(May) Electors meet in Prague (Kurfürstentag) as Rudolf II attempts to limit Matthias; (December) Troops raised by Archduke Leopold ('Passauer Kriegsvolk') invade Upper Austria; Galileo publishes *Sidereal Messenger*; Kepler publishes commentary on it

1611 (January) 'Passauer Kriegsvolk' invade Bohemia and are
     repulsed at Prague; (March) Archduke Matthias drives them
     out; (23 May) Matthias crowned King of Bohemia, and also
     assumes rule in Silesia and Lusatia; Kepler publishes treatise
     on dioptrics containing discussion of the telescope

1612 (20 January) Rudolf II dies in Prague; Matthias elected and
     crowned emperor

1617 Archduke Ferdinand (of Styria) elected King of Bohemia

1618 Defenestration of Prague; beginning of the Thirty Years War

1619 Elector Fredrick V of the Palatinate King of Bohemia; death
     of Emperor Matthias; Archduke Ferdinand succeeds him as
     Emperor Ferdinand II

1620 Battle of White Mountain; defeat of Frederick V and the
     Bohemian estates

1627 Kepler publishes the *Rudolphine Tables*

1648 Treaties of Westphalia end Thirty Years War; Sack of Prague
     and dispersal of much of what was left there of Rudolf's
     collections

REFERENCES

Introduction: Countering the Black Legend of the Mad Emperor

1 The fall of Rudolf II has been a continuing focus in Czech historiography: see, for example, Jan Bedřich Novák, *Rudolf II a jeho pád* (Prague, 1935), and Josef Janáček, *Pád Rudolfa II* (Prague, 1995).

2 See, for example, Philippe Erlanger with Eric Neweklowsky, *L'Empereur insolite: Rodolphe II de Habsbourg* (Paris, 1971).

3 Robert J. W. Evans, 'Rudolf II', *Neue Deutsche Biographie*, XXII (2005), pp. 169–71 (online version), https://www.deutsche-biographie.de.

4 See H. Luxemberger, 'Psychiatrisch-erbbiologisches Gutachten über Don Julio d'Austria', *Mitteilungen des Vereins für Geschichte der Deutschen in Böhmen*, LXX (1932), pp. 41–54; Eugen Vencovský, 'Duševní choroba císaře Rudolf II', *Čtení o psychiatrii*, III (1983), pp. 166–172, and Eugen Vencovský, *Duševní život Rudolfa II, a jiných osobností* (Prague, 1993), pp. 47–54.

5 A key comment was that offered by Rudolf's personal confessor and confidant, Johannes Pistorius, who, on the occasion of one of his bouts with illness in 1599, said, 'Obsessus non est, quod quidam exstimant, sed melancholia laborat, quae longe temporis tractu radices nimium agit' (He is not possessed, as some think, but suffers from melancholy, which has for a long time struck deep roots in him), as quoted in R.J.W. Evans, *Rudolf II and His World: A Study in Intellectual History, 1576–1612* (Oxford, 1973), p. 91.

6 See Mary Quinlan-McGrath, *Influences: Art, Optics, and Astrology in the Italian Renaissance* (Chicago, IL, and London, 2013).

7 Gertrude von Schwarzenfeld, *Rudolf II, der saturnische Kaiser* (Munich, 1961).

8 Stephen Lesieur to Robert Cecil, Earl of Salisbury, 17 November 1610, cited in Natalia Neverová, 'The Emperor and Diplomatic Relations: Rudolf II through the Eyes of Foreign Ambassadors',

in *The Image and Perception of Monarchy in Medieval and Early Modern Europe*, ed. S. McGlynn and E. Woodacre (Cambridge, 2014), p. 133; Maurice Lee, *James I and Henri IV* (Urbana, IL, 1970), p. 136, had previously cited this quotation.

9 Aquilius is probably a play on the word *aquila*, Latin for eagle, a symbol of the German kingdom and Holy Roman Empire that Rudolf adopted as his personal device.

10 This comment is probably meant as a slander, as Jews were not allowed in England at the time, but it may reflect relations that Rudolf II had with the Jewish community in Prague, alluded to below.

11 The quotation is from Megan Williams, 'The Making of Rudolf II as a Mad Monarch', *Groniek*, CCXXVII (2021), pp. 135–6, whose review complements and expands on points made here. The expression 'buzzing and chaotic cloud of often ill-informed diplomatic rumors' comes from H. C. Erik Midelfort, *Mad Princes of Renaissance Germany* (Charlottesville, VA, 1994), p. 125.

12 For political propaganda at this time, see, in general, Karl Vocelka, *Die politische Propaganda Kaiser Rudolfs II. (1570–1612)* (Vienna, 1980), and, more pointedly, Karl Vocelka, 'Matthias contra Rudolf: Zur politischen Propaganda in der Zeit des Bruderzwistes', *Zeitschrift für Historische Forschung*, X/3 (1983), pp. 341–51.

13 Ludwig Albert Gebhard, *Genealogische Geschichte der erblichen Reichsstände in Teutschland*, 3 vols (Halle, 1776–85), vol. II, p. 462, cites Barclay and an unfavourable account by the Tuscan ambassador, Daniel Eremita, *Iter Germanicum*, who visited Prague in 1609. Daniel Eremita, *Iter Germanicum*, in *Aulicae Vitae ac Civilis Libri IV* (Utrecht, 1701), pp. 358–9.

14 R.J.W. Evans, 'Rudolf II and his Historians: The Nineteenth Century', in *Prag um 1600: Beiträge zur Kunst und Kultur am Hofe Rudolfs II*, ed. Eliška Fučíková (Freren, 1988), pp. 45–50.

15 Karl Vocelka, 'Dichtung und Wahrheit – Franz Grillparzers Drama Bruderzwist in Habsburg im Lichte neuerer Forschung', *Studia Rudolphina*, IX (2009), pp. 22–38; and, more generally, Karl Vocelka, 'Druhý život císaře Rudolfa II. v německy psané literatuře', in *Symbolické jednání v kultuře raného novověku*, ed. Josef Hrdlička, Pavel Král and Rostislav Smíšek (Prague, 2019), pp. 309–19.

16 W. Wostry, 'Rudolf II, der Sonderling in der Prager Burg', *Prager Jahrbuch* (1943), pp. 49–59; Evans, 'Rudolf II'.

17 For a summary of these claims and arguments against them, see Geoffrey Parker, *The Grand Strategy of Philip II* (New Haven, CT,

and London, 1998), and A. Wess Mitchell, *The Grand Strategy of the Habsburg Empire* (Princeton, NJ, and Oxford, 2018).

18 As expressed by Williams, 'The Making of Rudolf II as a Mad Monarch'.

19 Patricia Falguières, *Les Chambres des merveilles* (Paris, 2003), pp. 97–104, addresses several of the reversals of interpretation of Rudolf II that she also calls his black legend.

20 Benedikt Hopffer, *Stricturae historico-politicae ad iter Germanicum Danielis Eremitae* (Tübingen, 1682); Hopffer's work was presented as the dissertation of Marcus Christoph Merer.

21 Jan Matoušek, 'K problému osobností Rudolfa II', in *K dějinám Československým v období humanismu (Sborník prací věnovaných Janu Bedřichu Novákov)* (Prague, 1932), vol. I, pp. 343–62.

22 Ibid.; see, in general, Tomáš Černušák and Pavel Marek, *Gesandte und Klienten: Päpstliche und spanische Diplomaten im Umfeld von Kaiser Rudolf II* (Berlin and Boston, 2020).

23 Williams, 'The Making of Rudolf II as a Mad Monarch'.

24 Ibid. This may explain why Lesieur was better received by Archduke Maximilian III, who conspired with Matthias against Rudolf.

25 They may have drawn from Georg Ludwig von Leuchtenberg: see Elmer Weiss, 'Die kaiserliche Gesandtschaftsreise des Landgrafen Georg Ludwig von Leuchtenberg an Jakob I. von England (1605)', *Verhandlungen des Historischen Vereins für Oberpfalz und Regensburg*, CXVIII (1978), pp. 221–35. For the context in which Barclay may be interpreted, see further Mathew Grohoski, 'Soldier of Fortuna: John Barclay, England, and the European Wars of Interpretation', *Shakespeare Studies*, XLVIII (2020), pp. 87–93. For other sources of information, see E. H. Gombrich, '"My library was dukedom large enough": Shakespeare's Prospero and Prospero Visconti of Milan', in *England and the Continental Renaissance: Essays in Honor of J. B. Trapp*, ed. Edward Chaney and Peter Mack (Woodbridge and Rochester, NY, 1990), pp. 185–90. Gombrich cites a communication by Chaney providing rich information (p. 189, n. 1).

26 William Shaw and G. Dyfnallt Owen, eds, *Report on the Manuscripts of the Right Honourable Viscount De L'Isle Penshurst Place Kent (Sidney Papers, 1611–1626)* (London, 1961), vol. V, p. 131: 'His Matys Embassador, Mr. Le Sieurs, after his souer audience with the Emperor, went notwithstanding to see the Archduke Maximilian, of whom he had more courteous usage, he not approving that of the other Imperialists towerds him.' For the reaction of the imperial

court to the low status of Lesieur, see Weiss, 'Die kaiserliche
Gesandtschaftsreise'.

27 Herbert Haupt, 'Kaiser Rudolf II. in Prag: Persönlichkeit und
imperialer Anspruch', in *Prag um 1600*, ed. Fučíková, vol. I, pp. 47,
50. Compare Bernd Rill, *Kaiser Matthias: Bruderzwist und Glaubenskampf*
(Graz, Vienna and Cologne, 1999), for a more sympathetic opinion
of Matthias, which, however, does not contradict his rumour-
mongering and plotting.

28 Vocelka, 'Matthias contra Rudolf'; this is also a theme in Josef
Janáček, *Rudolf II. a jeho doba* (Prague, 1987).

29 Felix Stieve, *Vom Reichstag 1608 bis zur Gründung der Liga*, Briefe und
Acten zur Geschichte des Dreissigjährigen Krieges, vol. VI (Munich,
1895), pp. 48–53. Stieve hypothesizes quite reasonably that
Archbishop Melchior Khlesl, who was active in the recatholicization
of the Austrian lands and had engineered this meeting, was
responsible for writing this document. In any event it formed the
basis for the archdukes' agreement and actions.

30 Evans, *Rudolf II and His World*.

31 R. J. W. Evans, 'Culture and Politics at the Court of Rudolf II',
in R. J. W. Evans, Eliška Fučíková and Mungo Campbell, *The Stylish
Image: Printmakers to the Court of Rudolf II* (Edinburgh, 1991), p. 9.

32 Evans, *Rudolf II and His World*, p. 48: 'To call a man mad is as
meaningless as to call him sane: it acquires significance only
when put in the context of intellectual attitudes at the time,
and when the factors which have driven him into abnormality
are examined.'

33 Evans, 'Culture and Politics', pp. 9–15.

34 Evans, 'Rudolf II', seems to represent his latest comments on these
topics. See Arnold Hauser, *Mannerism: The Crisis of the Renaissance and
the Origin of Modern Art*, 2 vols (London, 1965). Evans continues to use
'Mannerism' and the 'Mannerist Age' in *The Making of the Habsburg
Monarchy, 1500–1700: An Interpretation* (Oxford, 1979).

35 See for example Janáček, *Rudolf II. a jeho doba*, pp. 343–4; and Peter
Marshall, *The Magic Circle of Rudolf II: Alchemy and Astrology in Renaissance
Prague* (New York and London, 2006).

36 Midelfort, *Mad Princes of Renaissance Germany*, pp. 125, 130.

37 Jan Paul Niederkorn, *Die europäischen Mächte und der 'Lange Türkenkrieg'
Kaiser Rudolfs II (1593–1606)* (Vienna, 1993), pp. 57–8; Karl Vocelka,
Rudolf II und seine Zeit (Vienna, 1985), pp. 9–10; Vencovský, 'Duševní
choroba císaře Rudolf II' and Vencovský, *Duševní život Rudolfa II*; Ivan

Lesný, 'Rudolf II. jako nemocný člověk', *Folia Historica Bohemica*, VII (1984), pp. 271–9.

38 See for example the slant of the informative Simone Bardazzi and Giulio Carrai, 'Constantino de' Servi architetto e informatore medíceo, alla corte di Rodolfo II: Nuovi documenti circa le relazioni tra Praga e le corti principesche italiane', *Studia Rudolphina*, XXI–XXII (2022), pp. 86–114.

39 As pointed out by Haupt, 'Kaiser Rudolf II'.

40 For example, Bardazzi and Carrai, 'Constantino de' Servi', relying on Vencovský, 'Duševní choroba císaře Rudolf II'.

41 Sigmund Freud, '"Wild" Psycho-Analysis', in *The Standard Edition of the Complete Psychological Works of Sigmund Freud*, vol. XI (London, 1910), p. 225 (available online at https://pep-web-org.ezproxy. princeton.edu/search/document/SE.011.0219A?page=P0223&-searchTerms=%5B%7B%22type%22%253A%22article%22%252C%22 term%22%253A%22Wild%20Analysis%22%7D).

42 Aaron Levin, 'Goldwater Rule's Origins Based on Long-Ago Controversy', 25 August 2016, https://psychnews.psychiatryonline. org.

43 Bardazzi and Carrai, 'Constantino de' Servi', p. 88.

44 Robert Burton, *The Anatomy of Melancholy*, ed. and intro. Holbrook Jackson (New York, 1977), p. 351.

45 Geoffrey Parker, *Imprudent King: A New Life of Philip II* (New Haven, CT, and London, 2014), especially pp. 369–72.

46 For the quotations and the discussion of this tradition see Raymond Klibansky, Erwin Panofsky and Fritz Saxl, *Saturn and Melancholy: Studies in the History of Natural Philosophy, Religion and Art* (London and New York, 1964), pp. 241–74.

47 For Agrippa, Maximilian I and Maximilian's interests in alchemy and the occult see Ivo Purš, 'The Habsburgs on the Bohemian Throne and their Interest in Alchemy and the Occult Sciences', in *Alchemy and Rudolf II: Exploring the Secrets of Nature in Central Europe in the 16th and 17th Centuries* (Prague, 2016), ed. Ivo Purš and Vladimír Karpenko, especially p. 99, and for the familiarity of Agrippa at Rudolf II's court see for example Alena Richterová, 'Alchemical Manuscripts in the Collection of Rudolf II', ibid., pp. 259–62, but the essays in *Alchemy and Rudolf II* contain much further information. For Maximilian I's interests, Agrippa and the magical tradition in general see most recently Anthony Grafton, *Magus: The Art of Magic from Faustus to Agrippa* (Cambridge, MA, 2023).

48 Klibansky et al., *Saturn and Melancholy*, pp. 284–373. Significantly for
    the interpretation offered in this book, the authors argue in regard to
    this image and in general that the end effect of positive melancholy
    (*melancolia generosa*) is an increase in power (of various kinds).

49 Václav Bůžek and Pavel Marek, *Smrt Rudolfa II* (Prague 2015), p. 10.

50 Luciano Berti, *Il principe dello studiolo* (Florence, 1967).

51 Martyn Rady, *The Habsburgs: To Rule the World* (New York, 2020),
    p. 111.

52 Williams, 'The Making of Rudolf II as a Mad Monarch', p. 147.

53 Compare Evans, 'Culture and Politics'.

54 Thomas DaCosta Kaufmann, *The Mastery of Nature: Aspects of Art,
    Science, and Humanism in the Renaissance* (Princeton, NJ, and London,
    1993), p. 193.

55 See, in general, Černušák and Marek, *Gesandte und Klienten*.

56 See *Sněmy České od léta 1526* [1877] (Prague, 1910), p. 97.

57 For information on the different conditions, see the article on the
    Medline Plus medical encyclopedia of the U.S. National Institute of
    Health: https://medlineplus.gov/ency/article/003093.htm.

58 Václav Bůžek and Pavel Marek, 'Krankheiten, Sterben und Tod
    Kaiser Rudolfs II in Prag', *Mitteilungen des Instituts für Österreichische
    Geschichtsforschung*, CXXV/1 (2017), pp. 40–67; see also Bůžek and
    Marek, *Smrt Rudolfa*.

59 There is no evidence that other causes, such as poisoning by
    medicine, liver failure, malaria or tuberculosis, caused his death, or
    for that matter syphilis, even if he suffered from it, as has variously
    been suggested.

60 Paula Sutter Fichtner, *Emperor Maximilian II* (New Haven, CT, and
    London, 2001).

61 This has, however, led to much speculation; compare the reasoned,
    but not convincing, account in Paula Sutter Fichtner, 'A Community
    of Illness: Ferdinand I and his Family', in *Kaiser Ferdinand I: Aspekte
    eines Herrscherlebens*, ed. Martina Fuchs and Alfred Kohler (Münster,
    2003), pp. 214–15.

62 See Bethany Aram, *La reina Juana: Gobierno, piedad y dinastía* (Madrid,
    2001) and *Juana the Mad: Sovereignty and Dynasty in Renaissance Europe*
    (Baltimore, MD, 2005); María A. Gómez, Santiago Juan-Navarro
    and Phyllis Zatlin, eds, *Juana the Mad: Sovereignty and Dynasty
    in Renaissance Europe* (Lewisburg, PA, 2008); Gillian B. Fleming,
    Juana I: Legitimacy and Conflict in Sixteenth-Century Castille (London,
    2018).

63 Antoine Schnapper, 'The King of France as Collector in the Seventeenth Century', *Journal of Interdisciplinary History*, XVII/1 (1986), pp. 185–202; Antoine Schnapper, *Le Géant, la licorne et la tulipe: Les Cabinets de curiosités en France au xviie siècle*, 2nd edn (Paris, 2012), pp. 23, 25.

64 See Frances A. Yates, review of Evans, *Rudolf II and His World*, originally published in 1973 in the *New Statesman*, reprinted in her *Ideals and Ideas in the North European Renaissance: Collected Essays, Volume III* (London, Boston, Melbourne and Henley, 1984), pp. 214–20, at p. 219, and the review by Thomas DaCosta Kaufmann of Hugh Trevor-Roper, *Princes and Artists, Patronage and Ideology at Four Habsburg Courts, 1507–1633*; A. G. Dickens, ed., *The Courts of Europe: Politics, Patronage and Royalty, 1400–1800*; and R.J.W. Evans, *The Making of the Habsburg Monarchy, 1500–1700*, *Journal of the Society of Architectural Historians*, XLI (1981), pp. 70–72, and further Thomas DaCosta Kaufmann, 'The Problem of Northern "Mannerism": A Critical Review', in *Mannerism: Essays in Music and the Arts*, ed. S. E. Murray and Ruth I. Weidner (West Chester, PA, 1980), pp. 89–115.

65 Joaquim Oliveira Caetano, 'Francisco de Hollanda (1517–1584): The Fascination of Rome and the Times in Portugal', in Franciso de Hollanda, *On Antique Painting*, trans. Alice Sedgwick Wohl (University Park, PA, 2013), p. 16.

66 For instance, the production and performance of music: see the review in Erika Supria Honisch, 'Encounters with Music in Rudolf II's Prague', *Austrian History Yearbook*, LII (2021), pp. 64–80, who, however, emphasizes the difficulty of relating it to the patronage (and implicitly the interests) of the emperor.

1 Rudolf II: Politics and Religion

1 Geoffrey Parker, *Emperor: A New Life of Charles V* (New Haven, CT, and London, 2020), is the most comprehensive recent biography.

2 See Frances A. Yates, *Astraea: The Imperial Theme in the Sixteenth Century* (London and Boston, MA, 1975).

3 Alphons Lhotsky, 'Die sogenannte Devise Kaiser Friedrichs III. und sein Notizbuch cod. vind. Palat. n. 2674', *Jahrbuch der kunsthistorischen Sammlungen in Wien*, XIII (1944), pp. 71–112; Alphons Lhotsky, 'AEIOU: Die "Devise" Kaiser Friedrichs III. und sein Notizbuch', *Mitteilungen des Instituts für Österreichische Geschichtsforschung*, LX (1952), pp. 155–93.

4 Yates, *Astraea*.

5   Franz Bosbach, *Monarchia Universalis: Ein politischer Leitbegriff der frühen Neuzeit* (Göttingen, 1988); for the response to the Turkish threat, see p. 51.

6   This is a theme developed by Heinz Schilling and presented in many of his writings: pertinent here are *Konfessionalisierung und Staatsinteressen: Internationale Beziehungen 1559–1660* (Paderborn, 2007), and *Konfessioneller Fundamentalismus: Religion als politischer Faktor im europäischen Mächtesystem um 1600* (Munich and Vienna, 2007).

7   Géraud Poumarède, 'Le Voyage de Tunis et d'Italie de Charles Quint ou l'exploitation politique du mythe de la Croisade (1535–1536)', *Bibliothèque d'Humanisme et Renaissance*, LXVII/2 (2005), pp. 247–85: https://www.jstor.org/stable/29729395 (accessed 27 August 2023).

8   Parker, *Emperor*, and Geoffrey Parker, *Imprudent King: A New Life of Philip II* (New Haven, CT, and London, 2014), place Charles and Philip in a larger context, for which see further the surveys by J. H. Elliott, *Europe Divided, 1559–1598* (London, 1968), and Geoffrey Parker, *Europe in Crisis, 1598–1648* (Bridgton and Ithaca, NY, 1979).

9   See most recently Lars Larsson, 'Adriaen de Vries (1555?–1626)', in *Bellum et Artes: Mitteleuropa im Dreissigjährigen Krieg*, ed. Claudia Brink, Susanne Jaeger and Marius Winzeler (Dresden, 2021), pp. 331–2. It has often been pointed out the type of a ruler on curvetting horse derives from a print of Henri IV of France that was frequently used for depictions of field marshals and rulers: see Amandine Souvré, 'Le Roi et le prince: Copies cavalières dans la collection d'estampes', *Numelyo*, https://numelyo.bm-lyon.fr (accessed 24 August 2023).

10 Winfried Eberhard, *Monarchie und Widerstand: Zur ständischen Oppositionsbildung im Herrschaftssystem Ferdinands I. in Böhmen* (Munich, 1985).

11 Abrecht P. Luttenberger, *Kurfürsten, Kaiser und Reich: Politische Führung und Friedenssicherung unter Ferdinand I. und Maximilian II* (Mainz, 1994), provides a detailed analysis of Ferdinand I's policies on which this account draws.

12 Geoffrey Parker, *The Grand Strategy of Philip II* (New Haven, CT, and London, 1998), and A. Wess Mitchell, *The Grand Strategy of the Habsburg Empire* (Princeton, NJ, and Oxford, 2018).

13 Geoffrey Parker, *The World Is Not Enough: The Imperial Vision of Philip II of Spain* (Waco, TX, 2001).

14 Stanley J. Stein and Barbara H. Stein, *Silver, Trade, and War: Spain and America in the Making of Early Modern Europe* (Baltimore, MD, 2000), offers a broad view.

15 Barbara Stollberg-Rilinger, *The Emperor's Old Clothes: Constitutional History and the Symbolic Language of the Holy Roman Empire*, trans. Thomas Dunlap (New York and Oxford, 2015), and Barbara Stollberg-Rilinger, *The Holy Roman Empire: A Short History*, trans. Yair Mintzker (Princeton, NJ, and Oxford, 2018).

16 See the references cited in Jan Paul Niederkorn, *Die europäischen Mächte und der 'Lange Türkenkrieg' Kaiser Rudolf II. (1563–1606)* (Vienna, 1993), p. 60.

17 Dirk Syndram, 'Vorwort – Prag und Dresden', in *Dresden – Prag um 1600*, ed. Beket Bukovinská and Lubomír Konečný (Prague, 2018), p. 7. Syndram also mentions the relation of Augustus to Ferdinand discussed above. Syndram considers some gift exchanges: for more aspects of this interchange, see Thomas DaCosta Kaufmann, 'Arcimboldo and the Elector of Saxony', in *Scambio culturale con il nemico religioso: Italia e Sassonia attorno 1600*, ed. Sybille Ebert-Schifferer (Rome, 2007), pp. 27–36.

18 See Krzystof Baczkowski, 'Der Polnische Adel und das Haus Österreich: Zur zeitgenössischen Diskussion über die habsburgische Kandidatur für den polnischen Thron während des Ersten und Zweiten Interregnums', in *Kaiser Maximilian II: Kultur und Politik im 16. Jahrhundert*, ed. Friedrich Edelmayer and Alfred Kohler (Vienna and Munich, 1992), pp. 70–83, with references to previous bibliography. Norman Davies, *God's Playground: A History of Poland* (Oxford, 1981), pp. 421–3; Jan Zamoyski, *The Polish Way* (London, 1989), pp. 128, 129.

19 See Howard Louthan, *The Quest for Compromise: Peacemakers in Counter-Reformation Vienna* (Cambridge, 1997); Viktor Bibl, *Maximilian II: Der Rätselhafte Kaiser* (Hellerau bei Dresden, 1929).

20 Paula Sutter Fichtner, *Emperor Maximilian II* (New Haven, CT, and London, 2001); Maximilian Lanzinner, *Friedenssicherung und politische Einheit des Reiches unter Kaiser Maximilian II. (1564–1576)* (Göttingen, 1994); Luttenberger, *Kurfürsten, Kaiser, und Reich*; Conrad Bierman, *S. Imperii Romani Ius Publicum, Hoc Est, De Romani Imperatoris Electione, Vicaria Imperii Administratione, Principum Electorum sessione, successione, tutela, privilegiis, &c. De S. Caesareae Maiestatis, Camerae, Potentissimorum Imperii principum & Ordinum, aliorumque Magistratuum Iurisdictione . . .* (Hanau, 1615), p. 277.

21 Félix Labrador Arroyo, ed., *Diario de Hans Khevenhüller: Embajador Imperial en la Corte de Felipe II* (Madrid, 2001), pp. 31–2, 61. For Maximilian II and Spain, see, in general, Fichtner, *Emperor Maximilian II*.

22 Ernst Mayer-Löwenschwerdt, *Der Aufenthalt der Erzherzöge Rudolf und Ernst in Spanien 1564–1571* (Vienna, 1927).

23 Parker, *The World Is Not Enough*, p. 30, and Parker, *Imprudent King*, pp. 365–7.

24 See José Manuel Guirau Cabas and José Luis del Valle Merlino, eds, *Catálogo de impresos de los siglos XVI al XVIII de la Real Bibliotheca del Monasterio de San Lorenzo de el Escorial* (Madrid, 2011), vol. II, pp. 17–18, nos 6423, 6425, 6427, 6428 and 6433.

25 See Vera Keller, *Knowledge and the Public Interest, 1575–1725* (Cambridge, 2015), pp. 106–10.

26 Parker, *Imprudent King*.

27 Paula Sutter Fichtner, *The Habsburgs: Dynasty, Culture, and Politics* (London, 2014), p. 143. Hubert Ch. Ehalt, *Ausdrucksformen absolutistischer Herrschaft: Der Wiener Hof im 17. und 18. Jahrhundert* (Munich, 1980), discusses the situation at the Austrian (Central European) court.

28 See Parker, *Imprudent King*, p. 96 and plate 19,

29 Parker, *The Grand Strategy of Philip II*, p. 15.

30 See Ernst H. Kantorowicz, 'Mysteries of State: An Absolutist Concept and its Late Mediaeval Origins', *Harvard Theological Review*, XLVIII/1 (1955), pp. 65–91.

31 See Michael Stolleis, *Arcana imperii und Ratio status* (Göttingen, 1980).

32 For the fate of Don Carlos, who it now seems suffered brain damage from a fall that may have accounted for his erratic behaviour and development, see Parker, *Imprudent King*, pp. 175–91, who, however, points out that contemporaries were unable to analyse such situations or perhaps birth defects.

33 Philip's choice must be given weight in assessing the attempt to judge Rudolf II's 'melancholy' by Simone Bardazzi and Giulio Carrai, 'Costantino de' Servi architetto e informatore mediceo, alla corte di Rodolfo II: Nuovi documenti circa le relazioni tra Praga e le corti principesche italiane', *Studia Rudolphina*, XXI–XXII (2022), p. 87, on the basis of the report of a Venetian ambassador from March 1568 who explicitly describes Rudolf as not mad but desperate, and says that he sought to throw himself out of a window. Like many other ambassadorial reports that contributed to the rumour mill around the Habsburgs, this remains uncorroborated and isolated. Such an incident could not have been kept from the Spanish king. Would Philip have chosen Rudolf as a son-in-law if he created the problems that Don Carlos, whom Philip had to restrain

and who died in 1568, did? Could the ambassador even be
extrapolating from the situation with Don Carlos?

34 Joseph Fiedler, ed., *Relationen Ventianischer Botschafter über Deutschland und Österreich*, Fontes Rerum Austriacarum 30 (Vienna, 1870), p. 284.

35 For the events of 1571, see Karl Vocelka, *Habsburgische Hochzeiten 1550–1600* (Vienna, Cologne and Graz, 1976), pp. 63–74, and Thomas DaCosta Kaufmann, *Variations on the Imperial Theme in the Age of Maximilian II and Rudolf II* (Boston and London, 1978), pp. 33–40, and for other tournaments of the 1570s, pp. 28–33 and 40–45; see further Thomas DaCosta Kaufmann, 'The Festival Designs of Jacopo Strada Reconsidered', *Artibus et Historiae*, LXII (2010), pp. 173–87.

36 See Stollberg-Rilinger, *The Emperor's Old Clothes*, pp. 111–13.

37 See Karl Vocelka, *Die poltische Propaganda Kaiser Rudolfs II. (1570–1612)* (Vienna, 1980).

38 See Hermann Fillitz, *Die Österreichische Kaiserkrone und die Insignien des Kaisertums Österreich* (Vienna, 1959).

39 Gülru Necipoğlu, 'Süleyman the Magnificent and the Representation of Power in the Context of Ottoman-Hapsburg-Papal Rivalry', *Art Bulletin*, LXXI/3 (September 1989), pp. 401–27.

40 See D. P. Snoep, *Praal en propaganda: Triumfalia in de Noordelijke Nederlanden in de 16de en 17de eeuw* (Alphen aan den Rijn, 1975).

41 See the large compendium J. R. Mulryne, Krista De Jonge, R.L.M. Morris and Pieter Martens, eds, *Occasions of State: Early Modern European Festivals and the Negotiation of Power* (New York, 2019), but there is much earlier literature, too.

42 See Harriet Rudolph, *Da Reich als Ereignis: Formen und Funktionen der Herrschaftsinszenierung bei Kaisereinzügen (1558–1618)* (Cologne, Weimar and Vienna, 2011).

43 Bohuslav Balbin, *Epitome Historica* (Prague, 1677), pp. 603–4.

44 Jaroslava Hausenblasová, *Der Hof Kaiser Rudolfs II* (Prague, 2002), p. 395, no. 139/6. Kaufmann, *Variations on the Imperial Theme*, pp. 49–50; for the 1579 tournament, see further Bardazzi and Carrai, 'Costantino de' Servi', p. 89.

45 See, in general, J. R. Mulryne and Elizabeth Goldring, eds, *Court Festivals of the Renaissance: Art, Politics and Performance* (New York and London, 2017); for the Habsburgs, Wilfried Seipel, ed., *Wir sind Helden: Habsburgische Feste in der Renaissance* (Innsbruck, 2005), and Vocelka, *Politische Propaganda*, pp. 56–63, 84–95.

46 Wácslaw Wladiwoj Tomek, *Dějepis města Prahy* (Prague, 1901), vol. XII, pp. 321–2.

47 See Thomas DaCosta Kaufmann, 'Hand-Colored Prints and Pseudo-Manuscripts: The Curious Case of Codex 7906 of the Österreichische Nationalbibliothek Wien', *Codices Manuscripti*, 11 (1976), pp. 26–31.

48 Tomáš Černušák and Pavel Marek, *Gesandte und Klienten: Päpstliche und spanische Diplomaten im Umfeld von Kaiser Rudolf II* (Berlin and Boston, MA, 2020), p. 240.

49 Kaufmann, *Variations on the Imperial Theme*, pp. 140–44, provides sources for these events.

50 'Reichspolizeiordnung' (1577), at http://ra.smixx.de/media/files/Reichspolizeiordnung-1577.pdf.

51 Summarized in Herbert Haupt, 'Kaiser Rudolf II. in Prag: Personlichkeit und imperialer Anspruch', in *Prag um 1600: Beiträge zur Kunst und Kultur am Hofe Rudolfs II*, 2 vols, ed. Eliška Fučíková (Freren, 1988), vol. 1, pp. 47, 50.

52 Megan Williams, 'The Making of Rudolf II as a Mad Monarch', *Groniek*, CCXXVII (2021), pp. 134–55.

53 Ibid., p. 138, quoting Grillparzer.

54 This is a theme of R.J.W. Evans, *Rudolf II and His World: A Study in Intellectual History, 1576–1612* (Oxford, 1973).

55 Thomas Fusenig, '"Wollen mit vleis euch erkundigen, ob ir nicht derselbige kunststueck zu wege zu bringen vermöchte": Graf Simon VI. zur Lippe kauft niederländische Gemälde für Kaiser Rudolf II.', in *Kunst und Repräsentation*, ed. Heiner Borggrefe and Barbara Uppenkamp (Lemgo, 2002), pp. 109–49, and more recently Heiner Borggrefe, 'Arte et Marte: Simon VI. am Prager Kaiserhof', in *Im Dienst des Kaisers Simon VI zur Lippe (1554–1613)*, ed. Michael Bischoff (Lemgo, 2014), pp. 72–107.

56 Evans, *Rudolf II and His World*, pp. 239–42.

57 See Herbert Karner, ed., *Die Wiener Hofburg 1521–1705: Baugeschichte, Funktion und Etablierung also Kaiserresidenz* (Vienna, 2014), pp. 131–3 and 336–45.

58 Hilda Lietzmann, *Das Neugebäude in Wien: Sultan Süleymans Zelt – Kaiser Maximilians II. Lustschloß* (Munich and Berlin, 1987).

59 Quoted by R.J.W. Evans, 'Culture and Politics at the Court of Rudolf II', in R.J.W. Evans, Eliška Fučíková and Mungo Campbell, *The Stylish Image: Printmakers to the Court of Rudolf II* (Edinburgh, 1991), p. 10.

60 Petr Uličný, 'Erotica & Sapientia: Rudolf II's Early Years at Prague Castle', *Umění*, LXIX/4 (2021), pp. 390–415.

61 For groundbreaking essays that contradicted this older opinion,
    see Jarmila Krčálová, 'Poznámky k rudolfinské architektuře', *Umění*,
    XXIII (1975), pp. 499–525; Jarmila Krčálová, 'Die rudolfinische
    Architektur', *Leids Kunsthistorische Jaarboek*, I (1982), pp. 271–308; Ivan
    Muchka, 'Die Architektur unter Rudolf II., gezeigt am Beispiel der
    Prager Burg', in *Prag um 1600*, ed. Fučíková, vol. I, pp. 85–93.

62 Compare Jürgen Zimmer, *Die Schatz- und Kunstkammer Kaiser Rudolf
    II. in Prag: Inventare und Listen im Kontext weiterer Quellen von 1576 bis 1860*,
    Studia Rudolphina XXIII (Prague, 2021), p. 16.

63 See, in general, Mario Müller, Karl-Heinz Spieß and Uwe Tresp,
    eds, *Erbeinigungen und Erbverbrüderungen in Spätmittelalter und Früher
    Neuzeit: Generationsübergreifende Verträge und Strategien im europäischen
    Vergleich* (= *Studien zur brandenburgischen und vergleichenden Landesgeschichte*,
    XVII) (Berlin, 2014).

64 For their services, see Stefan Ehrenpreis, *Kaiserliche Gerichtsbarkeit und
    Konfessionskonflkt: Der Reichshofrat unter Rudolf II. 1576–1512* (Göttingen,
    2006).

65 As pointed out by Haupt, 'Kaiser Rudolf II. in Prag', p. 54, n. 18,
    who says that the older monograph works on the topic – Victor
    Bibl, *Die Einführung der katholischen Gegenreformation in Niederösterreich
    unter Kaiser Rudolf II. (1576–1589)* (Innsbruck, 1900), and Bibl, 'Die
    Religionsreformation Kaiser Rudolfs II. in Oberösterreich', *Archiv
    für Österreichische Geschichte*, CIX/I (1921), pp. 374–446 – are to be used
    with caution.

66 Compare Bibl, *Die Einführung der katholischen Gegenreformatoin*.

67 Parker, *Political Strategy*, p. 80.

68 Arroyo, *Diario de Hans Khevenhüller*, p. 315.

69 See William Eamon, 'The Scientific Education of a Renaissance
    Prince: Archduke Rudolf II at the Spanish Court', in *Alchemy and
    Rudolf II: Exploring the Secrets of Nature in Central Europe in the 16th and
    17th centuries*, ed. Ivo Purš and Vladimír Karpenko (Prague, 2016),
    pp. 129–38.

70 Vocelka, *Politische Propaganda*, pp. 184–5.

71 See Evans, *Rudolf II and His World*, pp. 57–8.

72 See Franz Bosbach, 'Köln, Erzstift und Freie Reichsstadt', in *Die
    Territorien des Reichs im Zeitalter der Reformation und Konfessionalisierung,
    1500–1650*, ed. A. Schindling and W. Ziegler (Münster, 1991), vol. III,
    pp. 58–85.

73 Peter H. Wilson, *Europe's Tragedy: A New History of the Thirty Years War*
    (New York, 2010), is the most recent comprehensive treatment in

English of the war and its causes and consequences, with, however, a differing interpretation of Rudolf II's role than that offered here.

74 Josef Leeb, *Der Magdeburger Sessionsstreit von 1582: Voraussetzungen, Problematik und Konsequenzen für Reichstag und Reichskammergericht* (Wetzlar, 2000).

75 Henri IV of France also became involved in the Strasbourg conflict: see Ehrenpreis, *Kaiserliche Gerichtsbarkeit und Konfessionskonflkt*, pp. 173–83.

76 D. C. Peck, ed., *Leicester's Commonwealth: The Copy of a Letter Written by Master of Art of Cambridge (1584) and Related Documents* (Athens, OH, and London, 1985), p. 184.

77 Evans, 'Culture and Politics at the Court of Rudolf II', p. 10.

78 Elmer Weiss, 'Die kaiserliche Gesandtschaftsreise des Landgrafen Georg Ludwig von Leuchtenberg an Jakob I. von England (1605)', *Verhandlungen des Historischen Vereins für Oberpfalz und Regensburg*, CXVIII (1978), pp. 221–35. The confusion and supposed mishandling that Weiss attributes to the conduct of diplomacy by the imperial court was most likely due to the intrigues that he notes occurred at court. These, as suggested, were caused by the new teams assembled after 1601.

79 See Thomas DaCosta Kaufmann, 'The Imperial Theme in Art and Architecture of the Polish Vasas' ('Motywy imperialne w sztuce i architekturze polskich Wazów'), *Biuletyn Historii Sztuki*, LXXXIII/2 (2021), pp. 323–49, especially pp. 331–2, with further references; the essay discusses the impact of the Austrian (and through them the Spanish) Habsburgs on Vasa art and architecture.

80 Vocelka, *Die politische Propaganda*, pp. 233, 235, 259.

81 Niederkorn, 'Lange Turkenkrieg', pp. 52–8.

82 See Rotraud Bauer and Herbert Haupt, eds, 'Das Kunstkammer-inventar Kaiser Rudolfs II., 1607–1611', *Jahrbuch der Kunsthistorischen Sammlungen in Wien*, LXXII (1976), p. 33, fol. 56v, no. 590; p. 19, fol. 39v, no. 327; p. 30, fol. 53, nos 504–10; p. 72, fol. 209r, no. 1330 [170].

83 'His Majesty is interested only in wizards, alchemists, kabbalists and the like, sparing no expense to find all kinds of treasures, learn secrets and use scandalous ways of harming his enemies . . . He also has a whole library of magic books. He strives all the time to eliminate God completely so that he may in future serve a different master' (translated by Evans, *Rudolf II and His World*, p. 196, who, however, does not give his reference).

84 Felix Stieve, *Von der Abreise Erzherog Leopolds nach Jülich bis zu den Werbungen Herzog Maximilians von Bayern im März 1610*, Briefe und Akten zur Geschichte des Dreissigjährigen Krieges, vol. VII (Munich, 1905), p. 49.

85 Alexander Wied, ed., *Die Profanen Bau- und Kunstdenkmäler der Stadt Linz* (Vienna, 1977), p. 506: 'er beabsichtige nach Linz zu kommen und im Schloß zu residieren'.

86 See Evans, *Rudolf II and His World*, who quotes Eremita, pp. 44–5.

87 For information on the design of the stalls and what took place there, see Eliška Fučíková, 'Der Wladislawsaal als öffentlicher Raum', in *Dresden – Prag um 1600*, ed. Bukovinská and Konečný, pp. 55–63.

88 See Evans, Fučíková and Campbell, *The Stylish Image*, p. 52, cat. no. 39 (entry by Mungo Campbell; Campbell, however, misidentifies the emissaries as Turkish and the crown as Rudolf's – it is imaginary and varies the crown of St Wenzel); Bert W. Meijer, *Arte grafica alla corte di Praga al tempo di Arcimboldo e Rodolfo II / Graphic Arts at the Prague Court in the Time of Giuseppe Arcimboldo and Rudolf II*, exh. cat. (Milan, 2011), pp. 32–34, cat. no. 18; Alena Volrábová and Blanka Kubíková, eds, *Rudolf II. a mistři grafického umění / Rudolf II and Masters of Printmaking*, exh. cat. (Prague, 2012), pp. 54, 161, cat. no. II 15 (entry by Dalibor Leškový); Blanka Kubíková, 'Portraits and the Art Patronage of Kryštof Popel the Younger of Lobkowicz, a Courtier of Rudolf II', *Studia Rudolphina*, XVI (2016), p. 14.

89 That the staff is a sign of office or authority, and not used as a means of support, is confirmed by a portrait of Kryštof Popel the Younger of Lobkowicz: see Kubíková, 'Portraits and the Art Patronage'.

90 Kaufmann, *Variations on the Imperial Theme*, pp. 111–13.

91 See Felix Stieve, *Vom Reichstag 1608 bis zur Gründung der Liga*, Briefe und Acten zur Geschichte des Dreissigjährigen Krieges, vol. VI (Munich, 1895), pp. 230ff, 246ff and passim.

92 In general, for gifts received by Johann Georg I, see Dirk Syndram, 'Johann Georg I von Sachsen: Für das Reich und den Glauben', in *Bellum et Artes: Sachsen und Mitteleuropa im Dreissigjährigen Krieg*, ed. Theda Jürjens and Dirk Syndram, exh. cat. (Dresden, 2021), pp. 29–41, especially p. 31.

93 See Hilda Lietzmann, *Herzog Heinrich Julius zur Braunschweig und Lüneburg, 1564–1613: Persönlichkeit und Wirken für Kaiser und Reich* (Braunschweig, 1993).

94 Stieve, *Briefe und Akten*, vol. VI, pp. 718, 709 and passim.

95 Ibid., pp. 176, 177, 703 (for the audience), 679 and passim.
96 Williams, 'The Making of Rudolf II as a Mad Monarch'; Černušák and Marek, *Gesandte und Klienten.*
97 Vocelka, *Politische Propaganda*, p. 141, and Gertrude von Schwarzenfeld, *Rudolf II, der saturnische Kaiser* (Munich, 1961), p. 242.
98 See A. D. Anderson, *On the Verge of War: International Relations and the Jülich-Cleve Succession Crisis (1609–1614)* (Boston, 1999), for a recent account of this crisis and the events described in the next paragraphs.
99 Bardazzi and Carrai, 'Constantino de' Servi', p. 113.

2 Rudolf II as Collector

1 Julius von Schlosser, *Art and Curiosity Cabinets of the Late Renaissance: A Contribution to the History of Collecting*, ed. Thomas DaCosta Kaufmann, trans. Jonathan Blower (Los Angeles, CA, 2021); for the background and reception of the book, see Thomas DaCosta Kaufmann, '*Die Kunst- und Wunderkammer der Spätrenaissance*: A Landmark Reconsidered', ibid., pp. 1–50.
2 See Friedrich Polleroß, '"Kayserliche Schatz-und Kunstkammer": Die habsburgischen Sammlungen und ihre Öffentlichkeit im 17. Jahrhundert', in *Das Haus Habsburg und die Welt der fürstlichen Kunstkammern im 16. und 17. Jahrhundert*, ed. Sabine Haag, Franz Kirchweger and Paulus Rainer (Vienna, 2015), pp. 255–7.
3 For this information as for many other details in this chapter, the account is based on Alphons Lhotsky, *Festschrift des Kunsthistorischen Museums zur Feier des fünfzigjährigen Bestandes: Zweiter Teil – Die Geschichte der Sammlungen. Erste Hälfte: Von den Anfängen bis zum Tode Kaiser Karls VI.* (Vienna, 1941–5).
4 This last detail is of importance because it is another piece of evidence that suggests Juana was not mad, as was noted in an account of the provenance of these collections by Karl Rudolf, 'Die Kunstbestrebungen Kaiser Maximilian II. und Rudolf II. im Spannungsfeld zwischen Madrid und Wien: Untersuchungen zu den Sammlungen der österreichischen und spanischen Habsburger im 16. Jahrhundert', *Jahrbuch der kunsthistorischen Sammlungen in Wien*, XCI (1995), p. 199.
5 This is a theme in much of the work of Matthew Canepa, whose observation is here paraphrased. See, for example, Matthew Canepa, 'Distant Displays of Power: Understanding Cross-Cultural Interaction among the Elites of Rome, Sasanian Iran, and Sui-Tang China', *Ars Orientalis*, XXXVII/1 (2010), pp. 121–54.

6 This collection, known as the *Burgunderschatz*, was a focus of an exhibition in the Historisches Museum, Bern, where much of it is held: see *Kunst, Krieg, und Hofkultur*, exh. cat. (Bern, 2008).

7 Still central for this discussion is Jan-Dirk Müller, *Gedechnus: Literatur und Hofgesellschaft um Maximilian I* (Munich, 1982).

8 Larry Silver, *Marketing Maximilian: The Visual Ideology of a Holy Roman Emperor* (Princeton, NJ, 2008), discusses this print and others in reference to their use in regard to spreading imperial ideology.

9 See Carina L. Johnson, 'Aztec Regalia and the Reformation of Display', in *Collecting across Cultures: Material Exchanges in the Early Modern Atlantic World*, ed. Daniela Bleichmar and Peter C. Mancall (Philadelphia, PA, 2011), pp. 83–98.

10 Earl Rosenthal, 'Die "Reichskrone", die "Wiener Krone" und die "Krone Karls des Großen" um 1520', *Jahrbuch der Kunsthistorischen Sammlungen in Wien*, LXVI (1970), pp. 7–48.

11 See Karl Friedrich Rudolf, '"Yo el infante – ich der Infant": Ferdinand, Prinz in Hispanien', in *Kaiser Ferdinand I 1503–1564: Das Werden der Habsburgermnoarchie*, ed. Wilfried Seipel (Vienna, 2003), especially pp. 45–7.

12 For these bequests, see the discussion and the texts quoted in Lhotsky, *Festschrift*, pp. 154–5.

13 For a discussion of this work, see Gert Van der Osten and Horst Vey, *Painting and Sculpture in Germany and the Netherlands* (Harmondsworth, 1969), pp. 254–5, and Jeffrey Chipps Smith, *German Sculpture of the Later Renaissance c. 1520–1580: Art in an Age of Uncertainty* (Princeton, NJ, 1994), p. 304. The translation is taken from Jennifer Montagu, *Bronzes* (New York, 1965), pp. 67–9, with the word *Artlichkeit* taken from the original text as quoted in Van der Osten and Vey, *Painting and Sculpture*.

14 Rudolf, 'Kunstbestrebungen', p. 169, n. 38.

15 Johnson, 'Aztec Regalia'.

16 Lhotsky, *Festschrift*, and Karl Rudolf, 'Arcimboldo im kulinarischen Wissensraum: Die Kunstkammer Kaiser Ferdinands I (1503–1564)', in *Das Haus Habsburg und die Welt der fürstlichen Kunstkammern*, ed. Haag, Kirchweger and Rainer, pp. 133–66.

17 Paulus Rainer, 'Facetten Habsburgischen Sammelwesen betrachtet anhand des Bestandes der Kunstkammer und der Schatzkammer des Kunsthistorischen Museums Wien', PhD thesis, University of Vienna, 2017.

18 See Lhotsky, *Festschrift*, p. 145.
19 Renate Holzschuh-Hofer, 'Galerie, Kunstkammergebäude und Ballhaus, 1521–1619', in *Die Wiener Hofburg 1521–1705: Baugeschichte, Funktion und Etablierung als Kaiserresidenz*, ed. Herbert Karner (Vienna, 2014), pp. 205–10.
20 Rudolf, 'Arcimboldo im kulinarischen Wissensraum'.
21 Thomas DaCosta Kaufmann, 'Arcimboldo's Imperial Allegories', *Zeitschrift für Kunstgeschichte*, XXXIX (1976), pp. 275–96; for the room in which they were probably hung, and the presence of representative tapestries there, see Renate Holzschuh-Hofer, 'Die Alte Burg', in *Die Wiener Hofburg*, ed. Karner, pp. 124–9.
22 Petr Uličný, 'Bella & rara armaria di sua Altezza: Zbrojnice Pražského hradu v době Ferdinanda Tyrolského', *Průzkumy Památek*, XXV/1 (2018), pp. 25–46.
23 Ibid.
24 For the Ambras armoury, see most recently Thomas Kuster, '"Dises heroische thatrum": The Heldenrüstkammer at Ambras Castle', in *Ferdinand II: 450 Years Sovereign Ruler of Tyrol*, ed. Sabine Haag and Veronika Sandbichler (Innsbruck, 2017), pp. 83–8.
25 See the summary in Veronika Sandbichler, 'sovil schönen, kostlichen und verwunderlichen zeugs, das ainer vil monat zu schaffen hette, alles recht zu besichtigen vnd zu contemplieren.' 'Die Kunst- und Wunderkammer Herzog Ferdinands II. auf Schloss Ambras', in *Das Haus Habsburg und die Welt der fürstlichen Kunstkammern*, ed. Haag, Kirchweger and Rainer, pp. 195–228.
26 A drawing by Joris Hoefnagel of Innsbruck and Ambras Castle based on a model by the sculptor Alexander Colin and used for an engraving in Georg Braun and Franz Hohenberg, *Civitates Orbis Terrarum, Gesamtausgabe der kolorierten Tafeln 1582–1617*, ed. Stephan Füssel (Hong Kong, Cologne, etc., 2008 [facsimile edition; as in Vignau Wilberg]), vol. V, p. 58, illustrates the library (*bibliotheca*) and museum (*musaeum*) of Ambras: see Thea Vignau Wilberg, *Joris and Jacob Hoefnagel: Art and Science around 1600* (Berlin, 2017), pp. 316–17, cat. no. F-g 4.
27 See primarily Elisabeth Scheicher, *Die Kunstkammer* (Innsbruck, 1977); Elisabeth Scheicher, *Die Kunst- und Wunderkammer der Habsburger*, ed. Christian Brandstätter (Vienna, Munich, Innsbruck and Zurich, 1979), pp. 73–136; and Sandbichler, '"Sovil schönen, kostlichen und verwunderlichen zeugs"'.
28 See in general Rudolf, 'Kunstbestrebungen'.
29 See, for example, ibid., pp. 234, no. 69, and 236, no. 127 and 148.

30 Almudena Pérez de Tudela and Annemarie Jordan Gschwend, 'Luxury Goods for Royal Collectors: Exotica, Princely Gifts and Rare Animals exchanged between the Iberian Courts and Central Europe in the Renaissance (1560–1612)', in *Exotica: Portugal Entdeckungen im Spiegel fürstlicher Kunst- und Wunderkammern der Renaissance*, ed. Helmut Trnek and Sabine Haag, Jahrbuch des Kunsthistorischen Museums Wien, III (Mainz, 2001), p. 8.

31 Ibid. and, in general, Thomas DaCosta Kaufmann, *Arcimboldo: Visual Jokes, Natural History, and Still-Life Painting* (Chicago, IL, and London, 2009).

32 My thanks to Elizabeth Pilliod for this reference, which will be presented in a forthcoming article.

33 Strada is treated in numerous essays by Dirk Jacob Jansen, most comprehensively in his *Jacopo Strada and Cultural Patronage at the Imperial Court: The Antique as Innovation* (Boston, MA, and Leiden, 2019).

34 See Lhotsky, *Festschrift*, p. 172.

35 See Kaufmann, *Arcimboldo*; Lhotsky, *Festschrift*, p. 165; and similarly Rudolf, 'Kunstbestrebungen', pp. 218–19.

36 For the Stallburg, see Renate Holzschuh-Hofer and Sibylle Grün, 'Die Stallburg 1559–1619', in *Die Wiener Hofburg*, ed. Karner, pp. 294–304; for the attribution of this building and its treatment in context, see Janson, *Jacopo Strada*.

37 Hilda Lietzmann, *Das Neugebäude in Wien: Sultan Süleymans Zelt — Kaiser Maximilians II. Lustschloß* (Munich and Berlin, 1987).

38 Rudolf, 'Kunstbestrebungen', pp. 166–7.

39 Thomas DaCosta Kaufmann, 'Arcimboldo and the Elector of Saxony', in *Scambio culturale con il nemico religioso: Italia e Sassonia attorno 1600*, ed. Sybille Ebert-Schifferer (Rome, 2007), pp. 27–36, and Kaufmann, *Arcimboldo*.

40 For the gifts to Maximilian, see Dorothea Diemer, 'Giambologna in Deutschland', in *Giambologna: Triumph des Körpers*, ed. Wilfried Seipel (Vienna, 2006); for those to Dresden, see Dirk Syndram, Moritz Woelk and Martina Minning, eds, *Giambologna in Dresden: Die Geschenke der Medici* (Dresden, 2006).

41 De Tudela and Jordan Gschwend, 'Luxury Goods for Royal Collectors', p. 11.

42 Thomas DaCosta Kaufmann, 'The *Kunstkammer* as a Form of *Representatio*: Remarks on the Collections of Rudolf II', *Art Journal*, XXXVIII (1978), pp. 22–8 (republished in Donald Preziosi and Claire Farago, eds, *Grasping the World* (Aldershot, 2004), pp. 526–37).

43 According to 'Art for Display: The Painting Collection of Emperor
   Rudolf II within the Context of Collecting Practices circa 1600', an
   ongoing project of the Institute for the History of Art, Prague: see
   'Inventaria Rudolphina', available at www.inventariarudolphina.com.

44 See Eliška Fučíková, 'The Collection of Rudolf II at Prague: Cabinet
   of Curiosities or Scientific Museum?', in *The Origins of Museums: The
   Cabinet of Curiosities in Sixteenth- and Seventeenth-Century Europe*, ed.
   Oliver Impey and Arthur MacGregor (Oxford, 2017), pp. 49–51.

45 Lawrence W. Nichols, 'The "Pen Works" of Hendrick Goltzius',
   Philadelphia Museum of Art Bulletin, LXXXVIII/373–4 (Winter 1992),
   pp. 4–56.

46 For a relatively recent overview, see Michael Eichberg, 'Zu den
   Antiken in de Prager Kunstkammer Kaiser Rudolfs II', *Studia
   Rudolphina*, XIV (2014), pp. 7–14. Earlier studies include Lhotsky,
   Festschrift, pp. 241–5. For the history of the *Ilioneus* and the *Gemma
   Augustea*, see Gabriel Hejzlar, 'Dvě antiky z Rudolfových sbírek',
   Sborník prací Filozofické Fakulty Brněnské Univerzity, F, Řada uměnovědná,
   X/5 (1961), pp. 113–34; for the latter and its impact on Rudolfine art,
   see Rudolf Chadraba, 'Die Gemma Augustea und die rudolfinische
   Allegorie', *Umění*, XVIII/3 (1970), pp. 289–97, and Jürgen Zimmer,
   'Aus der Sammlungen Kaiser Rudolfs II: "Der Kameo"', *Studia
   Rudolphina*, IX (2009), pp. 110–26.

47 The category of *scientifica* as a designation for objects in Rudolf's
   collection seems to originate with Erwin Neumann, 'Das Inventar
   der rudolfinischen Kunstkammer von 1607–1611', in *Queen Christina
   of Sweden: Documents and Studies*, ed. Magnus von Platen, Analecta
   Reginensia, I (Stockholm, 1966), p. 263.

48 Léopold Chatenay, ed., *Vie de Jacques Esprinchard, Rochelais, et journal de ses
   voyages au XVIe siècle* (Paris, 1957), pp. 168–9.

49 Sylva Dobalová, *Zahrady Rudolfa II. Jejích vznik a vývoj* (Prague, 2009),
   pp. 128–41.

50 Emanuel Sweerts, *Early Flower Engravings*, ed. E. F. Bleiler (New York,
   1976), p. xi. The various versions of Sweerts's text and the reliability
   of his comments are discussed in Chapter 4.

51 Dobalová, *Zahrady Rudolfa II.*, pp. 121–7.

52 These are discussed in the next chapter.

53 Renate Holzschuh-Hofer, 'Die Neue Burg (Amalienburg)',
   in *Die Wiener Hofburg*, ed. Karner, pp. 335–41.

54 Petr Uličný, 'Erotica & Sapientia: Rudolf II's Early Years at
   Prague Castle', *Umění*, LXIX/4 (2021), pp. 390–415, traces the

early history of construction of rooms for collections under Rudolf, with references (especially note 1) to previous literature on the building of the castle; his interpretation of the collection and description of the Summer House as a *Kunstkammer* cannot, however, be accepted.

55 The arguments in the paragraph reprise part of Thomas DaCosta Kaufmann, '*Zur Zierd*: Revisiting the Prague *Kunstkammer*', *Studia Rudolphina*, XVII–XVIII (2018), pp. 140–54.

56 See Thomas DaCosta Kaufmann, *The School of Prague: Painting at the Court of Rudolf II* (Chicago, IL, and London, 1988), pp. 20–21.

57 Jeffrey Chipps Smith, *Kunstkammer: Early Modern Art and Curiosity Cabinets in the Holy Roman Empire* (London, 2022), provides an accessible introduction to these collections, with bibliography.

58 See Herbert Brunner, *Schatzkammer der Residenz* (Munich, 1979), pp. 7–18.

59 See Barbara Gutfleisch-Ziche and Joachim Menzhausen, 'How a Kunstkammer Should be Formed: Gabriel Kaltemarckt's Advice to Christian I of Saxony on the Formation of an Art Collection', *Journal of the History of Collections*, 1 (1989), pp. 3–32.

60 Jakob Bornitz, *Tractatus Politicus* (Tampach, 1625 [but composed earlier]), p. 61.

61 These comments represent a summary of Thomas DaCosta Kaufmann, 'Artes ante Bellum: The Arts before the Thirty Years' War in Central Europe and Beyond', in *Bellum et Artes: Central Europe in the Thirty Years' War*, ed. Claudia Brink, Susanne Jaeger and Marius Winzeler (Dresden, 2021), pp. 17–39.

62 The text is accessible in *The First Treatise on Museums: Samuel Quiccheberg's Inscriptiones, 1565*, ed. and trans. Mark A. Meadow and Bruce Robertson (Los Angeles, CA, 2013). The importance of the connection with Giulio Camillo was first emphasized in Thomas DaCosta Kaufmann, *Variations on the Imperial Theme in the Age of Maximilian II and Rudolf II* (Boston, MA, and London, 1978), p. 122.

63 For this discussion of Bornitz, see Kaufmann, 'Artes ante Bellum'.

64 For the information in these paragraphs, see Kaufmann, *Variations on the Imperial Theme*, pp. 104–13. The relations with Saxony are discussed further in Thomas DaCosta Kaufmann, 'Arcimboldo au Louvre', *Revue du Louvre et des Musées de France*, XXVII (1977), pp. 337–42, and Thomas DaCosta Kaufmann, 'Arcimboldo and the Elector of Saxony', in *Scambio culturale con il nemico religioso: Italia e Sassonia attorno 1600*, ed. Sybille Ebert-Schifferer (Rome, 2007), pp. 27–36.

65 I owe this information on the display of tapestries in the so-called Trabantensaal of Prague Castle to a presentation of Marta Ježková at a seminar in the Institute of the History of Art, Prague, October 2022, at which she summarized the findings of 'Art for Display'.

66 See Simone Bardazzi and Guido Carrai, 'Costantino de' Servi, architetto e informatore mediceo, alla corte di Rodolfo II: Nuovi documenti circa le relazioni tra Praga le corti principesce italiane', *Studia Rudolphina*, XX–XXI (2022), pp. 86–114.

67 These are located in the Museum der bildenden Künste, Leipzig, *Graphische Sammlung, Rensi Sammlung*, vol. III and VIII, but remain to be thoroughly studied.

68 The translation here is taken from R.J.W. Evans, *Rudolf II and His World: A Study in Intellectual History, 1576–1612* (Oxford, 1973), p. 162.

69 Joachim von Sandrart, *L'academia Todesca oder Teutsche Academie . . .* (Nuremberg, 1675), vol. I, p. 356.

70 See Thomas DaCosta Kaufmann, 'In the Imperial Orbit: Art at the German Princely Courts in the Era of Rudolf II', in *The Eloquent Artist: Essays on Art, Art Theory and Architecture, Sixteenth to Nineteenth Century* (London, 2004), pp. 174–207.

71 Discussed in Kaufmann, 'The *Kunstkammer* as a Form of *Representatio*', pp. 22–3.

72 Gertrude von Schwarzenfeld, *Rudolf II, der saturnische Kaiser* (Munich, 1961), p. 94.

73 Annemarie Jordan Gschwend, ed., *Hans Khevenhüller at the Court of Philip II of Spain: Diplomacy and Consumerism in a Global Empire* (London, forthcoming).

74 See Eliška Fučíková, 'The Fate of Rudolf II's Collections in Light of the History of the Thirty Years' War', in *1648: War and Peace in Europe*, ed. Klaus Bussmann and Heinz Schilling, Art and Culture II (Münster and Osnabrück, 1998), pp. 173–80.

3 Rudolf II as Patron of Art and Architecture

1 Karel van Mander, *Het Schilder-boeck* (Haarlem, 1604), 'Voorreden', fol. IIIIv, as cited in translation by R.J.W. Evans, *Rudolf II and His World: A Study in Intellectual History, 1576–1612* (Oxford, 1973), p. 162.

2 Impressions of the collections are scattered through the literature, including older overviews such as Jaromír Neumann, *The Picture Gallery of Prague Castle* (Prague, 1967), and Eliška Fučíková, 'Rudolf

ii — Einige Bemerkungen zu seinen Sammlungen', *Umění*, XVIII/2 (1970), pp. 128–32, but this large subject surprisingly lacks a dedicated comprehensive study. The ongoing project 'Art for Display' (see note 78 below) promises to remedy this situation.

3 Eliška Fučíková, 'Prague Castle under Rudolf II, his predecessors and Successors, 1530–1648', in *Rudolf II and Prague: The Court and the City*, ed. Eliška Fučíková et al. (Prague, 1997), pp. 2–71, offers an introduction that, among other things, relates the production of art to collecting.

4 In 1592 Rudolf II made Giuseppe Arcimboldo a count palatine, one of only three such artists to receive this title in the sixteenth century. In 1588 he improved the coat of arms of Bartholomeus Spranger, to whom he granted a hereditary title in 1595. And in 1605 he knighted Hans von Aachen.

5 Eri Kawakami, 'Bartholomeus Spranger's *Triumph of Wisdom* as an Allegory of the Re-Evaluation of the Art of Painting in Sixteenth-Century Prague', *Studia Rudolphina*, XVII–XVIII (2018), pp. 66–78, relates the increased status of the imperial artists to the more general re-evaluation of the arts in Prague, and Spranger's involvement in both.

6 K. D. Haszler, ed., *Reisen und Gefangenschaft Hans Ulrich Kraffts aus der Originalhandschrift* (Stuttgart, 1861), p. 389. Probably on the basis of a report from Spranger that he received directly when Spranger visited Holland in 1602, van Mander, *Het Schilder-boeck*, fol. 273r also says that Rudolf had the artist work in his presence.

7 Roderigo Alidosi, *Relazione di Germania e delle cose della corte di Rodolfo II imperatore negli anni 1605–1607*, ed. C. and G. Campori (Modena, 1872), p. 7. As discussed in the present book, rumours about Rudolf's supposed isolation and avoidance of matters of state are contradicted by his holding audiences like this one. Audiences were regularly accorded, for example, to ambassadors who were leaving the court: see Thomas DaCosta Kaufmann, *Variations on the Imperial Theme in the Age of Maximilian II and Rudolf II* (Boston, MA, and London, 1978), p. 108.

8 Thomas DaCosta Kaufmann, 'Artes ante Bellum: The Arts before the Thirty Years' War in Central Europe and Beyond', in *Bellum et Artes: Central Europe in the Thirty Years' War*, ed. Claudia Brink, Susanne Jaeger and Marius Winzeler (Dresden, 2021), pp. 19–20.

9 See Inv. no. 2 D 406. See Bente Gudestrup, *Det kongelige danske Kunstkammer 1737/The Royal Danish Kunstkammer 1737* (Copenhagen, 1981), vol. I, p. 301, no. 766/339, illustrated.

10 A good brief summary of arguments for the social status of the artist is still to be found in Anthony Blunt, *Artistic Theory in Italy, 1450–1600* (Oxford, 1940), pp. 48–57.

11 Peter Burke, *The Fortunes of the Courtier: The European Reception of Castiglione's Courtier* (University Park, PA, 1996).

12 See Thomas DaCosta Kaufmann, *The School of Prague: Painting at the Court of Rudolf II* (Chicago, IL, and London, 1988), pp. 24–5, for rulers who practised arts – for which drawing was in general basic.

13 Martin Warnke, *The Court Artist: On the Ancestry of the Modern Artist*, trans. David Maclintock (Cambridge and New York, 1993), relates many such stories; for Philip II's correcting plans for the Escorial, see Geoffrey Parker, *Imprudent King: A New Life of Philip II* (New Haven, CT, and London, 2014), p. 20; for Arcimboldo's copies for Ferdinand, see Manfred Staudinger, 'Sources on Arcimboldo at the Habsburg Court', in *Arcimboldo 1526–1593*, ed. Sylvia Ferino-Pagden, exh. cat. (Milan, 2007), pp. 303–4.

14 Rotraud Bauer and Herbert Haupt, eds, 'Das Kunstkammerinventar Kaiser Rudolfs II., 1607–1611', *Jahrbuch der Kunsthistorischen Sammlungen in Wien*, LXXII (1976), p. 50, fol. 96v, no. 922, p. 53, fol. 99r, no. 982.

15 Kaufmann, *The School of Prague*, pp. 24–5.

16 Balthasar Exner de Hirschberg, *Valerius Maximus Christianus* (Hanau, 1620), p. 31.

17 See Werner L. Gundersheimer, *Ferrara: The Style of a Renaissance Despotism* (Princeton, NJ, 1973), pp. 268ff; Pogius Bracciolini, 'De nobilitate', in *Opera Omnia* (Basel, 1538 [repr. Turin, 1964]), pp. 65ff; Giovanni Gioviano Pontano, 'De magnificentia' and 'De splendore', in *Trattati delle virtù sociale* (Rome, 1965), especially pp. 131ff.

18 Most easily accessible in Jeffrey Ashcroft, ed., *Albrecht Dürer, Documentary Biography* (New Haven, CT, and London, 2017), vol. II, p. 838.

19 Bauer and Haupt, 'Kunstkammerinventar Kaiser Rudolfs II', p. 137, fol. 383v, no. 2754.

20 Giovanni Botero, *The Reason of State*, ed. Robert Bireley (Cambridge, 2017).

21 Vera Keller, *Knowledge and the Public Interest, 1575–1725* (Cambridge, 2015), pp. 125–6.

22 James Fishburne, 'Newly Discovered Monetary Characteristics of Rudolf II's Gold Portrait Medal', *Getty Research Journal*, VIII (2016), pp. 209–16.

23 Viktor Fleischer, *Karl Eusebius von Liechtenstein as Bauherr und Sammler* (Vienna, 1919), p. 89.

24 Thomas DaCosta Kaufmann, *Court, Cloister, and City: The Art and Culture of Central Europe, 1450–1800* (Chicago, IL, and London, 1995).

25 Antoine Schnapper, 'The King of France as Collector in the Seventeenth Century', *Journal of Interdisciplinary History*, XVII/I (1986), pp. 185–202.

26 See the basic monographs by George Kubler, *Building the Escorial* (Princeton, NJ, 1982), and Catherine Wilkinson-Zerner, *Juan de Herrera: Architect to Philip II of Spain* (New Haven, CT, and London, 1992).

27 See Ivan Muchka, 'Architectural Styles in the Reign of Rudolf II: Italian and Hispanic Influences', in *Rudolf II and Prague*, ed. Fučíková et al., pp. 90–95; Pablo Jiménez Diaz, 'Spain, Prague, and the Habsburg Ideology: Some Aspects of the Architecture of Rudolf II', in *Rudolf II, Prague and the World*, ed. Lubomír Konečný, Beket Bukovinská and Ivan Muchka (Prague, 1998), pp. 11–15.

28 See the documents discussed in Alexander Wied, ed., *Die Profanen Bau- und Kunstdenkmäler der Stadt Linz* (Vienna, 1977), pp. 501, 506, 492. See further a document dated 15 June 1607 published in Hans von Voltelini, 'Urkunden und Regesten aus dem k. k. Haus-, Hof- und Staatsarchiv in Wien. Nachträge und Forschungen', *Jahrbuch der kunsthistorischen Sammlungen des allerhöchsten Kaiserhauses*, vol. XIX (1898), p. LXXV, reg. no. 16705.

29 See Wied, *Die Profanen Bau- und Kunstdenkmäler*, p. 501.

30 For an account of Rudolf II and the role of the Habsburgs in the Linz Schloss, see further Thomas DaCosta Kaufmann, 'Linz – Des Kaisers Kulturhauptstadt um 1600? Ein Escorial in Oberösterreich?', in *Linz – Des Kaisers Kulturhauptstadt um 1600?* (Weitra, 2012), pp. 39–54.

31 Amalienburg and Ambras are still more or less recognizable as they were, but Ebersdorf has been altered substantially: for its earlier appearance, see Hilda Lietzmann, *Das Neugebäude in Wien: Sultan Süleymans Zelt – Kaiser Maximilians II. Lustschloß* (Munich and Berlin, 1987), p. 31, fig. 5.

32 See Muchka, 'Architectural Styles', and the plan illustrated in Petr Uličný, *Architektura Albrechta z Valdštejna: Italská stavební kultura v Čechách v letech 1600–1635 (Architecture of Albrecht of Wallenstein: Italian Building Culture in Bohemia in 1600–1635)* (Prague, 2017), vol. I (vol. II), pp. 838–9.

33 Bruce Edelstein et al., eds, *Eleonora di Toledo e l'invenzione della corte dei Medici a Firenze* (Florence, 2023), and Bruce Edelstein, *Eleonora di Toledo and the Creation of the Boboli Gardens* (Livorno, 2022).

34 Guido Carrai, 'Architettura italiana a Praga alla fine del '500', *Critica d'arte*, VIII (2008), pp. 34–50; Adriana Concin, 'Splendid Gifts and a Florentine Architect for Emperor Rudolf II: Antonio Lupicini at the Imperial Court in Prague (1578–1580)', *Studia Rudolphina*, XX (2020), pp. 25–50.

35 Guido Carrai, 'I fiorentini al Castello: Il progetto di Bernardo Buontalenti e Giovanni Gargiolli per la nuova galleria di Rodolfo II', *Umění*, LI (2003), pp. 370–84.

36 Simone Bardazzi and Giulio Carrai, 'Constantino de' Servi architetto e informatore mediceo alla corte di Rodolfo II: Nuovi documenti circa le relazioni tra Praga e le corti principesche italiane', *Studia Rudolphina*, XXI–XXII (2022), pp. 86–114.

37 Muchka, 'Architectural Styles in the Reign of Rudolf II: Italian and Hispanic Influences', in Fučíková et al., *Rudolf II and Prague*, pp. 94–5, also relates the Matthias Gateway to the Escorial.

38 Roy Strong, *Splendor at Court: Renaissance Spectacle and the Theater of Power* (Boston, MA, and London, 1973).

39 As discussed in Thomas DaCosta Kaufmann, *Arcimboldo: Visual Jokes, Natural History, and Still-Life Painting* (Chicago, IL, and London, 2009).

40 See Thomas DaCosta Kaufmann, 'Representation, Replication, Reproduction: The Legacy of Charles V in Sculpted Rulers' Portraits of the Sixteenth and Early Seventeenth Century', *Austrian History Yearbook*, XLIII (2012), pp. 1–18.

41 An accessible overview is available in Dorothy Limouze, 'Engraving at the Court of Prague', in *Rudolf II and Prague*, ed. Fučíková et al., pp. 17–28.

42 See Sabine Haag and Katja Schmitz von Ledebur, eds, *Kaiser Karl V. erobert Tunis: Dokumentation eines Kreuzuges in Cartons und Tapisserien* (Vienna, 2013).

43 Felix Stieve, *Von der Abreise Erzherog Leopolds nach Jülich bis zu den Werbungen Herzog Maximilians von Bayern im März 1610*, Briefe und Akten zur Geschichte des Dreissigjährigen Krieges, vol. VII (Munich, 1905), pp. 185, 202.

44 See Kaufmann, *The School of Prague*, pp. 149–53, with further references.

45 Heinrich Zimmermern, 'Das Inventar der Prager Schatz und Kunstkammer vom 6. Dezember 1621', *Jahrbuch der Kunthistorischen Sammlungen des Allerhöchsten Kaiserahuses*, XXV (1905), no. 691.

46 Karl Vocelka, *Die politische Propaganda Kaiser Rudolfs II. (1570–1612)*
    (Vienna, 1980), treats the anti-Turkish imagery and processions
    at length.

47 Ibid.; for individual works related to paintings on this theme,
    see Kaufmann, *The School of Prague*, especially pp. 222–3 for the
    interpretation of the painting by van Ravesteyn presented here.

48 The interpretation offered here was presented first in Thomas
    DaCosta Kaufmann, 'Arcimboldo's Imperial Allegories', *Zeitschrift
    für Kunstgeschichte*, XXXIX (1976), pp. 275–96, and Thomas DaCosta
    Kaufmann, 'Arcimboldo and Propertius: A Classical Source for *Rudolf
    II as Vertumnus*', *Zeitschrift für Kunstgeschichte*, XLVIII (1985), pp. 117–23.

49 Kaufmann, *Arcimboldo*, pp. 125, 130, 134–40; see further Thomas
    DaCosta Kaufmann, 'Arcimboldo and the Elector of Saxony', in
    Scambio culturale con il nemico religioso: Italia e Sassonia attorno 1600, ed.
    Sybille Ebert-Schifferer (Rome, 2007), pp. 27–36.

50 Kaufmann, *Variations on the Imperial Theme*, p. 40.

51 The classic interpretation of this painting is Anthony Blunt, 'El
    Greco's "Dream of Philip II": An Allegory of the Holy League',
    Journal of the Warburg and Courtauld Institutes, III (1939–40), pp.
    58–69. A catalogue entry by William B. Jordan in Jonathan Brown
    et al., *El Greco of Toledo* (Boston, MA, 1982), pp. 231–2, provides
    comprehensive information on this painting.

52 For a good discussion of these paintings with previous literature,
    see Rosemarie Mulcahy, 'Celebrar o no celebrar: Felipe II e las
    representaciones de la Batalla de Lepanto', *Reales sitios*, XLIII (2006),
    pp. 2–15, no. 168.

53 Kaufmann, *The School of Prague*, p. 151.

54 See Anna Coreth, *Pietas Austriaca*, trans. Wiliam Bowman and Anna
    Maria Leitgeb (West Lafayette, IN, 2004).

55 See Jarmila Krčálová, 'Poznámky k Rudolfínské Architektuře', *Umění*,
    XXIII (1975), pp. 499–526; Jürgen Zimmer, *Hofkirche und Rathaus in
    Neuburg, Donau: Die Bauplanungen von 1591 bis 1630* (Weissenhorn, 1971).

56 See Rosemarie Mulcahy, *Philip II as Patron of the Arts* (Dublin, 2004),
    pp. 215ff. De Vries made a bronze group of *Christ at the Column* (1604)
    for the epitaph of the court official Adam Hanniwald in Rothsurben/
    Żórawina in Silesia, and a *Christ as Man of Sorrows* (1607) for Karl von
    Liechtenstein, whom the sculpture links with the court by calling
    him *palati praefectus* on the base. Larger works with religious content
    include his standing figure of St Sebastian, also created for Karl
    von Liechtenstein, and an important tomb in Stadthagen as well as

a baptismal font in Bückeburg executed for Ernst of Schaumburg-Holstein-Lippe, all made, however, after Rudolf's death. These works are discussed in Frits Scholten, ed., *Adriaen de Vries, 1556–1626, Imperial Sculptor* (Amsterdam, Stockholm and Los Angeles, 1998), and in L. O. Larsson, *Adrian de Vries in Schaumburg: Die Werke für Fürst Ernst zu Holstein-Schaumburg 1613–1621* (Ostfildern-Ruit, 1998).

57 See the documents published in Eliška Fučíková, 'Adriaen de Vries, die Prager Burg, und das Waldstein-Palais', *Studia Rudolphina*, VI (2006), pp. 33–4.

58 In the early 1590s Spranger painted an epitaph for his father-in-law that also had a sculpted frame by de Vries. In the early 1600s he painted another epitaph for an imperial counsellor. Van Mander says the artist gave a painting of St Sebastian to the devout Duke of Bavaria; a second version replaced it in the Augustinian church of St Thomas in the Malá Strana, Prague. See Sally Metzler, *Bartholomeus Spranger: Splendor and Eroticism in Imperial Prague* (New York, New Haven, CT, and London, 2014), for these works.

59 Von Aachen designed many devotional works and altarpieces, but these were made largely before he came to Prague, and for patrons in Catholic Munich (for one possible exception, see Kaufmann, *The School of Prague*, p. 46, cat. no. 1.48). It has now been established that another important late altarpiece of the *Annunciation* by von Aachen was commissioned by the imperial counsellor Johann Anton Barvitius, who was responsible for several other religious commissions, not Rudolf II. See Michal Šroněk, 'Johann Barvitius als Mäzen in rudolfinischen Prag', *Studia Rudolphina*, VIII (2008), pp. 49–57, and further Michal Šroněk, *De sacris imaginibus: Patroni, malíři a obrazy předbělohorské Prahy* (Prague, 2013).

60 Noteworthy is an altarpiece for the burial chapel of the Italian community in Prague (Kaufmann, *The School of Prague*, p. 191, cat. no. 7.27). Similar differences are found in works done in Prague by Matthias Gundelach: see Fučíková et al., *Rudolf II and Prague*, pp. 46, 60–62, 394–5, 466–7.

61 For the paintings of Heintz, see primarily the many publications of Jürgen Zimmer, especially *Joseph Heintz der Ältere als Maler* (Weissenhorn, 1971), and *Joseph Heintz der Ältere: Zeichnungen und Dokumente* (Berlin and Munich, 1988).

62 Marie Tanner, *The Last Descendant of Aeneas: The Hapsburgs and the Mythic Image of the Emperor* (New Haven, CT, and London, 1993). The appearance of Neptune in the background of Titian's painting of

Spain Succouring Religion may be related to the antagonism of Neptune/ Poseidon to Aeneas known from the *Aeneid*, and thus meaningfully deployed in this picture, for which see Rosemarie Mulcahy, 'Celebrar o no celebrar', *Reales sitios*, XLIII (2006), pp. 2–15, no. 168.

63 R.J.W. Evans, Eliška Fučíková and Mungo Campbell, *The Stylish Image: Printmakers to the Court of Rudolf II* (Edinburgh, 1991), and Alena Volrábová and Blanka Kubíková, eds, *Rudolf II and Masters of Printmaking* (Prague, 2012), provide overviews.

64 Bardazzi and Carrai, 'Constantino de' Servi', p. 92.

65 This and the following paragraphs enlarge on arguments presented in Thomas DaCosta Kaufmann, 'Éros et poesia: La Peinture à la cour de Rodolphe II', *Revue de l'art*, XVIII, (1985), pp. 29–46.

66 Kaufmann, 'Éros et poesia', and more recently L. O. Larsson, 'Humor und Utopie in den mythologischen Darstellungen der Malerei am Hofe Rudolfs II.', in *Hans von Aachen in Context: Proceedings of the International Conference, Prague 22–25 September 2010*, ed. Lubomír Konečný and Štěpán Vácha (Prague, 2012), pp. 63–71, and Lubomír Konečný, 'A Note on Two "Rudolfine" Gestures', *Studia Rudolphina*, XV (2015), pp. 132–5.

67 As discussed in Kaufmann, *The School of Prague*, with further notes, p. 146, no. 1.39; p. 265, no. 20–48 and 20.49 for the former subject; and for the latter subject pp. 137–8, no. 1.12.

68 Bardazzi and Carrai, 'Constantino de' Servi', p. 92: 'Si diletta ora Sua Maestà grandemente di cose di pittura et però in questo, con ogni cosella piccola et specialmente lasciva ma fatta si maestra mano'.

69 See Pablo Jiménez Díaz, *El coleccionismo manierista de los Austrias: Entre Felipe II y Rodolfo II* (Madrid, 2001). The most recent treatment of these pictures was in an exhibition ('Titian: Women, Myth and Power') held at the Gardner Museum, Boston, 2021–2, for which see the wall labels and commentary at www.gardnermuseum.org.

70 See Görel Cavalli-Björkman, 'Mythologische themen am Hofe des Kaisers', in *Prag um 1600: Beiträge zur Kunst und Kultur am Hofe Rudolfs II*, 2 vols, ed. Eliška Fučíková (Freren, 1988) vol. 1, pp. 61–8.

71 Compare Gudrun Swoboda, ed., *Idole und Rivalen: Künstlerischer Wettstreit in Antke und früher Neuzeit*, exh. cat. (Vienna, 2022), for the Parmigianino, pp. 181–3, with notes; Spranger's emulation of other artists, and the reaction to Titian, are discussed elsewhere in the catalogue.

72 Lubomír Konečný, 'Sources and Significance of Two Mythological Paintings by Bartholomäus Spranger', *Jahrbuch der Kunsthistorischen Sammlungen in Wien*, LXXXV–LXXXVI (1989–90), pp. 47–56.

73 Bernhard Schnackenburg, 'Beobachtungen zu einem neuen Bild von Bartholomäus Spranger', *Niederdeutsche Beiträge zur Kunstgeschichte*, IX (1970), pp. 143–60.

74 See Thomas DaCosta Kaufmann, 'A "Modern" Sculptor in Prague: Adriaen de Vries and the *Paragone* of the Arts', in *Festschrift Konrad Oberhuber*, ed. Achim Gnann and Heinz Widauer (Milan, 2000), pp. 283–92, and Swoboda, *Idole und Rivalen*.

75 Swoboda, *Idole und Rivalen*, pp. 184–9.

76 Thomas DaCosta Kaufmann, 'Empire Triumphant: Notes on an Imperial Allegory by Adriaen de Vries in the National Gallery of Art', *Studies in the History of Art*, VIII (1978), pp. 63–75.

77 These works are illustrated or discussed in Kaufmann, *The School of Prague*, and in Fučíková et al., *Rudolf II and Prague*.

78 I would again like to express my gratitude to the Institute of the History of Art of the Czech Academy for holding a seminar for me in October 2022, at which were presented the preliminary results of 'Art for Display', to which reference is made here.

79 For the initial identification of van Ravesteyn's studies, see the contributions by Thea Wilberg-Vignau Schuurman to *Le Bestiaire de Rodolphe II: Cod. min. 129 et 130 de la Bibliothèque nationale d'Autriche*, ed. Herbert Haupt et al., trans. Léa Marcou (Paris, 1990), with good illustrations.

4 Rudolf II as Patron of Science

1 The classic account in English remains Frances A. Yates, *Giordano Bruno and the Hermetic Tradition* (London, 1964). See the assessment by Guido Giglioni, 'Who's Afraid of Frances Yates? "Giordano Bruno and the Hermetic Tradition" Fifty Years Later', *Bruniana & Campanelliana*, XX/2 (2014), pp. 421–32.

2 R.J.W. Evans, *Rudolf II and His World: A Study in Intellectual History, 1576–1612* (Oxford, 1973), p. 212. See further M.E.H.N. Mout, 'Hermes Trismegistos Germaniae: Rudolf II en de arcane wetenschappen', *Leids Kunsthistorisch Jaarboek*, I (1982), pp. 161–91, but the idea has been adopted by others: see note 4.

3 Anthony Grafton, 'Protestant versus Prophet: Isaac Casaubon on Hermes Trismegistus', *Journal of the Warburg and Courtauld Institutes*, XLVI (1983), pp. 78–93.

4 Some recent interpretations of Shakespeare regard Rudolf II as a prototype for Prospero, the exiled prince and wizard in *The Tempest*, and point out the association of natural magic (the

animation of a statue) with Hermeticism in *The Winter's Tale* – the second half of which takes places in Bohemia: Robert Grudin, 'Rudolf II of Prague and Cornelis Drebbel: Shakespearean Archetypes?', *Huntington Library Quarterly*, LIV/3 (Summer 1991), pp. 181–205; see further Frances A. Yates, *Majesty and Magic in Shakespeare's Last Plays* (Boulder, CO, 1978), pp. 87–106. Sally Metzler has argued that alchemy and magic are important features of the work of the imperial artists Spranger and Arcimboldo: 'The Alchemy of Drawing: Bartholomaus Spranger at the Court of Rudolf II', PhD thesis, Princeton University, 1997; Sally Metzler, 'Artists, Alchemists, and Mannerists in Courtly Prague', in *Art and Alchemy*, ed. Jacob Wamberg (Copenhagen, 2006), pp. 129–48; Sally Metzler, *Bartholomeus Spranger: Splendor and Eroticism in Imperial Prague*, exh. cat., Metropolitan Museum of Art, New York (New Haven, CT, and London, 2014), pp. 14, 50–51. Aldo delle Rose, *La grande Opera di Giuseppe Arcimboldo: Un discorso sul Metodo per non iniziati all'Alchimia*, preface Andrea Zucconi and Guido Buffo (Milan, 2018), expands these speculations to over four hundred pages.

5 As translated by Evans, *Rudolf II and His World*, p. 195, without, however, citing the source in Felix Stieve, *Vom Reichstag 1608 bis zur Gründung der Liga*, Briefe und Acten zur Geschichte des Dreissigjährigen Krieges, vol. VI (Munich, 1895), pp. 49–50.

6 Angelo Maria Ripellino, *Praga magica* (Turin, 1973); Leo Perutz, *By Night Under the Stone Bridge*, trans. Eric Mosbacher (London, 1989).

7 Evans, *Rudolf II and His World*, p. 198.

8 Ivo Purš and Vladimír Karpenko, 'Materielle, schriftliche und ikonographische Quellen der Laboratorien Kaiser rudolf II.', *Studia Rudolphina*, XX (2020), pp. 102–33.

9 This is a theme in many of the essays in Ivo Purš and Vladimír Karpenko, eds, *Alchemy and Rudolf II: Exploring the Secrets of Nature in Central Europe in the 16th and 17th Centuries*, (Prague, 2016), and in Sven Dupré, Dedo Kerssenbrock-Krosigk and Beat Wismer, *Art and Alchemy: The Mystery of Transformation* (Düsseldorf, 2014).

10 See Anthony Grafton, *Cardano's Cosmos: The Worlds and Works of a Renaissance Astrologer* (Cambridge, MA, 1999).

11 See Vladimír Karpenko and Ivo Purš, 'Tycho Brahe: Between Astronomy and Alchemy', in Purš and Karpenko, *Alchemy and Rudolf II*, pp. 459–88.

12 John Robert Christianson, *Tycho Brahe* (London, 2020).

13 For court salaries, see Jaroslava Hausenblasová, *Der Hof Rudolfs II.* (Prague, 2002).

14 See variously Lorraine Daston and Katharine Park, *Wonders and the Order of Nature, 1150–1750* (New York, 1998); R. J.W. Evans and Alexander Marr, eds, *Curiosity and Wonder from the Renaissance to the Enlightenment* (Aldershot and Burlington, VT, 2006); Wolfram Koeppe, ed., *Making Marvels: Science and Splendor at the Courts of Europe*, exh. cat., Metropolitan Museum of Art, New York (New Haven, CT, and London, 2019).

15 Jaroslava Hausenblasová and Ivo Purš, 'Simon Thadeas Budek und Christoph Harant von Polžice unter der Alchemisten Kaiser Rudolfs II.', *Studia Rudolphina*, IX (2009), p. 70, and p. 71 for the spread of interest in alchemy in society.

16 See Tara Nummedal, *Alchemy and Authority in the Holy Roman Empire* (Chicago, IL, 2007), pp. 73–95, and for a later historical example, Pamela H. Smith, *The Business of Alchemy: Science and Culture in the Holy Roman Empire* (Princeton, NJ, 1994).

17 The classic work of Eugenio Garin, *Astrology in the Renaissance: The Zodiac of Life* (London, Boston, Melbourne and Henley, 1983), Grafton, *Cardano's Cosmos*, and Mary Quinlan McGrath, *Influences, Art, Optics, and Astrology in the Italian Renaissance* (Chicago, IL, 2013), provide good introductions to astrology as understood in the early modern era.

18 The pioneering work of Suzanna Ivanič, *Cosmos and Materiality in Early Modern Prague* (Oxford, 2021), hints at the broader reception of beliefs usually associated with the court.

19 For an overview of Maximilian I's interests in the occult sciences and in general those of Rudolf II's predecessors see Ivo Purš, 'The Habsburgs on the Bohemian Throne and Their Interest in Alchemy and the Occult Sciences', in *Alchemy and Rudolf II*, pp. 93–127.

20 For Fabritius, see most accessibly Thomas DaCosta Kaufmann, *The Mastery of Nature: Aspects of Art, Science, and Humanism in the Renaissance* (Princeton, NJ, 1993), pp. 136–50.

21 Ivo Purš, 'Erzherzog Ferdinand II., Astrologie, und das Lustschloss Hvězda (Stern)', *Studia Rudolphina*, XIV (2014), p. 16.

22 Karl Rudolf, 'Arcimboldo im kulinarischen Wissensraum: Die Kunstkammer Kaiser Ferdinands I. (1503–1564)', in *Das Haus Habsburg und die Welt der fürstlichen Kunstkammern im 16. und 17. Jahrhundert*, ed. Sabine Haag, Franz Kirchweger and Paulus Rainer (Vienna, 2015), pp. 133–65.

23 Hilda Lietzmann, 'Ferdinands I. Verdienst um die Gartenkunst', in *Kaiser Ferdinand I 1503–1564: Das Werden der Habsburgermonarchie*, ed. Wilfried Seipel (Vienna, 2003), pp. 259–63; Sylva Dobalova, *Zahrady*

Rudolf II. Jejích Vznik a Vývoj (Prague, 2006), pp. 57–82; Sylva Dobalova and Jaroslava Hausenblasová, 'Die Zitruskultur am Hofe Ferdinands I. und Anna Jagiellos: Import und Anbau von Zitruskultur in Prag 1526–1564', *Studia Rudolphina*, xv (2015), pp. 9–36.

24 Karl Rudolf, '"Quanta rariora tanta Meliora": Die Kunstbestrebungen Kaiser Maximilians II. im Spannungsfeld zwischen Madrid und Wien', *Jahrbuch der kunsthistorischen Sammlungen in Wien*, xci (2000), p. 170.

25 For these, see the analyses and summaries in Dobalová, *Zahrady Rudolfa II.*

26 Anna Pavord, *The Tulip: The Story of a Flower that has Made Men Mad* (New York and London, 1999), pp. 53–5.

27 Kurt Mühlberger, 'Bildung und Wissenschaft: Kaiser Maximilian II und die Universität Wien', in *Kaiser Maximilian II: Kultur und Politik im 16. Jarhundert*, ed. Friedrich Edelmayer and Alfred Kohler (Vienna and Munich, 1992), pp. 212–13.

28 For example, Rembert Dodoens, *De Sphaera*, 2nd edn (Antwerp, 1584).

29 Ivo Purš, 'Tadeaš Hájek or Hájek and his Alchemical Circle', in Purš and Karpenko, *Alchemy and Rudolf II*, pp. 423–57.

30 See the original text of Dee's work in the translation and interpretation by C. H. Josten, 'A Translation of John Dee's "Monas Hieroglyphica" (Antwerp, 1564), with an Introduction and Annotations', *Ambix*, xii/2–3 (1964), pp. 84–221, DOI:10.1179/000269864790223101, accessed 21 November 2023.

31 Ivo Purš, 'Das Interesse Erzherzog Ferdinands II. an Alchemie und Bergbau und seine Widerspiegelung in seiner Bibliothek', *Studia Rudophina*, vii (2007), pp. 76, 105, n. 10.

32 Sven Alfons, 'The Museum as Image of the World', in *The Arcimboldo Effect: Transformations of the Face from the Sixteenth to the Twentieth Century* (Milan, 1987), p. 68.

33 Pamela H. Smith, 'Between Nature and Art: Casting from Life in Sixteenth-Century Europe', in *Making and Growing: Anthropological Studies of Organisms and Artefacts*, ed. Elizabeth Hallam and Tim Ingold (Farnham and Burlington, vt, 2014), pp. 45–64.

34 See Madelon Simons, 'Theatrum van Representatie? Aartshertog Ferdinand von Oostenrijk stadhouder in Praag tussen 1547 en 1567', PhD thesis, University of Amsterdam, 2009, pp. 134–54; Katherine Seidl, '. . . how to assuage all outer and inner malady . . .": Medicine at the Court of Archduke Ferdinand II', in *Ferdinand II: 450 Years Sovereign Ruler of Tyrol*, ed. Sabine Haag and Veronika Sandbichler (Innsbruck, 2017), pp. 67–75; Ivo Purš, 'Scientific and Literary

Activity Linked with the Influence of Ferdinand II (1529–1595) in the Bohemian Lands and in Tyrol', in *Archduke Ferdinand II of Austria: A Second-Born Son in Renaissance Europe*, ed. Sylva Dobalová and Jaroslava Hausenblasová (Vienna, 2021), especially pp. 341–9.

35 Petr Uličný, 'The Garden of Archduke Ferdinand II at Prague Castle', *Studia Rudolphina*, XVII–XVIII (2018), pp. 23–34.

36 Purš, 'Das Interesse Erzherzog Ferdinands II. an Alchemie'.

37 Purš, 'Erzherzog Ferdinand II., Astrologie, und das Lustschloss Hvězda'.

38 Books by Regiomontanus and also by Copernican astronomers were present in the library of Philip II: see José Manuel Guirau Cabas and José Luis del Valle Merlino, eds, *Catálogo de impresos de los siglos XVI al XVIII de la Real Bibliotheca del Monasterio de San Lorenzo de el Escorial* (Madrid, 2011), and the discussion in William Eamon, 'The Scientific Education of a Renaissance Prince: Archduke Rudolf at the Spanish Court', in Purš and Karpenko, *Alchemy and Rudolf II*, pp. 129–38.

39 Eamon, 'The Scientific Education of a Renaissance Prince'.

40 René Taylor, 'Architecture and Magic: Considerations on the "Idea" of the Escorial', in *Essays in the History of Architecture presented to Rudolf Wittkower*, ed. Douglas Fraser, Howard Hibbard and Milton J. Lewine (New York and London, 1967), pp. 81–109.

41 Eamon, 'The Scientific Education of a Renaissance Prince'.

42 Rotraud Bauer and Herbert Haupt, eds, 'Das Kunstkammerinventar Kaiser Rudolfs II., 1607–1611', *Jahrbuch der Kunsthistorischen Sammlungen in Wien*, LXXII (1976), no. 2748 (p. 137 [fol. 383v]).

43 See Taylor, 'Architecture and Magic'.

44 Mout, 'Hermes Trismegistos Germaniae', p. 161.

45 Alfonzo E. Perez Sanchez, 'The Madrid–Prague Axis', in *The Arcimboldo Effect*, p. 58.

46 Marco Beretta, 'Material and Temporal Powers at the Casino di San Marco (1574–1621)', in *Laboratories of Art: Alchemy and Art Technology from Antiquity to the 18th Century*, ed. Sven Dupré (Cham, 2014), pp. 129–54.

47 See, in general, Luciano Berti, *Il principe dello studiolo: Francesco I dei Medici e la fine del Rinascimento fiorentino* (Florence, 1967).

48 See Peter J. French, *John Dee: The World of an Elizabethan Magus* (London, 1972), and Frances A. Yates, 'John Dee and the Elizabethan Age', in *Theatre of the World* (Chicago, IL, 1969).

49 See Jennifer M. Rampling, *The Experimental Fire: Inventing English Alchemy, 1300–1700* (Chicago, IL, and London, 2020).

50 See, for example, James's treatise *Daemonologie* (Edinburgh, 1597).

51 Evans, *Rudolf II and His World*, p. 238.

52 See Hilda Lietzmann, *Herzog Heinrich Julius zur Braunschweig und Lüneburg, 1564–1613: Persönlichkeit und Wirken für Kaiser und Reich* (Braunschweig, 1993).

53 See Bruce T. Moran, *The Alchemical World of the German Court: Occult Philosophy and Chemical Medicine in the Circle of Moritz of Hessen (1572–1632)* (Stuttgart, 1991); Heiner Borggrefe, Vera Lüpkes and Hans Ottomeyer, eds, *Moritz der Gelehrte: Ein Renaissancefürst in Europa* (Eurasberg, 1997). See, in general, Frances A. Yates, *The Rosacrucian Enlightenment* (London, 1972), who traces the origins of the movement to a Calvinist court, but to the wrong one.

54 See Michael Korey, *Die Geometrie der Macht: Mathemathische Instrumente und fürstliche Mechanik um 1600* (Munich and Berlin, 2007), and Wolfram Dolz, 'Die scientifica in der Dresdner Kunstkammer: Messinstrumente der Landesvermessung und des Artilleriewesens als Werkzeuge des tätigen Fürsten, Karten sowie Erd-und Himmelsmodelle als Repräsentationsobjekte seiner weltlichen Macht', in *Die kurfürstliche sächsische Kunstkammer in Dresden: Geschichte einer Sammlung*, ed. Dirk Syndram and Martina Minning (Dresden, 2012), pp. 184–99.

55 For a balanced treatment, see Martina Minning, 'Werkzeug in der Dresdner Kunstkammer', in *Die kurfürstliche sächsische Kunstkiammer*, ed. Syndram and Minning, pp. 166–83.

56 Nummedal, *Alchemy and Authority*, pp. 81–4 and 91–4.

57 See, in general, John Robert Christianson, *Tycho Brahe and the Measure of the Heavens* (London and Chicago, IL, 2020).

58 Lars Olof Larsson, 'Bemerkungen zur Bildhauerkunst am dänischen Hofe', *Münchener Jahrbuch der bildenden Kunst*, XXVI (1975), pp. 177–92.

59 See Ksenija Tschetschik-Hammerl, *Nach Dürer: Kunst begegnet Natur bei Hans Hoffmann und Daniel Fröschel* (Petersberg, 2023), pp. 23–7; p. 25, fig. 14; and p. 299, no. 16.

60 Vladimír Karpenko, 'Martin Rulands *Lexicon alchemiae* im Kontext der chemischen Spranche und System', *Studia Rudolphina*, XI (2011), pp. 102–26.

61 See Ivo Purš, 'Oswald Croll und die Symbolik des Titelblattes seines Werkes *Basilica chymica*', *Studia Rudolphina*, XV (2015), pp. 64–87.

62 Jakub Hlaváček, 'The Theory of Signatures in the Works of the Physician and Paracelsian Oswald Croll (1560–1608)', *Studia Rudolphina*, XIX (2019), pp. 98–113.

63 Ralf Töllner, *Das unendliche Kommentar: Untersuchungen zu vier ausgewählten Kupferstichen aus Heinrich Khunraths 'Ampitheatrum Sapientiae Aeternae Solius Verae' (Hanau 1609)* (Ammersbek bei Hamburg, 1991).

64 For Della Porta and Prague see the summary (and partial publication of Della Porta's text) in Luisa Muraro, *Giambattista Della Porta mago e scienziato. In appendice l'indice della Taumatologia* (Milan, 1978), pp. 18, 21–2, 49.

65 Giordano Bruno, *Božskému Rudolfovi II = To the Divine Rudolphus II* (with the Latin original), trans. Jan Kalivoda (into Czech) and Petr Smolka (into English) (Prague, 2001).

66 Evans, *Rudolf II and His World*, pp. 218–28, 235–41, and more fully Rampling, *Experimental Fire*, pp. 284–316.

67 In addition to Rampling, *Experimental Fire*, see the comprehensive account in Vladimír Karpenko and Ivo Purš, 'Edward Kelly: A Star of the Rudolfine Era', in Purš and Karpenko, *Alchemy and Rudolf II*, pp. 489–534.

68 See Corinna Gannon, 'The Alchemical Hand Bell of Rudolf II: A Touchstone of Art and Alchemy', *Studia Rudolphina*, XIX (2019), pp. 81–98, illustration on p. 80.

69 Corinna Gannon, 'The Amulet of Rudolf II: Kabbalistic Talisman and Pansophic Collectible', *Studia Rudolphina*, XX (2020), pp. 83–101, illustration on p. 82.

70 Erich Trunz, *Wissenschaft und Kunst im Kreise Kaiser Rudolfs II. 1576–1612* (Neumünster, 1992).

71 William Eamon, *Science and the Secrets of Nature: Books of Secrets in Medieval and Early Modern Culture* (Princeton, NJ, 1996), and for the sources of ideas of secrets of nature, see Georg Luck, *Arcana Mundi: Magic and the Occult in the Greek and Roman Worlds* (Baltimore, MD, and London, 1985).

72 See Kaufmann, *Mastery of Nature*, especially p. 145.

73 Earth was associated with the cube, air with the octahedron, water with the icosahedron and fire with the tetrahedron.

74 Dedre Gentner, 'Analogy in Scientific Discovery: The Case of Johannes Kepler', in *Model-Based Reasoning: Science, Technology, Values*, ed. L. Magnani and N. J. Nersessian (New York, 2002), pp. 21–39.

75 For Kepler's place in the history of optics, see (most comprehensively) David C. Lindberg, *Theories of Vision from al-Kindi to Kepler* (Chicago, IL, 1976).

76 See Gentner, 'Analogy', and Fernand Hallyn, *The Poetic Structure of the World: Copernicus and Kepler*, trans. Donald M. Leslie (New York, 1990). There is extensive literature on Kepler: Zdeněk Horský,

Kepler v Praze (Prague, 1980), and Mechthild Lemcke, *Johannes Kepler* (Hamburg, 1995), provide good concise overviews.

77 Hausenblasová, *Hof Rudolfs II.*, p. 421, no. 178/3.

78 Giambattista della Porta, *Magiae Naturalis Libri Viginti* (Naples, 1589); English translation *Natural Magick by John Baptista Porta* (London, 1669 [repr. New York, 1957]), Book Five, Chapter 17.

79 Kaufmann, *Mastery of Nature*, pp. 191ff, provides a summary of this development; see further Lindberg, *Theories of Vision*, and Sven Dupré, 'Kepler's Optics without Hypotheses', *Synthese*, CLXXXV (2012), pp. 501–25.

80 Hallyn, *Poetic Structure*.

81 See fully Vera Keller, 'Cornelis Drebbel (1572–1633): Fame and the Making of Modernity', PhD thesis, Princeton University, 2008, and Vladimír Karpenko and Ivo Purš, 'Cornelius Drebbel: Inventor, Mechanic, and Alchemist', in Purš and Karpenko, *Alchemy and Rudolf II*, pp. 625–45.

82 Ivo Purš, 'Anselm Boëtius de Boodt a alchymie', *Studia Rudolphina*, IV (2004), pp. 44–53, and Ivo Purš, 'Anselm Boëthius de Boodt: Physician, Mineralogist and Alchemist', in Purš and Karpenko, *Alchemy and Rudolf II*, pp. 535–79.

83 Charles Parkhurst, 'A Color Theory from Prague: Anselm de Boodt, 1609', *Bulletin of the Allen Memorial Art Museum*, XXIX (1971), pp. 3–10.

84 Thoroughly discussed most recently in Purš, 'Anselm Boëthius de Boodt', pp. 561–78.

85 Brian W. Ogilvie, *The Science of Describing: The Study of Natural History in Renaissance Europe* (Chicago, IL, and London, 2006).

86 See Marie-Christiane Maselis, Arnout Balis and Roger H. Marijnissen, *The Albums of Anselmus de Boodt (1550–1632): Natural History Painting at the Court of Rudolph II in Prague* (Tielt, 1999).

87 Lee Hendrix, whose many outstanding studies on Hoefnagel should also be noted, provides an overview in 'Natural History Illustration at the Court of Rudolf II', in *Rudolf II and Prague: The Court and the City*, ed. Eliška Fučíková et al. (Prague, 1997), pp. 157–7.

88 Fritz Koreny, *Albrecht Dürer and the Animal and Plant Studies of the Renaissance*, trans. Pamela Marwood and Yehuda Shapiro (Boston, 1988); Yasmin Doosry, ed., *Hans Hoffmann, Ein europäischer Künstler der Renaissance* (Nuremberg, 2022); Tschetschik-Hammerl, *Nach Dürer*.

89 See the many studies of Thea Wilberg Vignau, most fully in *Joris and Jacob Hoefnagel: Art and Science around 1600* (Berlin, 2017), and Marisa Anne

Bass, *Insect Artifice: Nature and Art in the Dutch Revolt* (Princeton, NJ, and Oxford, 2019). See also Janice Neri, *The Insect and the Image: Visualizing Nature in Early Modern Europe, 1500–1700* (Minneapolis, MN, and London, 2011). It is moot whether or not Hoefnagel painted the *Four Elements* for Rudolf; according to van Mander, he owned it; several other works by him were in the *Kunstkammer*, and other works by Hoefnagel were made for him or allude to the emperor and the empire.

90 See Thomas DaCosta Kaufmann, *Arcimboldo: Visual Jokes, Natural History, and Still-Life Painting* (Chicago, IL, and London, 2009), and Sylvia Ferino-Pagden, ed., *Arcimboldo, 1526–1593*, exh. cat. (Milan, 2007).

91 Kaufmann, *Arcimboldo*, offers a thorough account of these issues.

92 Clusius, *Fungorum in Pannonniis Observatorum Brevis Historia*, published in *Rarorium Plantarum Historia* (1601); this is a topic of ongoing research by John White.

93 Florence Hopper, 'Jacques de Gheyn II and Rudolf II's Collection of Nature Drawings', in *Prag um 1600:Beiträge zur Kunst und Kultur am Hofe Rudolfs II*, ed. Eliška Fučíková (Freren, 1988), pp. 124–31, and 'Science and Art at Leiden: Carolus Clusius and Jacques De Gheyn II's Flower drawings for Rudolf II', in *Rudolf II, Prague and the World*, ed. Lubomír Konečný, Beket Bukovinská and Ivan Muchka (Prague, 1998), pp. 128–33.

94 Van Mander, *Het Schilder-boeck*, fol. 233r. The translation is from Karel van Mander, *The Lives of the Illustrious Netherlandish and German Painters*, ed. intro. and trans. Hessel Miedema (Doornspijk, 1994), vol. I, p. 294.

95 For a magisterial overview, see Teréz Gerszi, 'Landscapes and City Views of Prague', in *Rudolf II and Prague*, ed. Fučíková et al., pp. 130–45. The question of 'after life' in Savery is most recently discussed in Olga Kotková, ed., *Roelandt Savery: A Painter in the Services of Emperor Rudolf II* (Prague, 2010).

96 Kotková, *Roelandt Savery*, provides a reliable overview of the artist, his relations to Prague and the questions addressed here, as well references to previous bibliography on these topics.

97 The translations here are ibid., p. 29.

98 Emanuel Sweerts, *Florilegium Amplissimum et Selectissimum* (Frankfurt am Main, 1612); the Latin foreword appears on fol. 4r, with forewords in German, Dutch and French on succeeding unnumbered folios. The easily available English-language edition, Emanuel Sweerts, *Early Floral Engravings: All the Plates from the 1612 'Florilegium'*, ed. E. F. Bleiler (New York, 1976), does not include or refer to the differences in the various forewords, and translates only the Latin.

99 'Ih bin mit der Rögel inss khaiser garten gewösen, bin beim
     lusthauss auh gewösen, wo die istrament sint gestanten. Mier sint
     die garten ale aussgangen, es ist fierwar ein schener garten. Der
     khaiser geth ale Dag vmb 3vr drein, der gertner hats vnss gesagt.
     Mier sint zun leben gangen, haben sie auch geschaut, wier haben
     3 leben esehen, sie haben gar häslich prillt, das hauss hat ales zitert,
     wan sie prilt haben, wier haben sonst auch seltzame Diere gesehen'
     (quoted in Trunz, *Wissenschaft und Kunst*, p. 121).
100 Della Porta, *Natural Magick*, Book v, Chapter 17.
101 Kaufmann, *Mastery of Nature*, p. 191. The account in *Mastery of Nature*
     unfortunately escaped several later publications by Czech scholars
     about the telescope and observations of the moon.
102 As quoted in translation in Thomas DaCosta Kaufmann, *The School
     of Prague: Painting at the Court of Rudolf II* (Chicago, IL, and London,
     1988), p. 5. The excerpt is translated slightly differently in Evans,
     Rudolf II and His World, p. 196, in which, crucially, the second sentence
     is not included.
103 See, for example, Jennifer Powell McNutt, 'Hesitant Steps:
     Acceptance of the Gregorian Calendar in Eighteenth-Century
     Geneva', *Church History*, LXXV/3 (September 2006), pp. 544–64.

5 Rudolf II and the Wider World

  1 This is the author's paraphrase and partial translation of part
     of a document first published in Thomas DaCosta Kaufmann,
     Arcimboldo: Visual Jokes, Natural History, and Still-Life Painting (Chicago, IL,
     and London, 2009), p. 268, n. 47. For the fact that they had to be
     made from life, and for further documents, see pp. 122–5, with
     related notes.
  2 The fullest treatment and identification of Arcimboldo's nature
     studies, with references, is ibid. For Savery and exotic birds, see
     most recently Jiří Milíkovský, 'Zoological Note: The Dodo of
     Emperor Rudolf II', in *Roelandt Savery: A Painter in the Services of
     Emperor Rudolf II*, ed. Olga Kotková (Prague, 2010), pp. 325–31. For
     van Ravesteyn and other artists, see the next note.
  3 See most thoroughly Ksenija Tschetschik-Hammerl, *Nach Dürer:
     Kunst begegnet Natur bei Hans Hoffmann und Daniel Fröschel* (Petersberg,
     2023), with references to earlier literature.
  4 See Herbert Haupt et al., eds, *Le Bestiaire de Rodolphe II: Cod. min. 129
     et 130 de la Bibliothèque nationale d'Autriche*, trans. Léa Marcou (Paris,

1990), with comments by Thea Wilberg-Vignau Schuurman.

5 Rotraud Bauer and Herbert Haupt, eds, 'Das Kunstkammerinventar Kaiser Rudolfs II., 1607–1611', *Jahrbuch der Kunsthistorischen Sammlungen in Wien*, LXXII (1976).

6 Ibid., p. 59, fol. 127, no. 1103.

7 Jessica Keating and Lia Markey, 'Indian Objects in Medici and Austrian-Habsburg Inventories: A Case-Study of the Sixteenth-Century Term', *Journal of the History of Collections*, XXIII/2 (2011), pp. 283–300.

8 See Barbara Karl, '"Marvelous things are made with needles": Bengal *Colchas* in European Inventories, c. 1580–1630', *Journal of the History of Collections*, XXIII/2 (2011), pp. 301–14, here especially p. 309. For the distinction of the display of the Prague *Kunstkammer* and the inventory listings, see Bauer and Haupt, 'Kunstkammerinventar Kaiser Rudolfs II.' (introduction), p. xxix. For various aspects of the organization of the Dresden *Kunstkammer*, see the essays in Dirk Syndram and Martina Minning, eds, *Die kurfürstliche sächsische Kunstkammer in Dresden: Geschichte einer Sammlung* (Dresden, 2012).

9 Bauer and Haupt, 'Kunstkammerinventar Kaiser Rudolfs II.', p. xxix.

10 For Vasari and the relation to geography to historiography in general, see Thomas DaCosta Kaufmann, *Toward a Geography of Art* (Chicago, IL, and London, 2004).

11 See Almudena Perez de Tudela and Annemarie Jordan-Gschwend, 'Luxury Goods for Royal Collectors: Exotica, Princely Gifts and Rare Animals Exchanged Between the Iberian Courts and Central Europe in the Renaissance (1560–1612)', *Jahrbuch des Kunsthistorischen Museums Wien*, III (2001), pp. 1–127.

12 Bauer and Haupt, 'Kunstkammerinventar Kaiser Rudolfs II.', pp. 1, 28–9 fol. 52–3.

13 Ibid., p. 56, fols 108 and 111.

14 As discussed in Thomas DaCosta Kaufmann, 'In the Imperial Orbit: Prague and Art at the German Courts in the Era of Rudolf II', in *The Eloquent Artist: Essays on Art, Art Theory and Architecture, Sixteenth to Nineteenth Century* (London, 2004), pp. 194–206.

15 As quoted ibid., p. 206.

16 Cited ibid., pp. 206–7.

17 See Karl Vocelka, *Die politische Propaganda Kaiser Rudolfs II. (1570–1612)* (Vienna, 1980), pp. 275–9.

18 Bauer and Haupt, 'Kunstkammerinventar Kaiser Rudolfs II.', p. 38,

fol. 63r, no. 684, p. 45, fol. 80v, no. 820.

19 Barbara Karl, 'Objects of Prestige and Spoils of War: Ottoman
    Objects in the Habsburg Networks of Gift-Giving in the Sixteenth
    Century', in *Global Gifts*, ed. Zoltán Biedermann, Anne Gerritsen and
    Giorgio Riello (Cambridge, 2018), pp. 119–49.

20 Otto Kurz, *European Clocks and Watches in the Near East* (London, 1975),
    pp. 30–42.

21 Jessica Keating, *Animating Empire: Automata, the Holy Roman Empire, and the
    Early Modern World* (University Park, PA, 2018), p. 93.

22 Ibid., p. 193.

23 Thomas DaCosta Kaufmann, *The School of Prague: Painting at the Court of
    Rudolf II* (Chicago, IL, and London, 1988), pp. 106–15.

24 See in general Keating, *Animating Empire*.

25 Otto Kurz, 'Umělecké vztahy mezi Prahou a Persií za Rudolfa II',
    Umění, XIV (1966), pp. 461–87.

26 See Ali Bakhtiar, 'The Royal Bazaar of Isfahan', *Iranian Studies*, VII/1–2,
    Studies on Isfahan: Proceedings of the Isfahan Colloquium, Part I
    (Winter–Spring 1974), pp. 320–47.

27 Ebba Koch, *Mughal Art and Imperial Ideology* (New Delhi, 2001).

28 British Museum, London, inv. 2006,0422,0.1.

29 Ebba Koch, 'Jahangir as Francis Bacon's Ideal of the King as an
    Observer and Investigator of Nature', *Journal of the Royal Asiatic
    Society*, 3rd series, XIX/3 (July 2009), pp. 293–338; Ebba Koch,
    'The Mughal Emperor as Solomon, Majnun and Orpheus, or the
    Album as a Think Tank for Allegory', *Muqarnas*, XXVII/1 (2010),
    pp. 277–311.

30 See Ebba Koch, *Dara-Shikoh Shooting Nilgais: Hunt and Landscape in Mughal
    Painting* (Washington, DC, 1998).

31 Keating, *Animating Empire*, pp. 95–119.

32 Thomas DaCosta Kaufmann, 'Scratching the Surface: On the
    Dutch in Taiwan and China', in *Mediating Netherlandish Art and Material
    Culture in Asia*, ed. Michael North and Thomas DaCosta Kaufmann
    (Amsterdam, Chicago, IL, and London, 2014), pp. 183–214.

33 In frescoes in the convent of Santa Monica, Velha Goa.

34 Thomas DaCosta Kaufmann, 'Global Aspects of Habsburg Imperial
    Collecting', in *Collecting and Empires*, ed. Maia Wellington Gahtan et
    al. (London and Leuven, 2019), pp. 162–81.

35 Mary W. Helms, *Craft and the Kingly Ideal: Art, Trade, and Power* (Austin,
    TX, 1993), p. 165, as quoted by Joan Aruz, 'Art and Interconnections
    in the Third Millenium B.C.', in *Art of The First Cities: The Third*

Millennium B.C. from the Mediterranean to the Indus, exh. cat., Metropolitan Museum of Art, New York (New Haven, CT, and London, 2003), p. 239.

Conclusion

1 Geoffrey Parker, *Imprudent King: A New Life of Philip II* (New Haven, CT, and London, 2014).
2 For this subject, see Peter H. Wilson, 'The Stuarts, the Palatinate and the Thirty Years' War', in *Stuart Marriage Diplomacy: Dynastic Politics in their European Context, 1604–1630*, ed. Valentina Caldari and Sara J. Wolfson (Martlesham, 2018), pp. 140–54.
3 'Unter die Haupt Tugenden eines Regenten . . . wird auch gezehlt die Mässigkeit . . . Diese tugend/ zierte auch gegenwärtigen Keyser Rudolff/ diss Nahmens den Andern gleichwie nicht weniger seine höchstlobliche Vorfahren/ von welche sie gleichsam auf ihn fortgepflantzet worden. Sonsten ware er/ wie ihr zum theil an seiner Bildniss sehe so Mäjestätischen Angesichtes/ unter andern löblichen Beschaffenheiten/ daß mehrmals fremde Abgesandten erstaunten und verstummelten . . . Die 37 Jahre seiner Regirung/ waren lauter güldene FridensJahre, Jahre der Freuden und des Wolstandes/ in welchen das/ von den vorigen Kriegen zerrüttelt und ausgemärgelte Reich sich wieder erholen und ausruhen konde. Er liess aber gleichwol seine Waffen nicht rasten und rosten sonder schützteete mit selbigen/ ausser dem Reiche kriegend/dessen Gränzen wider die Mahometischen Ein- und Uberfälle . . . Unterdessen ware sein Hof ein rechter Erzschrein der Musen und ein Auftenthalt der Gelehrten und Künstler, sonderlich aber der Kunstmahler und Gestrirnwweißen, welche an diesem Keyser nit allein einen gnädigsten Patron, sondern auch einen grundkündignen KunstGesellen hatten'. Sigmund von Birken, *Ostländischen Lorbeerhayn: Ein Ehrengedicht von dem höchstlöblichen Erzhaus Oesterreich; Einen Fürsten-Spiegel in XII. Sinnbildern* (Nuremberg, 1657), pp. 226–8; quoted in part; but without full citation and leaving out some important sections, in Erich Trunz, *Wissenschaft und Kunst im Kreise Kaiser Rudolfs II. 1576–1612* (Neumünster, 1992), p. 133. Author's translation.

SELECT BIBLIOGRAPHY

Bardazzi, Simone, and Giulio Carrai, 'Constantino de' Servi architetto e informatore medico, alla corte di Rodolfo II: Nuovi documenti circa le relazioni tra Praga e le corti principesche italiane', *Studia Rudolphina*, XXI–XXII (2022), pp. 86–114

Bauer, Rotraud, and Herbert Haupt, eds, 'Das Kunstkammerinventar Kaiser Rudolfs II., 1607–1611', *Jahrbuch der Kunsthistorischen Sammlungen in Wien*, LXXII (1976)

Brink, Claudia, Susanne Jaeger and Marius Winzeler, *Bellum et Artes: Central Europe in the Thirty Years War* (Dresden, 2021)

Carrai, Guido, 'I fiorentini al Castello: Il progetto di Bernardo Buonatalenti e Giovanni Gargiolli per la nuova galleria di Rodolfo II', *Umení*, LI (2003), pp. 370–84

Concin, Adriana, 'Splendid Gifts and a Florentine Architect for Emperor Rudolf II: Antonio Lupicini at the Imperial Court in Prague (1578–1580)', *Studia Rudolphina*, XX (2020), pp. 25–50

Coreth, Anna, *Pietas Austriaca*, trans. Wiliam Bowman and Anna Maria Leitgeb (West Lafayette, IN, 2004)

Dobalová, Sylva, and Jaroslava Hausenblasová, eds, *Archduke Ferdinand II of Austria: A Second-Born Son in Renaissance Europe* (Vienna, 2021)

Doosry, Yasmin, ed., *Hans Hoffmann, Ein Europäischer Künstler der Renaissance* (Nuremberg, 2022)

Dupré, Sven, 'Kepler's Optics without Hypotheses', *Synthese*, CLXXXV (2012), pp. 501–25

Eamon, William, *Science and the Secrets of Nature: Books of Secrets in Medieval and Early Modern Culture* (Princeton, NJ, 1996)

—, 'The Scientific Education of a Renaissance Prince: Archduke Rudolf at the Spanish Court', in *Alchemy and Rudolf II: Exploring the Secrets of*

Nature in Central Europe in the 16th and 17th Centuries, ed. Ivo Purš and Vladimír Karpenko (Prague, 2016), pp. 129–38

Edelmayr, Friecrich, and Alfred Kohler, eds, *Kaiser Maximilian II: Kultur und Politik im 16. Jahrhundert* (Vienna and Munich, 1992)

Evans, R.J.W., 'Culture and Politics at the Court of Rudolf II', in R.J.W. Evans, Eliška Fučíková and Mungo Campbell, *The Stylish Image: Printmakers to the Court of Rudolf II* (Edinburgh, 1991), pp. 9–15

——, *The Making of the Habsburg Monarchy 1500–1700: An Interpretation* (Oxford, 1979)

——, 'Rudolf II', *Neue Deutsche Biographie*, XXII (2005), pp. 169–71 (online version), www.deutsche-biographie.de

——, *Rudolf II and His World: A Study in Intellectual History, 1576–1612* (Oxford, 1973)

——, and T. V. Thomas, eds, *Crown, Church and Estates: Central European Politics in the Sixteenth and Seventeenth Centuries* (London, 1991)

Fichtner, Paula Sutter, *Emperor Maximilian II* (New Haven, CT, and London, 2001)

Fučíková, Eliška, 'The Collection of Rudolf II at Prague: Cabinet of Curiosities or Scientific Museum?', in *The Origins of Museums: The Cabinet of Curiosities in Sixteenth- and Seventeenth-Century Europe*, ed. Oliver Impey and Arthur MacGregor (Oxford, 2017), pp. 47–53

——, 'The Fate of Rudolf II's Collections in Light of the History of the Thirty Years War', in *1648: War and Peace in Europe*, ed. Klaus Bussmann and Heinz Schilling, Art and Culture II (Münster and Osnabrück, 1998), pp. 173–80

——, 'Prague Castle under Rudolf II, his Predecessors and Successors, 1530–1648', in *Rudolf II and Prague: The Court and the City*, ed. Eliška Fučíková et al. (Prague, 1997), pp. 2–71

——, Rudolf II as Patron and Collector', in R.J.W. Evans, Eliška Fučíková and Mungo Campbell, *The Stylish Image: Printmakers to the Court of Rudolf II* (Edinburgh, 1991), pp. 17–21

——, ed., *Prag um 1600: Beiträge zur Kunst und Kultur am Hofe Rudolfs II*, 2 vols (Freren, 1988)

——, et al., eds, *Rudolf II and Prague: The Court and the City* (Prague, 1997)

Fusenig, Thomas, ed., *Hans von Aachen (1552–1615): Court Artist in Europe* (Berlin, 2010)

Gannon, Corinna, 'The Alchemical Hand Bell of Rudolf II: A Touchstone of Art and Alchemy', *Studia Rudolphina*, XIX (2019), pp. 81–98

—, 'The Amulet of Rudolf II: Kabbalistic Talisman and Pansophic Collectible', *Studia Rudolphina*, XX (2020), pp. 83–101

Gordon, Rona Johnston, 'Controlling Time in the Habsburg Lands: The Introduction of the Gregorian Calendar in Austria below the Enns', *Austrian History Yearbook*, XL (2009), pp. 28–36

Haag, Sabine, and Veronika Sandbichler, eds, *Ferdinand II: 450 Years Sovereign Ruler of Tyrol* (Innsbruck, 2017)

Hallyn, Ferdinand, *The Poetic Structure of the World: Copernicus and Kepler*, trans. Donald M. Leslie (New York, 1990)

Haupt, Herbert, et al., eds, *Le Bestiaire de Rodolphe II: Cod. min. 129 et 130 de la Bibliothèque nationale d'Autriche*, trans. Léa Marcou (Paris, 1990)

Hendrix, Lee, and Thea Vignau-Wilberg, *Mira Calligraphiae Monumenta: A Sixteenth-Century Calligraphic Manuscript Inscribed by Georg Bocskay and Illuminated by Joris Hoefnagel* (Los Angeles, CA, 1992)

Honisch, Erika Supria, 'Encounters with Music in Rudolf II's Prague', *Austrian History Yearbook*, LII (2021), pp. 64–80

Hopper, Florence, 'Jacques de Gheyn II and Rudolf II's Collection of Nature Drawings', in Fučíková, *Prag um 1600*, pp. 124–31

Jansen, Dirk Jacob, *Jacopo Strada and Cultural Patronage at the Imperial Court: The Antique as Innovation* (Boston and Leiden, 2019)

Jiménez Diaz, Pablo, 'Spain, Prague, and the Habsburg Ideology: Some Aspects of the Architecture of Rudolf II', in *Rudolf II, Prague and the World*, ed. Lubomír Konečný, Beket Bukovinská and Ivan Muchka (Prague, 1998), pp. 11–15

Kantorowicz, Ernst H., 'Mysteries of State: An Absolutist Concept and its Late Mediaeval Origins', *Harvard Theological Review*, XLVIII/1 (1955), pp. 65–91

Karl, Barbara, 'Objects of Prestige and Spoils of War: Ottoman Objects in the Habsburg Networks of Gift-Giving in the Sixteenth Century', in *Global Gifts*, ed. Zoltán Biedermann, Anne Gerritsen and Giorgio Riello (Cambridge, 2018), pp. 119–49

Karner, Herbert, ed., *Die Wiener Hofburg 1521–1705: Baugeschichte, Funktion und Etablierung als Kaiserresidenz* (Vienna, 2014)

Kaufmann, Thomas DaCosta, 'Arcimboldo au Louvre', *Revue du Louvre et des Musées de France*, XXVII (1977), pp. 337–42

—, *Arcimboldo: Visual Jokes, Natural History, and Still-Life Painting* (Chicago, IL, and London, 2009)

—, 'Arcimboldo's Imperial Allegories', *Zeitschrift für Kunstgeschichte*, XXXIX (1976), pp. 275–96

—, *Court, Cloister, and City: The Art and Culture of Central Europe, 1450–1800* (London and Chicago, IL, 1995)

—, *Drawings from the Holy Roman Empire, 1540–1680: A Selection from North American Collections* (Princeton, NJ, 1982)

—, 'The Eloquent Artist: Towards an Understanding of the Stylistics of Painting at the Court of Rudolf II', *Leids Kunsthistorisch Jaarboek*, I (1982), pp. 119–48

—, 'Empire Triumphant: Notes on an Imperial Allegory by Adriaen de Vries in the National Gallery of Art', *Studies in the History of Art*, VIII (1978), pp. 63–75

—, 'From Treasury to Museum: The Collections of the Austrian Habsburgs', in *The Cultures of Collecting*, ed. Roger Cardinal and John Elsner (London, 1994)

—, 'The *Kunstkammer* as a Form of *Representatio*: Remarks on the Collections of Rudolf II', *Art Journal*, XXXVIII (1978), pp. 22–8 (republished in *Grasping the World*, ed. Donald Preziosi and Claire Farago (Aldershot, 2004), pp. 526–37)

—, 'Linz – Des Kaisers Kulturhauptstadt um 1600? Ein Escorial in Oberösterreich?', in *Linz – Des Kaisers Kulturhauptstadt um 1600?* (Weitra, 2012), pp. 39–54

—, *The Mastery of Nature: Aspects of Art, Science, and Humanism in the Renaissance* (Princeton, NJ, and London, 1993)

—, 'Representation, Replication, Reproduction: The Legacy of Charles V in Sculpted Rulers' Portraits of the Sixteenth and Early Seventeenth Century', *Austrian History Yearbook*, XLIII (2012), pp. 1–18

—, 'Rudolf II Habsburg', in *The Dictionary of Art*, ed. J. Turner (New York, 1996), vol. XIII, pp. 912–15

—, *The School of Prague: Painting at the Court of Rudolf II* (Chicago, IL, and London, 1988)

—, '*Zur Zierd*: Revisiting the Prague *Kunstkammer*', *Studia Rudolphina*, XVII–XVIII (2018), pp. 140–54

Kawakami, Eri, 'Bartholomeus Spranger's *Triumph of Wisdom* as an Allegory of the Re-Evaluation of the Art of Painting in Sixteenth-Century Prague', *Studia Rudolphina*, XVII–XVIII (2018), pp. 66–78

Keating, Jessica, *Animating Empire: Automata, the Holy Roman Empire, and the Early Modern World* (University Park, PA, 2018)

Koeppe, Wolfram, ed., *Making Marvels: Science and Splendor at the Courts of Europe*, exh. cat., Metropolitan Museum of Art, New York (New Haven, CT, and London, 2019)

Konečný, Lubomír, and Štěpán Vácha, eds, *Hans von Aachen in Context: Proceedings of the International Conference Prague 22–25 September 2010* (Prague, 2012)

Konečný, Lubomír, Beket Bukovinska and Ivan Muchka, ed., *Rudolf II, Prague and the World* (Prague, 1998)

Koreny, Fritz, *Albrecht Dürer and the Animal and Plant Studies of the Renaissance*, trans. Pamela Marwood and Yehuda Shapiro (Boston, MA, 1988)

Korey, Michael, *The Geometry of Power* (Munich and Berlin, 2007)

Kotková, Olga, ed., *Roelandt Savery: A Painter in the Services of Emperor Rudolf II* (Prague, 2010)

Kurz, Otto, *European Clocks and Watches in the Near East* (London, 1975)

Louthan, Howard, *The Quest for Compromise: Peacemakers in Counter-Reformation Vienna* (Cambridge, 1997)

Marshall, Peter, *The Magic Circle of Rudolf II: Alchemy and Astrology in Renaissance Prague* (New York and London, 2006)

Maselis, Marie-Christiane, Arnout Balis and Roger H. Marijnissen, *The Albums of Anselmus de Boodt (1550–1632): Natural History Painting at the Court of Rudolph II in Prague* (Tielt, 1999)

Metzler, Sally, *Bartholomeus Spranger: Splendor and Eroticism in Imperial Prague*, exh. cat., Metropolitan Museum of Art, New York (New Haven, CT, and London, 2014)

Mitchell, A. Wess, *The Grand Strategy of the Habsburg Empire* (Princeton, NJ, and Oxford, 2018)

Muchka, Ivan, 'Architectural Styles in the Reign of Rudolf II: Italian and Hispanic Influences', in *Rudolf II and Prague*, ed. Fučíková et al., pp. 90–95

Neumann, Jaromír, *The Picture Gallery of Prague Castle* (Prague, 1967)

Neverová, Natalia, 'The Emperor and Diplomatic Relations: Rudolf II through the Eyes of Foreign Ambassadors', in *The Image and Perception of Monarchy in Medieval and Early Modern Europe,* ed. S. McGlynn and E. Woodacre (Cambridge, 2014), pp. 131–45

Nummedal, Tara, *Alchemy and Authority in the Holy Roman Empire* (Chicago, IL, 2007)

Ogilvie, Brian W., *The Science of Describing: The Study of Natural History in Renaissance Europe* (Chicago, IL, and London, 2006)

Parker, Geoffrey, *Imprudent King: A New Life of Philip II* (New Haven, CT, and London, 2014)

Perez Sanchez, Alfonzo E., 'The Madrid–Prague Axis', in *The Arcimboldo Effect. Transformations of the Face from the Sixteenth to the Twentieth Century* (Milan, 1987)

Polleross, Friedrich, *Prag um 1600: Kunst und Kultur am Hofe Rudolfs II*, 2 vols (Freren, 1988)

—, 'The (Re-)presentation of the Imperial Collections in the 17th Century', in *Espacios del coleccionismo en la Casa de Austria (Siglos XVI y XVII)*, ed. Fernando Checa Cremades (Aranjuez, 2023), pp. 219–48

Purš, Ivo, 'Anselm Boëthius de Boodt: Physician, Mineralogist and Alchemist', *Alchemy and Rudolf II: Exploring the Secrets of Nature in Central Europe in the 16th and 17th Centuries*, ed. Ivo Purš and Vladimír Karpenko (Prague, 2016), pp. 535–79

—, and Vladimír Karpenko, eds, *Alchemy and Rudolf II: Exploring the Secrets of Nature in Central Europe in the 16th and 17th centuries* (Prague, 2016)

Rady, Martyn, *The Habsburgs: To Rule the World* (New York, 2020)

Rainer, Paulus, 'Facetten Habsburgischen Sammelwesen betrachtet anhand des Bestandes der Kunstkammer und der Schatzkammer des Kunhistorischen Museums Wien', PhD thesis, University of Vienna, 2017

Reitz, Evelyn, *Discordia Concors. Kulturelle Differenzerfahrung und ästhetische Einheitsbildung in der Prager Kunst um 1600* (Berlin and Boston, MA, 2015)

Rudolf, Karl, 'Arcimboldo im kulinarischen Wissensraum: Die Kunstkammer Kaiser Ferdinands I (1503–1564)', in *Das Haus Habsburg und die Welt der fürstlichen Kunstkammern*, ed. Sabine Haag, Franz Kirchweger and Paulus Rainer (Vienna, 2016), pp. 133–66

—, 'Die Kunstbestrebungen Kaiser Maximilian II. und Rudolf II. im Spannungsfeld zwischen Madrid und Wien: Untersuchungen zu den Sammlungen der österreichischen und spanischen Habsburger im 16. Jahrhundert', *Jahrbuch der kunsthistorischen Sammlungen in Wien*, XCI (1995), pp. 165–256

Schlosser, Julius von, *The Cabinets of Art and Wonder of the Late Renaissance: A Contribution to the History of Collecting*, ed. Thomas DaCosta Kaufmann, trans. Jonathan Blower (Los Angeles, CA, 2021)

Scholten, Frits, ed., *Adriaen de Vries, 1556–1626, Imperial Sculptor* (Amsterdam, Stockholm and Los Angeles, CA, 1998)

Silver, Larry, *Marketing Maximilian: The Visual Ideology of a Holy Roman Emperor* (Princeton, NJ, 2008)

Smith, Jeffrey Chipps, *Kunstkammer: Early Modern Art and Curiosity Cabinets in the Holy Roman Empire* (London, 2022)

Stollberg-Rilinger, Barbara, *The Emperor's Old Clothes: Constitutional History and the Symbolic Language of the Holy Roman Empire*, trans. Thomas Dunlap (New York and Oxford, 2015)

—, *The Holy Roman Empire: A Short History*, trans. Yair Mintzker (Princeton, NJ, and Oxford, 2018)

Sweerts, Emanuel, *Early Floral Engravings: All the Plates from the 1612 'Florilegium'*, ed. E. F. Bleiler (New York, 1976)

Swoboda, Gudrun, ed., *Idole und Rivalen: Künstlerischer Wettstreit in Antke und früher Neuzeit*, exh. cat. (Vienna, 2022)

Tanner, Marie, *The Last Descendant of Aeneas: The Hapsburgs and the Mythic Image of the Emperor* (New Haven, CT, and London, 1993)

Trunz, Erich, *Wissenschaft und Kunst im Kreise Kaiser Rudolfs II. 1576–1612* (Neumunster, 1992)

Tschetschik-Hammerl, Ksenija, *Nach Dürer: Kunst begegnet Natur bei Hans Hoffmann und Daniel Fröschel* (Petersberg, 2023)

Uličný, Petr, 'Erotica & Sapientia: Rudolf II's Early Years at Prague Castle', *Umění*, LXIX/4 (2021), pp. 390–415

—, 'The Garden of Archduke Ferdinand II at Prague Castle', *Studia Rudolphina*, XVII–XVIII (2018), pp. 23–34

Vignau Wilberg, Thea, *Joris and Jacob Hoefnagel: Art and Science around 1600* (Berlin, 2017)

Vocelka, Karl, *Habsburgische Hochzeiten 1550–1600: Kulturgeschichtliche Studien zum manieristischen Repräsentationsfest* (Vienna, Cologne and Graz, 1976)

—, *Die politische Propaganda Kaiser Rudolfs II. (1570–1612)* (Vienna, 1980)

—, *Rudolf II und seine Zeit* (Vienna, 1985)

Volrábová, Alena, and Blanka Kubíková, eds, *Rudolf II and Masters of Printmaking* (Prague, 2012)

Williams, Megan, 'The Making of Rudolf II as a Mad Monarch', *Groniek*, CCVII (2021), pp. 134–55

Wilson, Peter H., *Europe's Tragedy: A New History of the Thirty Years War* (New York, 2010)

—, *The Holy Roman Empire* (London, 2017)

Yates, Frances A., *Astraea: The Imperial Theme in the Sixteenth Century* (London and Boston, MA, 1975)

—, *Giordano Bruno and the Hermetic Tradition* (London, 1964)

Zimmer, Jürgen, *Joseph Heintz der Ältere als Maler* (Weissenhorn, 1971)

—, *Joseph Heintz der Ältere: Zeichnungen und Dokumente* (Berlin and Munich, 1988)

ACKNOWLEDGEMENTS

I have been interested in Rudolf II and his milieu for more than five decades. During this time I have received assistance in various ways from numerous people. Here I wish first to thank the editors and staff of Reaktion Books for inviting me to return to the subject and to rethink what I and others have written about this fascinating figure, his impact and his reception, and for their help in the preparation of this volume.

Work on this book began during COVID, when in autumn 2020 Joseph Litts, Sharifa Lookman, Claire Sabitt, Sara Tridenti and John White participated in a lively graduate seminar at Princeton University devoted to Rudolfine Prague. In March 2023 Sofia Hernandez, Suzie Herrman, Sharifa Lookman, Olek Musiał, Claire Sabitt, Wenjie Su and John White accompanied Elizabeth Pilliod and me on a memorable trip to Bohemia, Moravia and Vienna on which many Rudolphina were seen and discussed.

While the book was being prepared the following scholars answered my requests for information or discussed issues with me, as well as in some cases facilitating access to collections: Jonathan Fine, Ondřej Jakubec, Markéta Ježková, Annemarie Jordan Gschwend, Jessica Keating, Vera Keller, Ebba Koch, Wolfram Koeppe, Miroslav Kindl, Martin Madl, Andrew Morrall, Elizabeth Pilliod, Friedrich Polleross, Ivo Purš, Paulus Rainer, Jennifer Rampling, Veronika Sandbichler, Konrad Schlegel, Jeffrey Chipps Smith and Štěpán Vácha.

I am grateful to all.

PHOTO ACKNOWLEDGEMENTS

The author and publishers wish to express their thanks to the sources listed below for illustrative material and/or permission to reproduce it. Some locations of artworks are also given below, in the interest of brevity:

AdobeStock: 30 (Matt), 34 (hdostal/fodo.media), 35 (diegograndi); The Albertina Museum, Vienna: 22; Alte Galerie – Universalmuseum Joanneum GmbH, Graz: 15 (P 120); Archivo General de Simancas: 31 (MPD XL-1.21); Bibliothèque de l'Institut national d'histoire de l'art (INHA): 6; Martin Herfurt/Pixabay: 19; Kunsthistorisches Museum, Vienna: 1 (GG 6438), 8 (KK 975), 38 (KK 5474), 42 (GG 6436), 45 (GG 1588), 46 (GG 2614), 52 (KK 5969, photo Daderot, public domain), 53 (ANSA XII 383); Kunsthistorisches Museum, Vienna, photos © KHM-Museumsverband: 7 (SK WS_XIa_I), 13 (KK 65), 17, 18 (KK 1118), 20 (KK 5898), 24 (KK 3709), 29 (KK 5506), 36 (KK 5504), 47 (KK 5979); The Metropolitan Museum of Art, New York: 2, 4, 9, 11, 12, 14, 37, 57; Musée des Beaux-Arts de Dijon: 44; Musée du Louvre, Paris, photo RMN-Grand Palais/Thierry Ollivier/RMN-GP/Dist. SCALA, Florence: 23; Museo Nacional del Prado, Madrid: 3, 5, 41; Národní Technické Muzeum (National Technical Museum), Prague: 25 (Inv. 24551); National Gallery of Art, Washington, DC: 33, 55; Nationalmuseet, Copenhagen (photo John Lee, CC BY-SA 4.0): 32; Österreichische Nationalbibliothek, Vienna: 26 (Cod. Min. 130, fol. 31r), 58 (Cod. Min. 129, fol. 10r); Philadelphia Museum of Art, PA: 21; Rijksmuseum, Amsterdam (on loan from a private collection): 54; courtesy Science History Institute, Philadelphia, PA: 49; Skoklosters slott/SHM: 40; photo © Správa Pražského hradu (Prague Castle Administration), photo Jan Gloc: 43; Staatliche Graphische Sammlung, Munich: 27; Staatliche Kunstsammlungen Dresden: 10 (Kupferstich-Kabinett, C 7042, photo A. Diesend), 28 (Skulpturensammlung, H4 001/004, photo E. Estel/H.-P. Klut), 56 (Kupferstich-Kabinett, CA 213/073, photo H. Boswank), 59

(Mathematisch-Physikalischer Salon, D V I, photo M. Lange); Strahovská obrazárna (Strahov Picture Gallery), Prague (O 786), photo Oto Palán, reproduced courtesy the Royal Canonry of Premonstratensians at Strahov – Strahov Picture Gallery: 39; University of Wisconsin–Madison, Department of Special Collections: 51; photo © Victoria and Albert Museum, London: 48; Wellcome Collection, London: 50; from Martin Zeiller, *Topographia provinciarum Austriacarum* (Frankfurt, 1649): 16.

INDEX

Illustration numbers are indicated by *italics*